Life and Letters in France

Life and Letters in France
General Editor
Austin Gill CBE, MA
Marshall Professor of French,
University of Glasgow

Other Volumes:

The Eighteenth Century
R Fargher B Lit, MA, D Phil

The Nineteenth Century
A W Raitt MA, D Phil

Life and Letters in France

The Seventeenth Century

W D Howarth, MA
Professor of Classical French Literature,
University of Bristol

Charles Scribner's Sons New York

A - 8.71ʳ (I)

Printed in Great Britain by Fletcher & Son Ltd. Norwich
Library of Congress Catalog Card Number 70-166298
SBN 684-12516-X (college paper)
SBN 684-12614-1 (trade cloth)

Preface

The type of commentary presented in this series is not meant to serve as an alternative to, and still less to compete with, the close analytical study known as *l'explication de textes*. It is intended rather as a complement, fulfilling a need which teachers of French literature in this country are acutely aware of, and which *la lecture expliquée* on the normal lines cannot conveniently satisfy. Our pupils are not equipped, like those brought up in French schools, with the knowledge of French history, political, social, economic and cultural, which should be brought to the understanding and appreciation of French authors. On that side of their study they need help which a method devised for teaching French literature in France does not afford. It is to the familiar problem of how best to give this help that the *Life and Letters in France* series suggests an answer. How good the answer may be, experience must decide, but *a priori* the method has some promising advantages. It places the historical facts not in an historian's arrangement, but in perspectives directly relevant to the study of literature. Also, since the historical commentary is always directed to the explanation of particular passages, the literary usefulness of a knowledge of history (about which students are often sceptical) is constantly illustrated.

The extent to which our understanding of literature is thus sharpened and deepened by systematic attention to what is conveniently called historical background depends a good deal on the nature of the works studied, and the choice of passages for commentary naturally reflects that fact. The passages are varied enough to show that the method is appropriate to many different kinds of work, but it is not claimed that they represent adequately the variety of French literature at any period in its history. Nor, on the other hand, do the commentaries in any of the volumes attempt to cover, taken together, all the main aspects of background for the century concerned. It was desirable to aim at diversity, but it would have been foolish to try to be complete.

Such, in rather bare outline, is what we have attempted. The authors of the different volumes, and I, are all tutors in French in Oxford colleges. That is a fair guarantee, I hope, that we have kept firmly in view the practical aim of teaching our compatriots to read French literature with profit and enjoyment. It is as tutors also that we particularly wish to guard against two possible misunderstandings. First, what we are proposing is a technique for teaching and learning; it has nothing to do with examining. Secondly, our concern here for historical aspects of the study of literature does not mean that those are the aspects which all or any of us are most interested in, or as teachers would stress most. The commentaries themselves make it quite clear, I believe, that their authors are alive to the strictly literary qualities of the passages they are discussing.

A.G.

Contents

List of Plates

Acknowledgments

For permission to reproduce photographs, the author makes grateful acknowledgment to the Bibliothèque Nationale (Plates I, II, IIIb, IV, V and VI); the Musée du Louvre (Plates IIIa and VIIa); the British Museum (Plate VIIb); and the Galleria Sabauda of Turin (Plate VIII).

Introduction

IN HIS *Port-Royal*, that immense survey of French intellectual life in the seventeenth century, Sainte-Beuve writes at one point that the age of Louis XIV is like 'un pont magnifique orné d'admirables statues'.[1] As far as the literature of the age is concerned, this image corresponds well enough to the impression fostered by the writers themselves: the aesthetic to which they subscribed was that of an art which preached universal truths and looked back to the ancient world for much of its inspiration. It is easy, therefore, to picture them as a privileged class living in dedicated isolation and producing their masterpieces in conditions unaffected by social, political or economic factors. They give the impression of being largely self-sufficient in another sense, too, for it seemed to them that they had turned their backs on their recent cultural and intellectual past, on the Renaissance with its ferment of ideas; those ideas which, says Sainte-Beuve, pursuing his image, 'ont traversé ce pont et passé dessous, pour reparaître aussitôt après'. This view of the literature of the Grand Siècle was strengthened in the eighteenth century; for the most part, the masterpieces of the preceding age soon came to be regarded as venerable classics, and eighteenth-century criticism gave little attention to the social conditions in which they had been produced. The nineteenth century, of course, had lost this reverence, and Romantic writers, where not positively iconoclastic, were at least able to show a real critical detachment towards seventeenth-century works. It is true that French academic criticism, even at the end of the nineteenth century, tended to take the classical aesthetic rather too much at its face value, and to judge works of literature in isolation from their social context; but this period saw the beginnings of a critical approach based on a greater awareness of the importance of historical background.

Taine's theories of 'la race, le milieu, le moment', indeed, foreshadow those of modern Marxist critics for whom everything in the context of literary history is reducible to social and material causes, leaving nothing

[1] *Port-Royal* (Paris, n.d.), III, p. 304.

to the chance development of individual genius. But although Taine is most conscientious in applying this new method, the historical background against which he seeks to place seventeenth-century literature is itself a mere stereotype. Take for instance a passage from his essay on Racine:

> La vie hasardeuse, solitaire et inventive a cessé avec l'indépendance et les guerres du seizième siècle . . . . La monarchie absolue et l'administration régulière ont amené les nobles oisifs et soumis dans les salons et à la cour; là règne un goût uniforme; il faut y plier son humeur; les convenances promènent leur niveau sur les singularités des esprits et des caractères . . . . L'architecture sèche et noble s'aligne avec la tenue, la gravité et la magnificence officielle d'un courtisan; les déesses à demi-nues qui se penchent au fond des allées ont le geste d'une grande dame qui plie son éventail ou retient d'un coup d'œil un assidu; les fleuves couchés sous leur voûte de rocaille ont l'air commandant et serein de Louis XIV ou de Thésée. Voilà les alentours de Racine; c'est cet esprit de la race et du siècle auquel s'est accommodé son esprit. S'il y a des climats dans le monde physique, il y en a aussi dans le monde moral.[1]

This is misleading, because it is based on such very selective evidence; as a result, the 'moral climate' to which Taine is trying to relate the characteristic qualities of Racine as a classical writer, is an artificial one largely derived from the reading of the major classical writers themselves, with the assistance of such unreliable aids as Louis Racine's filial *Mémoires sur la vie de Jean Racine*, and some rather vague historical generalisations. When he writes: 'Dans ce théâtre, qui ne parle ni de son temps ni de sa vie, je trouve l'histoire de sa vie et de son temps',[2] he is unconsciously pointing to the limitations of his method.

Thus the picture of the unbroken order and regularity of French literature, at any rate in the second half of the seventeenth century, continued to match the 'official' view of the Grand Siècle as a glorious period of national unity and social stability; both were considered to be the perfect expression of the national genius of the French people. Only gradually did the achievements of nineteenth-century historical scholarship modify this picture, and it was still possible for the historian Sorel to write in 1903:

> Malgré Saint-Simon, malgré Michelet, la plupart d'entre nous persistent à considérer l'histoire du Grand Siècle comme un spectacle pompeux et

[1] *Nouveaux Essais de critique et d'histoire* (Paris, 1865), pp. 212-14.   [2] Ibid., p. 269.

régulier, donné sur un théâtre qui n'aurait ni coulisses ni dessous. Le splendide décor de Versailles, l'incomparable ordonnance de la prose, la divine poésie de Racine, ont fait et feront encore longtemps ce prestige. Qui voudrait croire que ces beaux jardins étaient souillés d'ordures, que ce palais d'or et de marbre était traversé de couloirs obscurs, sales, de canaux nauséabonds qui l'empestaient ? [1]

However, thanks to much patient searching of archives, and the publication of countless volumes of memoirs and correspondence that has taken place over the last hundred years, a much more detailed, more intimate history of the period has been built up. Although this by no means entirely invalidates the traditional connection between classical literature and its social background, it is much easier now to recognise that this is only part of a more complex picture, and that beneath the outward splendour, the outward refinement and the outward orthodoxy of the age there were stresses and tensions of the most diverse kind, to which no writer of the time could escape being subjected.

This new view of seventeenth-century social history has in its turn helped discerning critics and literary historians to see new patterns in the literature of the period. The influence of social and intellectual movements such as *préciosité* and *libertinage* on a variety of writers has been explored, and the investigation of the affinities between baroque art and the literature of the time has thrown fresh light on seventeenth-century sensibility. The careful study of certain lesser literary figures has played its part here, and has increased the knowledge and understanding of the traditions and conventions which governed the writing of their greater contemporaries.

Nevertheless, the literary masterpieces from the second half of the century which have survived on their own account—as distinct from those less distinguished works which have been artificially resuscitated by scholars—do undoubtedly share certain common characteristics; and those characteristics do correspond to features in the historical background with which they have traditionally been linked. It is still legitimate, and still useful, to retain the term 'classical' to denote those masterpieces which obey a well-defined, fairly homogeneous aesthetic, and which express a contemporary social ideal just as certainly as they satisfied a contemporary taste. But it would be wrong to think that the social ideal was everywhere realised, and equally wrong to think that the

[1] Preface to F. Funck-Brentano, *Le Drame des poisons* (6th ed., 1903), p. viii.

refined taste which was satisfied by *Bérénice* or *La Princesse de Clèves* was a universal taste. When a modern literary historian writes:

> Nulle école littéraire mieux que le classicisme, fondé pourtant sur l'imitation de l'antiquité, ne justifie l'adage: 'la littérature est l'expression de la société'. Cette littérature de raison, d'ordre et de règle est la parfaite expression du siècle de Richelieu et de Louis XIV[1]

we may well feel that he is over-simplifying the picture, and nòt taking sufficient account of either the divergent trends in seventeenth-century literature or the disruptive forces at work within society. On the other hand, we may not be prepared to go to the lengths suggested by the late Daniel Mornet's somewhat cynical *boutade*:

> La vérité est qu'il y a eu un très bel effort littéraire et mondain vers la raison, l'ordre, la politesse, l'honnêteté. Mais on a fait l'effort parce que l'on vivait justement sans raison, sans ordre, sans politesse, sans honnêteté. L' «ordre classique» est un idéal dont la réalité reste fort éloignée.[2]

The truth surely lies somewhere between these two extremes: the literature of the Grand Siècle was neither the spontaneous expression of a society which carried the art of living to its highest level, nor was it produced by the 'escapist' idealism of a few refined spirits reacting against the anarchy and lack of refinement which they saw in the life around them.

The complex connection between literature and society cannot be defined by means of such simple formulae. The delicate relationship of the individual sensibility of an author to the 'period sensibility' of the age in which he lives; the relationship between inspiration of a bookish character, derived from ancient or modern literatures, and the less tangible, perhaps unconscious inspiration which comes from his life as a seventeenth-century Frenchman; his response to, or reaction against, a whole range of psychological influences, from the religious and philosophical movements which affected the conscience of an age, to the ephemeral fashions which affected only its speech or its dress; patronage, censorship, the social status of the writer and the political or ecclesiastical

---

[1] K. Loukovitch, *L'Évolution de la tragédie religieuse classique en France* (Paris, 1933), p. 146.

[2] Review of F. Gaiffe, *L'Envers du Grand Siècle* in *Revue d'histoire littéraire de la France*, vol. xxxiii (1926), p. 116.

obstacles to the free expression of his ideas: all these factors come into play, and help to determine the particular nature of each individual writer's 'classicism'.

Modern scholarship has done a great deal to overcome the handicap of a too schematic, doctrinaire critical approach to seventeenth-century literature, and to throw light on the unpredictable complexities of 'la création littéraire'. Daniel Mornet, who certainly did as much as any other scholar in this field, pointed out, in a stimulating short article published shortly before his death, how much more subtle and flexible the approach must be than that produced by the rigidly determinist theory of a Taine:

> Telle que Taine l'a appliquée, l'idée [d'étudier la race, le milieu et le moment] ne conduit à rien. D'abord, parce que l'information de Taine est tout à fait insuffisante et que l'image qu'il nous donne du milieu et du moment est trop souvent, du moins en ce qui concerne l'histoire de la littérature française, illusoire ou mensongère. Ensuite—et surtout—parce que Taine prétend trouver dans cette étude du milieu et du moment l'explication des œuvres de génie. Sainte-Beuve lui faisait déjà, dès le début, cette objection d'une éclatante évidence: tous les écrivains, ceux du 2e, du 3e ou du 10e ordre, ont vécu au même moment et dans le même milieu. Pourquoi n'ont-ils pas tous du génie et le même génie? Non, le résultat de la méthode est à l'inverse. Elle permet de déterminer ce qui, chez les grands écrivains, n'est pas leur véritable génie.... Quand on saura exactement, non pas par quelques citations, mais par tout un ensemble de faits et de textes, que telle façon de penser, telle sorte de curiosité, telle forme de goût est commune à un grand écrivain et à tous ses contemporains, ou du moins à un grand nombre de ses contemporains, on pourra dire avec certitude: 'Là n'est pas l'originalité de notre écrivain'. L'histoire complète de la pensée et du goût permet de tracer avec beaucoup plus de précision le cercle à l'intérieur duquel il faut seulement chercher le secret de son génie.[1]

I have quoted the paragraph at length because it helps to clarify the purpose of this volume. 'Tracer ... le cercle à l'intérieur duquel il faut ... chercher le secret de son génie' is a formula which comes near enough to defining my own approach in selecting the passages for commentary. Not that the commentaries are intended to add up to a comprehensive survey of every aspect, or even of the more important aspects, of the

---

[1] 'Méthode d'un cours sur l'histoire de la pensée et du goût en France au XVIIe siècle' in *Romanic Review*, vol. xxxix (1948), p. 205.

intellectual and social life of seventeenth-century France; to what Mornet calls 'l'histoire de la pensée et du goût'. Readers may perhaps be surprised to find certain authors represented here, and they will possibly regret the exclusion of others. The choice is, of course, a personal one; and my object has been less to pick out the most distinguished authors of the century than to select a score of passages by different authors, each worth studying as much for its subject-matter, reflecting some aspect of the times, as for the way in which the author has treated it. Having made a selection of representative passages, illustrating different literary genres and as far as possible a varied range of subject-matter, I have tried to 'situate' each passage in the sort of social and intellectual background which seemed to be relevant, in order to throw into relief the contemporary habits of thought and social influences which, just as surely as any purely literary conventions, helped to determine the form and the content of the works from which the passages were taken. Only a text which is so 'situated' can, I believe, be read with a sympathetic understanding.

The importance of such an approach increases with the remoteness in time of the period which is being studied; 'pure' literary criticism on its own cannot bridge a gap of three hundred years, and the student needs to be taught to read a seventeenth-century text. He has to try to make himself familiar with the habits of thought of the time, with the pressure of social forces as well as with the limits imposed by a narrower intellectual horizon; and it is doing him a disservice to write of any seventeenth-century writer as Giraudoux has written of Racine:

> Les commentaires littéraires sont les seuls qui permettent d'approcher et les seuls qu'eût volontiers écoutés le poète pour lequel on aurait pu graver l'épitaphe suivante: Ci-gît celui qui ne se posa jamais la question de Dieu, ni de la connaissance, ni des esprits animaux, celui pour qui n'existèrent ni les problèmes de la politique, ni ceux du blason, ni ceux de la morale: ci-gît Racine.[1]

The seventeenth century was an age in which men could still be burnt at the stake for impiety, and in which frightful atrocities were committed in the interests of a strong, authoritarian form of Christianity; an age in which the Divine Right of Kings was almost universally accepted without question; and in which modern science had hardly begun to take

---

[1] *Racine* (Paris, 1950), pp. 19–20.

shape. The theory of the circulation of the blood was still being chal-
lenged in the 1660s, and the Copernican revolution in astronomy was
still not accepted by Church and University even later in the century.
So we must not be surprised, for instance, to find the archaic physiology
based on the theory of the humours forming the basis for a play like
Le Misanthrope ou l'Atrabilaire amoureux; or that the philosophical
literature of the whole century takes an anthropocentric universe for
granted in a way which is quite impossible for modern thinkers. Professor
Butterfield has emphasised the immense gulf which separates a modern
reader from writers who were at work before this revolution in thought
really got under way:

> Since [the so-called 'scientific revolution'] overturned the authority in
> science not only of the Middle Ages but of the ancient world since it
> ended not only in the eclipse of scholastic philosophy but in the destruction
> of Aristotelian physics—it outshines everything since the rise of Christianity
> and reduces the Renaissance and Reformation to the rank of mere episodes,
> mere internal displacements, within the system of medieval Christendom.
> Since it changed the character of men's habitual mental operations even
> in the conduct of the non-material sciences, while transforming the whole
> diagram of the physical universe and the very texture of human life itself,
> it looms so large as the real origin both of the modern world and of the
> modern mentality that our customary periodisation of European history
> has become an anachronism and an encumbrance.[1]

'Revolution' in this context, as Professor Butterfield insists, is a misleading term: the change from the medieval to the modern mentality was
a gradual development spread over three centuries or more, and it was
far from complete in the period with which we are concerned. The
receptivity to new ideas shown by individual seventeenth-century
writers varies considerably, not only according to their own temperament but also to the education which they received and the milieu in
which they lived.

Looking at the century from a social and economic point of view, we
see the gradual emergence of the bourgeoisie starting to break down the
closed hierarchical structure of society, and the beginnings of a more
mobile class system nearer to that of our own day. A considerable change
can be observed between the opening years of the century and its close,
but it is easy to exaggerate the extent of such a change. By 1700 the

---

[1] H. Butterfield, *The Origins of Modern Science* (London, 1949), p. viii.

wealth of the country had largely passed into the hands of the 'grande bourgeoisie', but we must remember that there were limits to what money could do. The sale of offices carrying a title with them may have obscured the border-line between *bourgeoisie* and *noblesse de robe*, but the highest functions, and the right of entry to Court circles, were still the prerogative of the genuine nobility, the *noblesse d'épée*. Again, it is easy to obtain a false picture of the rise of the bourgeoisie if we merely consider the fact that most of the great writers of the classical age—Descartes, Pascal, Corneille, Molière, Racine, La Fontaine, Boileau, Bossuet— were of bourgeois origin, without at the same time reflecting on the social position of some of these writers. For the bourgeois was always conscious of being an outsider in the company of 'gens de qualité', even if he was not directly dependent on their patronage. Thus Racine's social ambitions are as important a factor in the development of his career as his Jansenism, to which historians have traditionally given much more importance; while La Bruyère's subservient status at Chantilly colours the whole of *Les Caractères*. It is ironical that another great writer of the end of the century, Saint-Simon, should have been spurred on to write his memoirs by the frustrated ambitions of a 'duc et pair' under what he scornfully terms 'un règne de vile bourgeoisie'; but if it is true that the great nobles had been systematically deprived of political power in the course of the century, if the political and economic administration of the country during Louis XIV's reign was in the hands of talented *roturiers*, the fact remains that socially there was an enormous gulf between the true 'gentilhomme' and the recently-ennobled bourgeois, however wealthy the latter might be.[1]

The Frenchman of the seventeenth century travelled abroad hardly at all, and took little interest in the culture of neighbouring countries. England, and English literature, were virtually unknown; and even in the case of Spain and Italy, the contacts were purely literary: there was a great decline in the speaking of both Italian and Spanish. Indeed, French seventeenth-century civilisation stands out as being remarkably insular, when one thinks of the artistic and intellectual cosmopolitanism which had distinguished the sixteenth century, and which was to be a prominent feature of the eighteenth. Only in the field of philosophy and

---

[1] The term *gentilhomme* was much more restricted in its application than the more general *noble*: 'Tout gentilhomme est noble, mais tout noble n'est pas gentilhomme. Le prince fait des nobles, mais le sang fait des gentilhommes'—*Dictionnaire de l'Académie* (1694), s.v. 'noble'.

the sciences was there a fertile interchange of ideas between Frenchmen and other scholars, and a readiness to transcend the limitations of a narrowly national culture: Descartes, for instance, died at Stockholm, where he had gone as the guest of Christine of Sweden; Pascal was in touch with foreign scientists at the time of his work on the nature of the vacuum; and there were regular exchanges at the end of the century between the Royal Society and the Académie des Sciences.

Indeed, this difference in outlook is perhaps symptomatic of a more general cleavage between literature and the sciences which was beginning to be apparent in the seventeenth century. The ideal of the 'honnête homme' attempted, it is true, to perpetuate the Italian Renaissance concept of the 'universal man'; but the 'honnête homme', even if he succeeded in living up to his own ideal, was merely the amateur, the spectator or the reader of the productions of others. As regards the 'professionals', the literary practitioners themselves, the age of the specialist had begun, even if there was nothing like the specialisation with which we are familiar today. On the one hand are the 'savants', cosmopolitan and forward-looking, themselves bourgeois in origin and making their appeal to a public largely drawn from the new, leisured bourgeoisie; on the other hand, the men of letters, whose writings tended to reflect the values of the traditional aristocratic culture in which they felt more at home.

It was of course a predominantly classical culture. Education in the colleges was above all linguistic and literary, and if the typical educated Frenchman of the seventeenth century was not taught very much about the world around him, at least he received a thorough grounding in the classics.[1] The educated classes, the élite for whom the literature of the period was written—the nobility, that is, and the educated bourgeois who modelled themselves on their social superiors—were not only imbued with a backward-looking classical culture, they also subscribed to a chivalric scale of values which was a survival from the Middle Ages, and according to which soldiering was the only occupation possible for a gentleman. These are two of the factors which help to make the themes, as well as the style, of so many seventeenth-century works appear so remote to a modern reader. On the one hand we have the prestige of certain genres, the fondness for mythology and allegory, and the

---

[1] This is particularly true of the Jesuit colleges; the Oratorians, whose first college was opened in 1614, made a serious attempt to teach some science. See R. Gal, *Histoire de l'éducation* (Paris, 2nd ed., 1953), pp. 81 ff.

chauvinistic attempt to rival or surpass the masterpieces of antiquity; on the other hand, the survival of the soldier as hero, and of military prowess as a favourite theme; while the heroic aristocratic ethic which inspired the generation of the Fronde finds its origin in a chivalric moral code inherited from an earlier age, combined with an idealised conception of Roman virtue.[1]

It is small wonder that literature written for this cultured élite should contain little in the nature of objective realism. These readers wanted their reading to entertain them or to instruct them, and if possible to flatter their self-esteem. Real life therefore tends either to be embellished or idealised, or else, by a contrary process, becomes the subject of satire or burlesque: the peasantry is excluded from literature, except for such instances as La Bruyère's 'animaux farouches', Molière's Pierrot or La Fontaine's woodcutter; and similarly the artisans and lower classes of the bourgeoisie appear only as comic subjects, in the works of such writers as Scarron, Molière or Dancourt. Even when they are writing about themselves and their own preoccupations, seventeenth-century writers are subject to the inhibitions of taste and breeding:

> Le XVIIᵉ siècle ne se livre guère, et même quand il paraît s'abandonner en confidences, il n'oublie pas une certaine réserve. Jamais alors un homme ne se fût peint sans réticences, à la Montaigne, par exemple, ou à la Jean-Jacques, pas plus qu'il ne se fût montré en public sans perruque et sans justaucorps.[2]

If this comparison seems somewhat facile, it is useful to reflect on the amount of selection and arrangement that has gone into the self-portraits of men like the Cardinal de Retz or La Rochefoucauld, who were trying to live up to a self-imposed ideal; or on the intellectual formation which led a Mme de Sévigné to write personal letters to her own daughter with such a very keen eye to literary effect. Indeed, the reading of certain seventeenth-century writers reveals only too clearly to what extent the spontaneous expression of personal feelings was replaced by the self-conscious cultivation of public attitudes.

Direct representation of reality for its own sake, then, was not to the taste of the seventeenth-century reader; the 'slice of life' is virtually unknown, with occasional exceptions such as Molière's theatrical conversation-piece, L'Impromptu de Versailles. The most characteristic

---

[1] See R. Bénichou, *Morales du Grand Siècle* (Paris, 1948).
[2] P. Bonnefon, *La Société française au XVIIᵉ siècle* (Paris, 1903), p. xiii.

works of the age of Louis XIV are distinguished, on the contrary, by a period style whose hallmarks are intellectual abstraction, a fondness for the dialectical approach even where it is not obviously called for by the subject, and an aspiration towards the indefinable goal of 'le sublime'.

But generalisations about a 'period style' can be misleading if they are applied uncritically to the works of individual writers. The exploration of the social and cultural ambiance should not only serve to illuminate common features in the works of different authors writing during the same period; it can also, most usefully, as Mornet suggests in the paragraph quoted above, help to indicate the limits of historical determinism, and to bring out the full extent of an author's individuality. On the one hand, for instance, a study of preciosity and the social life of the *salons* makes us aware of affinities between, say, Mme de Lafayette, Mme de Sévigné and Racine; yet on the other hand, the striking contrast between the ideas of Malherbe and his followers and their contemporary Théophile illustrates the extent to which we must allow for the effect of individual temperament, similar social circumstances producing both the orthodox conformist and the nonconformist rebel. It is dangerous, in short, to generalise about the influence of any social factors on the literature of a period, unless we bear in mind that individual writers vary considerably in their response to, or reaction against, such influences. The label 'Classical', nearly as much as its counterpart 'Romantic', needs to be interpreted and defined afresh in respect of every author to whom it is applied.

Finally, it is certainly not intended to suggest that the kind of approach to the literature of another century recommended here, through the social and intellectual background of the writers and their public, can ever take the place of the detailed critical analysis of the text itself. It is not a question of subordinating the study of the text to the study of the intellectual background, or of using a series of texts as so many pegs on which to hang a collection of discursive essays on seventeenth-century intellectual history. As in all literary studies, it is the text itself that is of prime importance; but we must make every effort to read the text with an informed and sympathetic understanding.

Bibliography

The following list of suggestions for reference and for further reading is confined to modern historical and critical works. Books devoted to individual authors of passages contained in this volume have not been listed, nor (on the whole) have those dealing with one particular, well-defined topic, treated in one or other of the commentaries; bibliographical information of this nature will be found in the notes to each commentary.

A note at the foot of each passage indicates the particular edition of the text from which it has been taken.

A. Adam, *Histoire de la littérature française au XVIIe siècle*, 5 vols. (Paris, 1948-56)

L. André, *Louis XIV et l'Europe* (Paris, 1950)

P. Barrière, *La Vie intellectuelle en France du XVIe siècle à l'époque contemporaine* (Paris, 1961)

P. Bénichou, *Morales du Grand Siècle* (Paris, 1948)

A. Blunt, *Art and Architecture in France*, 1500-1700 (London, 1953)

P. Bonnefon, *La Société française au XVIIe siècle* (Paris, 1903)

J. Boulenger, *Le Grand Siècle* (Paris, 1911)

H. Busson, *La Religion des classiques* (Paris, 1948)

H. Butterfield, *The Origins of Modern Science* (London, 1949)

G. Doutrepont, *La Littérature et la société* (Brussels, 1942)

ed. N. Edelman, *A Critical Bibliography of French Literature, Vol. III: Seventeenth Century* (Syracuse, New York, 1961)

F. Gaiffe, *L'Envers du Grand Siècle* (Paris, 1924)

B. Grœthuysen, *Origines de l'esprit bourgeois en France, Vol. I: L'Église et la bourgeoisie* (Paris, 1927)

H. A. Hatzfeld, *Literature through Art: a new approach to French Literature* (New York, 1952)

H. Hauser, *La Prépondérance espagnole*, 1559-1660—*Peuples et civilisations, Vol. IX* (Paris, 1933)

A. J. Krailsheimer, *Studies in Self-Interest* (Oxford, 1962)

P. Lacroix, *Le XVIIᵉ Siècle : Institutions, usages et costumes* (Paris, 1880)

J. Lough, *Introduction to Seventeenth-century France* (London, 1954)

E. Magne, *Images de Paris sous Louis XIV* (Paris, 1939)

G. Mongrédien, *La Vie littéraire au XVIIᵉ siècle* (Paris, 1947)

G. Mongrédien, *La Vie de société aux XVIIᵉ et XVIIIᵉ siècles* (Paris, 1950)

D. Mornet, *Histoire de la littérature française classique* (Paris, 3rd ed., 1947)

C. Normand, *La Bourgeoisie française au XVIIᵉ siècle*—1604-1661 (Paris, 1908)

G. Reynier, *La Femme au XVIIᵉ siècle* (Paris ,1929)

P. Sagnac, *La Formation de la société française moderne, Vol. I :* 1616-1715 (Paris, 1945)

A. de Saint-Léger and P. Sagnac, *La Prépondérance française*, 1660-1715—*Peuples et civilisations, Vol. X* (Paris, 1935)

C. A. Sainte-Beuve, *Port-Royal*, 7 vols. (Paris; Hachette, n.d.)

A. Tilley, *The Decline of the Age of Louis XIV* (Cambridge, 1929)

I

Malherbe

(1555–1628)

Pour Alcandre au retour d'Oranthe à Fontainebleau

Revenez, mes plaisirs, Madame est revenue,
Et les vœux que j'ai faits pour revoir ses beaux yeux,
Rendant par mes soupirs ma douleur reconnue,
  Ont eu grâce des Cieux.

Les voici de retour, ces astres adorables,
Où prend mon océan son flux et son reflux:
Soucis retirez-vous, cherchez les misérables:
  Je ne vous connais plus!

Peut-on voir ce miracle, où le soin de Nature
10 A semé comme fleurs tant d'aimables appas,
Et ne confesser point qu'il n'est pire aventure
  Que de ne la voir pas?

Certes, l'autre soleil d'une erreur vagabonde
Court inutilement par ses douze maisons;
C'est elle, et non pas lui, qui fait sentir au monde
  Le change des saisons.

Avecque sa beauté toutes beautés arrivent;
Ces déserts sont jardins de l'un à l'autre bout,
Tant l'extrême pouvoir des grâces qui la suivent
20   Les pénètre partout.

Ces bois en ont repris leur verdure nouvelle;
L'orage en est cessé, l'air en est éclairci,
Et même ces canaux ont leur course plus belle
  Depuis qu'elle est ici.

De moi, que les respects obligent au silence,
J'ai beau me contrefaire et beau dissimuler:
Les douceurs où je nage ont une violence
    Qui ne se peut celer.

Mais, ô rigueur du sort! tandis que je m'arrête
30 A chatouiller mon âme en ce contentement,
Je ne m'aperçois pas que le destin m'apprête
    Un autre partement.

Arrière ces pensers que la crainte m'envoie;
Je ne sais que trop bien l'inconstance du sort;
Mais de m'ôter le goût d'une si chère joie,
    C'est me donner la mort.

Les Poésies de M. de Malherbe, ed. J. Lavaud
(Paris, 1936-7), II, pp. 190-2

Malherbe's reputation has been more subject to legendary embellishment than that of most men of letters of his century. The picture of the literary tyrant, the pedantically meticulous critic of the poetry of the preceding generation, denouncing with brutal sarcasm any line of verse that did not conform to the rules of his own narrow aesthetic, yet himself producing little of any worth; of a man who lived frugally himself and condemned all vanity and ostentation in others—this image of Malherbe is familiar enough. It is based on his disciple Racan's *Mémoires pour la vie de Monsieur de Malherbe* and on Tallemant's portrait in the *Historiettes*, and there is no doubt that the poet himself did much to project it. Indeed, all the evidence suggests that the legend is authentic enough, at least as regards the latter period of Malherbe's life; but it does not provide us with the whole of the picture. The poet who could write scornfully of literary opportunism in others, and who could suggest to Racan that 'nous avons tous deux été bien fous de passer la meilleure partie de notre âge en un exercice si peu utile au public et à nous-mêmes', was certainly not without literary ambition himself, and had at an earlier stage of his career devoted a great deal of time and energy to establishing himself in the favour of Henri IV. Indeed, his career as a whole illustrates the position of the man of letters of his time, entirely dependent on royal or noble patronage.

Born into the petty nobility in Normandy in 1555, Malherbe did not attach himself to Henri's court until 1605, having lived and worked in the provinces until this date. He brought himself to the King's notice by a poem which is generally regarded as an example of his best 'occasional' verse, the 'Prière pour le Roi Henri le Grand allant en Limousin'; the King was sufficiently impressed to wish to retain his services, but not generous enough to offer him a pension right away: 'Par une épargne', says Tallemant, 'ou plutôt une lésine que je ne comprends point, il commanda à M. de Bellegarde, alors premier gentilhomme de la Chambre, de le garder jusqu'à ce qu'il l'eût mis sur l'état de ses pension-naires'.[1] Malherbe was to remain disappointed in his hopes of a royal pension, hard though he worked with this end in view. In 1606 he wrote to his friend Peiresc:

Vous verrez bientôt près de 400 vers que j'ai faits sur le Roi. J'y suis fort embesogné, parce qu'il m'a dit que je lui montre que je l'aime et qu'il me fera du bien. *Vedremo qual che ne seguira*;[2]

and in the following year:

Il m'a promis une pension sur la première abbaye ou évêché qui vaquera: cela me tiendra encore ici quelque temps; car sans cette espérance, j'aime trop la liberté pour m'en priver si longtemps.[3]

But in March 1608 the King was still making the same empty promise, and the poet's comment: 'Je ne sais quand j'en verrai l'effet; jusque-là il se faut contenter de sa bonne volonté' reveals a certain disillusionment. In fact, he remained a member of Bellegarde's household until the King's death in 1610, when Marie de Médicis gave him a pension of 500 *écus*.[4]

As well as producing 'official' verse in the form of odes to commemor-ate ceremonial occasions, any poet aspiring to the patronage of Henri IV

---

[1] Tallemant des Réaux, *Historiettes*, ed. A. Adam (Paris, 1960), I, p. 108.

[2] Letter of 15th October 1606. Malherbe's letters provide a particularly valuable com-mentary on events and affairs of current interest.

[3] Letter of 18th July 1607.

[4] In texts dating from the beginning of the century, the term *écu* refers to the *écu d'or*, later called a *demi-louis* and worth five *francs* or *livres*. From the 1640s onwards, the name designates the *écu d'argent*, whose value was three *livres*. For the sake of comparison with Malherbe's pension, we may note that when Colbert drew up the first list of royal pensions in 1663 (see commentary to passage no. XIX, p. 200), the pensions ranged from 4,000 to 600 *livres*. The real value of money, however, had declined during the intervening half-century.

had of necessity to be prepared to use his pen to further the King's numerous love-affairs. Not only Malherbe, but also Desportes, Vauquelin des Yveteaux, Régnier and others were pressed into service to celebrate the beauty, or to complain of the coldness, of a whole series of royal favourites from Gabrielle d'Estrées, who was Henri's mistress from 1591 until her death in 1599, to the young Charlotte de Montmorency, for whom he conceived an infatuation in the last year or so of his life. It is this attachment which provides the subject for the above poem.

Divorced from his first wife, the childless Marguerite de Valois, in 1599, Henri had been tempted to regularise the liaison with Gabrielle; but her death in childbirth in the same year removed that possibility. Almost immediately, he began a new liaison with Henriette d'Entragues, duchesse de Verneuil, and made her a secret promise of marriage if she should bear him a son within a certain time. This condition was not fulfilled, and in any case a conventional diplomatic marriage was already being negotiated with Marie de Médicis, whom he in fact married in 1600 and who bore him an heir in 1601. The King's second marriage produced almost continuous domestic discord, caused on the Queen's side by her indulgence towards Italian favourites, and on Henri's by a series of adulterous affairs in which he flaunted his infidelity more and more openly. The relationship with Charlotte de Montmorency was a stormy one, and more than a little humiliating for the elderly king. To begin with, she was not yet sixteen, while he was already well into his fifties; and the course of the affair illustrates the tyranny exercised over his whole life by this sort of passion. First, Henri engineered the breaking-off of her engagement to Bassompierre, his loyal friend, and then arranged a marriage with the prince de Condé, who was, he thought, so devoted to hunting and had so little interest in women, that he would not be too concerned about his wife's honour. He was mistaken in this, however, for while Charlotte's parents showed little reluctance to promote the liaison, Condé refused to fit in with the King's schemes, and removed his wife from the court: first to a property near the Flemish frontier, and then over the border to Brussels. Here the fugitive pair became a valuable counter in Spanish diplomatic intrigue against the French Crown, and the King's infatuation thus assumed considerable political importance. On a personal level, the King repeatedly went to ridiculous lengths to demonstrate his extravagant passion for Charlotte: ordinarily very neglectful of his personal appearance, he now took to dressing in youthful silks and satins, and on the occasion of his mistress's first flight he followed her in disguise, standing by the roadside with a patch over his eye to watch her pass. He acted, indeed, like a lovesick hero of one of the fashionable pastoral romances ('rendant par [ses] soupirs [sa] douleur reconnue'), and it is said that his passion was stimulated by having d'Urfé's novel *L'Astrée*[1] read to him while he lay in bed suffering from gout.

Among the resources at the King's command in his courtship of Charlotte was the talent of Malherbe and the other court poets. Régnier, for instance, produced an *Ode* and a stylised *Plainte* in thirty-six stanzas with the refrain 'Qu'est-elle devenue?':

> Mais Dieu! j'ai beau me plaindre et toujours soupirer,
> J'ai beau de mes deux yeux deux fontaines tirer,
> J'ai beau mourir d'amour et de regret pour elle,
>   Chacun me la recèle.
>
> Ô bois, ô prés, ô monts, ô vous qui la cachez,
> Et qui contre mon gré l'avez tant retenue,
> Si jamais de pitié vous vous vîtes touchés,
> Hélas, répondez-moi, qu'est-elle devenue?[2]

In Malherbe's own case, the first summons to collaborate in this rather sordid intrigue came in the form of an invitation to write some verses for a court ballet in which Charlotte was due to dance; the poet was perceptive enough, however, to see what his royal master was after: 'Le Roi m'a entretenu de quelque autre galanterie dépendante du ballet, qui était la vraie occasion pourquoi il m'a envoyé quérir exprès par un garçon de la chambre, et le ballet n'a servi que de prétexte'.[3] But courtier-poets could not afford moral scruples, and however unsavoury this pursuit of a mere child by an elderly satyr must have seemed, it had to be treated with the same conventional embellishment and refinement as other, more legitimate, themes of occasional verse.[4]

---

[1] The first part of the novel was published in 1607.

[2] Régnier, *Œuvres complètes*, ed. G. Raibaud (Paris, 1958), pp. 246-54. It was not only Malherbe and his disciples whose talents were available to the King: Régnier was Malherbe's bitterest critic in literary matters.

[3] Letter to Peiresc, 2nd February 1609.

[4] Cf. for example, Malherbe's odes "A la Reine sur sa bienvenue en France" or "Sur l'attentat commis en la personne de sa majesté"; or Vauquelin des Yveteaux's "Chant de louange au Roi pour la paix" and "Discours sur la naissance de monseigneur le Dauphin" alongside his *vers de commande* written in honour of Gabrielle d'Estrées.

The poem under discussion is one of five composed by Malherbe during the few months that the liaison lasted; it is clear from its subject-matter that it refers to the first separation of the King and Charlotte—Condé had prudently taken his wife away from the court within a month of his marriage (May 1609)—and her subsequent return, while in 'le destin m'apprête un autre partement' of lines 31-2 we have an allusion to the definitive separation at the end of July. It is possible that by the time the poem was completed, this final break had already taken place, since Malherbe was a notoriously slow worker: Lalanne comments appositely that 'pour qu'il pût être un poète de circonstance, il fallait que les circonstances marchassent bien lentement'[1] and it is said that his composition of a consolatory ode for a certain nobleman on the death of his wife was so lacking in spontaneity that by the time it was completed the bereaved man had married again.[2]

This laborious workmanship is reflected in the character of the poem. There is none of the fresh, spontaneous imagery which marks the best verse of the Pléiade, and which a nature-lover like Théophile was able to recapture. Malherbe's imagery is abstract and intellectualised (e.g. lines 5-6, 13-14), though it lacks the intellectual challenge of La Ceppède, to say nothing of his English contemporary Donne: the image in stanza 4 is a laboured development of a highly conventional comparison of the lover's mistress to the sun, and subsequent stanzas merely elaborate this traditional theme. When Charlotte is absent nature seems dull and lifeless, for she has taken the place of the 'other sun', which is reduced to an aimless wandering through the 'mansions' of the sky; but with her return everything blooms again. On the credit side, it can be said that the poem already shows the masterly control of the alexandrine and the fluency of Malherbe's mature verse: we may note the balancing of the two halves of the line round the caesura in lines 1, 17, 22 and the effective use of the half-line to end the stanza. At its best, the verse-form produced by the strict doctrine of Malherbe and his followers was to produce a dignified and harmonious vehicle for Corneille's rhetorical tragedy, but the effect of his 'reforms' on other types of poetry was not altogether a happy one: the emphasis on manner rather than on matter, on correctness rather than on vitality, tended to produce verses of a

[1] Malherbe, Œuvres, 'Grands Écrivains' edition (Paris, 1862-9), I, p. 156.
[2] For the dating of the five poems addressed to Alcandre, see the 'Grands Écrivains' edition, I, pp. 151 ff., and R. Fromilhague, La Vie de Malherbe : apprentissages et luttes (Paris, 1954), pp. 225 ff.

monotonous uniformity which may have been adequate for the majestic platitudes of the 'official' ode, but which killed any genuine lyrical inspiration.[1]

It would perhaps be wrong, however, to look for originality in this kind of formal verse. Convention dictated that the poet should put himself in the lover's place, and act as his mouthpiece; and even the names of Alcandre ('strong man') and Oranthe ('possessing the flower of beauty') were not of the poet's own invention: other poets had called Henri IV Alcandre, and a collection of anecdotes about the King's private life, published in 1657, bore the title *Les Amours du grand Alcandre*. One feature of the poem which does show the poet's creative imagination at work, however, is the attempt, in stanzas 5 and 6, to evoke the setting of the King's extravagant idyll at Fontainebleau. The attempt is a perfunctory one, it is true, but it reminds the modern reader that the setting may have had as much influence on the elderly lover's romanesque behaviour as the pastoral fashion in literature, and that the idyll might not have flourished in the same way if the Court had happened to be in residence at the Louvre at the time.

Built on the site of a hunting-lodge, Fontainebleau had been a royal palace throughout the Middle Ages. François I had rebuilt it between 1528 and 1540; the restoration was the work of the master mason Le Breton, and though Italian sculptors such as Primaticcio were employed, the design was in a generally simpler style than that of the Italianate Renaissance *châteaux* of the Loire valley, and looked forward to the great period of French classical architecture.[2] During the last forty years

[1] An interesting comment on Malherbe's verse-forms is made by Miss R. Winegarten: 'In Malherbe's day, lyricism was not associated with sentiment and sensibility . . . but with music. . . . It is not generally known that many (at least twenty-one) of Malherbe's lyrics were composed to fit a set air, or were given a musical setting afterwards. . . . The practice of setting poetry to music line by line imposed formal limitations on the lyric, and in the *air de cour* there was a tendency to end-stop the lines and to emphasise the rhyme and also to have a cadence in the middle of the line. The emphasis on rhyme corresponds to the importance given by Malherbe to rich, difficult rhyme; the end-stopping of lines corresponds to Malherbe's rule prohibiting *enjambement*; and the cadence in the middle of a line corresponds to his rule demanding a caesura at the hemistich'—*French Lyric Poetry in the Age of Malherbe* (Manchester, 1954), pp. 3-5.

[2] 'L'École de Fontainebleau reste un fait isolé et apparaît comme une inoculation' [*scil.* 'of a style imported from abroad'] 'faite à dose trop massive et qui n'eut pas de prise sur le tempérament français; les œuvres réalisées par elle, traduction plastique des œuvres des humanistes de la Renaissance, touffues comme les poèmes de Ronsard, seront comme eux vite incomprises, le Malherbe que fut pour elles Philibert Delorme devant remettre rapidement l'art décoratif français à une plus juste cadence'—A. Bray, *Le Château de Fontainebleau* (Paris, n.d.), p. 14.

of the sixteenth century Fontainebleau had been neglected, but it had a new lease of life under Henri IV, and was to be the principal residence of the court, when it was not in Paris at the Louvre, until the reign of Louis XIV. In Henri's reign further extensions and improvements were carried out, at a cost of 2½ million *livres;* French painters and sculptors were employed to embellish the interior of the palace, and although Fontainebleau was never to have such extensive formal gardens as Versailles or Vaux-le-Vicomte, the gardens were also enlarged at this period. The central feature of these works in the grounds of Fontaine-bleau was the immense canal, 1,200 metres long and 39 metres broad, which, together with a smaller canal to provide a water-supply for the palace, was constructed by the Italian engineer Francini. A letter from Malherbe to Peiresc comments on the King's enthusiasm for this enterprise:

> Il faut que vous sachiez que ce canal est aujourd'hui sa passion prédomi-nante, et qu'avec ces chaleurs qui ont été excessives s'il en fut jamais, il était ordinairement assis sur une pierre depuis cinq ou six heures du matin jusques à midi, sans parasol ni ombre quelconque, à voir travailler ses maçons,[1]

and stanza 6 of the poem evokes this feature of Fontainebleau, as well as the celebrated forest which extended all around, and whose abundant game made this royal palace popular with courtiers fond of hunting. Altogether, the atmosphere of Fontainebleau must have seemed spacious and sylvan indeed compared with the busy urban character of the Louvre. At the same time, in the severe regularity of the plan of both palace and gardens, it is perhaps not too fanciful to see a reflection of the same spirit which in the field of literature animates Malherbe's 'reforms'.[2]

The King's affair with the princesse de Condé, says M. Fromilhague, provided for Malherbe 'sa première consécration officielle: pour la première fois il apparaît véritablement comme le poète du Roi. En quelle occasion! Le voici promu en même temps au rôle de confident, dépositaire des secrets les plus intimes et les plus chers du souverain. Son prestige se trouve rehaussé auprès des courtisans, comme auprès de ses émules en poésie. Quelles heureuses perspectives s'ouvrent à lui!'[3] If

---

[1] Letter of 20th August 1608.
[2] See Plate I.
[3] Op. cit., p. 226.

the prospect of an assured position, after his long apprenticeship, had no time to bear fruit under Henri IV, it was to some extent realised under the Regency of Marie de Médicis. He repaid the long-awaited royal pension with devotion to the royal cause, and with his championship of the growth of absolutism and authoritarian central government under Richelieu; of his work written after Henri's death, a large part took the form of 'official' verse celebrating the virtues and the deeds of the Queen Mother, the young King, and the Cardinal. In this latter phase of his life he was recognised as a sound party man, who could be depended on for support of orthodoxy and disapproval of non-conformism, whether political and religious—cf. his ode 'Pour le Roi, allant châtier la rébellion des Rochelois' (1628):

> Assez de leurs complots l'infidèle malice
> A nourri le désordre et la sédition.
> Quitte le nom de Juste, ou fais voir ta justice
> En leur punition

—or social, in the form of *libertinage*.[1] Not that Malherbe was a puritan: he boasted of his womanising, and Racan informs us that in M. de Bellegarde's household he was known as 'le Père Luxure'.[2] But he knew better than to assert a positive Epicurean philosophy as a basis for licentious behaviour; and on the subject of religion, similarly, his preserved sayings go no further than a conventional, harmless anticlericalism. Whatever private reservations he may have had about the régime of which he was a servant—and his confident dogmatism on literary matters shows that he very definitely had a mind of his own—Malherbe was too much the courtier to allow them to interfere with his career. Whereas Ronsard and the other poets of the Pléiade had conceived a much loftier idea of the poet's function, and had deplored the necessity of obeying the wishes of a wealthy patron,[3] it is quite evident that the demands made on Malherbe the courtier did little violence to the artistic scruples of Malherbe the poet.

---

[1] See the commentary to passage no. II.

[2] Cf. the licentious verse published as an appendix to vol. II of *Les Poésies de M. de Malherbe*, ed. J. Lavaud (Paris, 1936).

[3] 'Et pour ce que les biens et faveurs viennent de tel endroit, il faut bien souvent ployer sous le jugement d'une demoiselle ou d'un jeune courtisan'—Ronsard, *Abrégé de l'art poétique*, passage added in 1567, in *Œuvres complètes*, ed. P. Laumonier (Paris, 1914-52), vol. XIV, p. 12.

What, finally, is the literary importance of this sort of occasional verse from the pen of a mercenary poet laureate? Should we not be justified in judging it to be as insignificant as the trivial verse of a twentieth-century counterpart? The answer must be, I think, that such a poem has considerably more importance in Malherbe's case. Firstly, because the *métier* of official poet in the seventeenth century was a much more demanding one; not only royal masters, but other noble patrons too, required complete allegiance from a writer in their pay, so that any *vers de commande* other than the merest trifles become a kind of 'littérature engagée', and bear witness to their author's way of life: at best a life of cautious opportunism, at worst one which imposed a humiliating need for hypocrisy and compromise. And secondly, because this sort of writing is in fact representative of the larger part of Malherbe's poetic output: his 'official' verse is all of a piece with his influential literary doctrine. His limited ideal of the poet's function, with creative originality subordinated to technical craftsmanship, emerges from these years of apprenticeship in which the formula for success was the expression of unadventurous, conventional banalities in an agreeably harmonious form.

II

Théophile de Viau

(1590–1626)

A Monsieur de L*** sur la mort de son père, lines 25-96

Mon Dieu que le soleil est beau!
Que les froides nuits du tombeau
Font d'outrages à la nature!
La mort, grosse de déplaisirs,
De ténèbres et de soupirs,
D'os, de vers et de pourriture,
Étouffe dans la sépulture
Et nos forces, et nos désirs.

Chez elle les géants sont nains,
10 Les Mores et les Africains
Sont aussi glacés que le Scythe;
Les Dieux y tirent l'aviron:
César comme le bûcheron,
Attendant que l'on ressuscite,
Tous les jours aux bords du Cocyte
Se trouve au lever de Charon.

Tircis, vous y viendrez un jour.
Alors les grâces et l'amour
Vous quitteront sur le passage,
20 Et dedans ces royaumes vains,
Effacé du rang des humains,
Sans mouvement et sans visage,
Vous ne trouverez plus l'usage
Ni de vos yeux ni de vos mains.

Votre père est enseveli,
Et dans les noirs flots de l'oubli
Où la Parque l'a fait descendre,
Il ne sait rien de votre ennui,
Et ne fût-il mort qu'aujourd'hui,
30 Puisqu'il n'est plus qu'os et que cendre,

11

Il est aussi mort qu'Alexandre
Et vous touche aussi peu que lui.

Saturne n'a plus ses maisons
Ni ses ailes ni ses saisons,
Les destins en ont fait une ombre.
Ce grand Mars n'est-il pas détruit?
Ses faits ne sont qu'un peu de bruit,
Jupiter n'est plus qu'un feu sombre
Qui se cache parmi le nombre
40 Des petits flambeaux de la nuit.

Le cours des ruisselets errants,
La fière chute des torrents,
Les rivières, les eaux salées,
Perdront et bruit et mouvement:
Le soleil insensiblement
Les ayant toutes avalées,
Dedans les voûtes étoilées
Transportera leur élément.

Le sable, le poisson, les flots,
50 La navire,[1] les matelots,
Tritons, et nymphes, et Neptune
A la fin se verront perclus;
Sur leur dos ne se fera plus
Rouler le char de la Fortune,
Et l'influence de la lune
Abandonnera le reflux.

Les planètes s'arrêteront,
Les éléments se mêleront
En cette admirable structure
60 Dont le ciel nous laisse jouir.
Ce qu'on voit, ce qu'on peut ouïr
Passera comme une peinture:
L'impuissance de la nature
Laissera tout évanouir.

Celui qui formant le soleil
Arracha d'un profond sommeil
L'air et le feu, la terre et l'onde,
Renversera d'un coup de main

---

[1] The gender of *navire* was variable in the seventeenth century. The grammarian Ménage comments that it was more commonly feminine in poetry, because the effect was more pleasing.

La demeure du genre humain
70 Et la base où le ciel se fonde;
Et ce grand désordre du monde
Peut-être arrivera demain.

Œuvres poétiques, seconde et troisième parties,
ed. J. Streicher (Geneva, 1958), pp. 215-17

These lines form part (stanzas 4-12) of an ode not published in the author's lifetime; found among his papers after his death, the poem was first published by Scudéry in the 1632 edition of Théophile's works. It is an example of the consolatory ode, one of the commonest forms of occasional verse at the time. Although editors of Théophile do not identify 'Monsieur de L.', it seems certain that the poem is addressed to Roger de Liancour, a noble patron and protector of the poet: he is addressed as Tircis elsewhere (although Théophile also uses this conventional name to address other friends), and the death of Liancour's father in 1620 inspired at least two other poems by Théophile.

However, this is far from being a conventional poetic exercise embodying the sort of banal sentiments which one expects of the consolatory ode (cf. for instance the famous *Consolation à Monsieur du Périer*, one of several such poems written by Malherbe). Théophile has used the 'consolation' as a pretext for the development of ideas on death very different from those conventionally offered to the bereaved, ideas which bear the stamp of the intellectual milieu in which he moved. For although he too was dependent like the great majority of men of letters of his time on the favours of noble patrons, and although the pursuit of these favours inevitably made of him something of an opportunist, he was never the complete court poet of the type represented by Malherbe, and he seems to have managed to preserve a large measure of independence and intellectual integrity.[1]

Théophile was born in 1590 into a Gascon Protestant family, and arrived in Paris in about 1615 after studying at Protestant academies in France and in Holland, and a period spent travelling with the itinerant theatrical company of Valleran Leconte. These early years had given him an independent, inquiring mind, critical of conventional morality

[1] Cf. his lines on the older poet:
Malherbe a très bien fait, mais il a fait pour lui . . .
J'approuve que chacun écrive à sa façon:
J'aime sa renommée et non pas sa leçon.
Œuvres poétiques, première partie, ed. J. Streicher (Geneva, 1958), pp. 9-10.

and of religious authority, and a taste for a life of complete sensual indulgence; in Paris he was able to satisfy these inclinations as a member of a group of young men, rich noblemen and men of letters, who lived a life free of all inhibitions. Their 'libertinage de mœurs'—complete moral licence—was allied to a thoroughgoing intellectual emancipation which took the form sometimes of deism, more often of atheism, but was always systematically opposed to the established Christian religion. Unlike the representatives of what M. Pintard has called the 'libertinage érudit' of this and the next generation,[1] these free-thinkers did not keep their opinions to themselves, but flaunted their godlessness, making of it a way of life; to quote M. Antoine Adam: 'L'athéisme à cette date ressortit bien plus à la sociologie qu'à l'histoire abstraite des idées philosophiques'.[2] Not that the philosophical basis was lacking: if they had not the highminded, scholarly seriousness of a La Mothe Le Vayer or a Gassendi, Théophile and his friends had studied under liberal teachers, their minds were emancipated from the scholastic respect for intellectual authority, and their free-thinking continues a tradition revived in Renaissance Italy, which shows the influence of Lucretius and other classical exponents of Epicureanism. In 1615, it seemed possible to practise an Epicurean way of life with impunity: these *libertin* poets had friends at court, the Church was still mustering its forces to attack, and for a brief spell there flourished a literary cult which foreshadows the excesses of 'bas-romantisme' in the nineteenth century.[3] In various licentious publications—*Le Cabinet satirique* (1618), *Les Délices satiriques* (1620), *Le Parnasse satirique* (1622)—and in other collections which remained unpublished, blasphemy is to be found side by side with obscenity; and M. Adam has somewhat imaginatively portrayed the milieu in which these works were composed:

> Ces poésies sont avant tout des œuvres de clan. C'est pour les agapes du groupe, c'est pour les joyeuses réunions autour d'une table chargée de bouteilles que ces vers ont été composés. Sorte de liturgies à rebours, opposées au culte de la religion officielle. Le poète se lève, chante son couplet, les confrères le reprennent en chœur: ainsi se transmet la libre doctrine.[4]

[1] Cf. *Le Libertinage érudit dans la première moitié du XVIIe siècle* (Paris, 1943).
[2] *Théophile de Viau et la libre pensée française en 1620* (Paris, 1935), p. 127.
[3] It is interesting, in this respect, to consider the admiration shown for his namesake by Théophile Gautier, himself the author of a lugubrious collection of poems entitled *La Comédie de la mort*.
[4] Op. cit., p. 128.

In this milieu, it is evident that Théophile played a leading part; M. Adam indeed puts forward the hypothesis that in Charles Sorel's novel *Francion* (1623), which we are told was written as 'le manuel du parfait libertin',[1] the hero is an embodiment of Théophile himself, for whom the younger writer is known to have had a great admiration. However, the *libertin* group was not to remain undisturbed for long, and the year 1619 brought with it two warnings. First, the Italian free-thinker Vanini, whose *De admirandis Naturae, reginae deaeque mortalium, arcanis*, published in Paris in 1616, had had a great influence in France, was arrested at Toulouse, convicted of practising black magic, had his tongue cut out and was burnt at the stake; and secondly, Théophile himself was sentenced to exile from Paris. The official reason, given by the *Mercure de France*, was that 'on fit entendre au Roi que le poète Théophile avait fait des vers indignes d'un chrétien tant en croyance qu'en saletés', though it is probable that this was only a pretext, the real reason being political disfavour; in any case the exile lasted less than a year. From this point onwards, however, Théophile was always suspect to authority, so suspect that in 1622 he judged it prudent to abjure his Protestantism and make a formal profession of the Catholic faith.

This is the background against which the passage should be read: a climate of provocative free thought, hostile to traditional Christian teaching; at the same time, a growing awareness of the need for caution in the expression of such ideas. It is true that the poem was not published during the poet's lifetime, but if, as is most likely, it was circulated in manuscript, there was still need for prudence. The poem strikes the reader immediately by the total absence of traditional Christian thought; there is no reference to the after-life as a haven from the storm and stress of this world, and in fact this 'Consolation' offers no consolation at all.[2] It is true that certain mythological references—'[les] bords du Cocyte', 'Charon'—might imply a conventional poetic substitution of the Greek

---

[1] See the introduction to the edition by E. Roy (Paris, 1924).

[2] The following anecdote provides an interesting commentary on this aspect of the poem: 'Quelque benêt, consolant [Mme de Rohan] de la mort de M. de Soubise dont elle ne se tourmentait guère, lui dit une stance de Théophile, où il y a:

Et dans les noirs flots de l'oubli
Où la Parque l'a fait descendre,
Ne fût-il mort qu'aujourd'hui
Il est aussi mort qu'Alexandre.

Elle acheva la stance en l'interrompant:

Et *me* touche aussi peu que lui'—Tallemant des Réaux, *Historiettes*, ed. cit., I, p. 625. M. de Soubise died in 1642; the poem was well enough known to be quoted in this way.

underworld for the Christian heaven, but I think a much more significant classical allusion, in this context, is the reference to the Fates (line 27) and to Destiny (line 35). Théophile was later to deny strenuously the rumours, circulated by his Jesuit persecutors—'des imposteurs, qu'une aveugle ignorance Oppose absolument aux libertés de France'—that 'mon sens libertin Confond l'Auteur du monde avecque le Destin',[1] but there seems little doubt that that is precisely what he is doing here. If any idea of a supernatural force ruling the world is to be found in this poem, it is an idea much closer to the blind Fates of Greek mythology than to the wise Providence of Christian teaching. All mortals, from the emperor to the woodcutter, are subject to the arbitrary power of death, which offers nothing but the 'froides nuits du tombeau'.

However, it is not the purely negative evidence of *libertin* ideas in the opening stanzas of the poem—the absence of an orthodox Christian view of the after-life—which is the most provocative feature; after all, the inevitability and unpredictability of death are something of a common-place in lyric poetry. In the second half of the poem (line 25 to the end) we find the much bolder expression of a positive philosophy, reflecting the ideas prevalent in the circle to which both Liancour and Théophile himself belonged. Broadly speaking, the metaphysical basis of these ideas is the pagan naturalism which Vanini helped to propagate in France, and of which the most distinguished modern exponent had been Giordano Bruno, also burnt at the stake, at Rome, in 1600. The particular form given to the exaltation of the forces of nature varied from a vague pantheism to the much more precise system of Epicurean materialism set forth by Lucretius in his *De rerum natura*, and of which, *pace* Professor Spink,[2] there seems to be more than a hint in this passage. According to Lucretius, the universe consists of an infinite number of atoms in perpetual movement, and the world is built up from the chance agglomeration of these particles. Man is not, therefore, the *raison d'être* of an anthropocentric cosmology, but the by-product of a system of cause and effect embracing the whole universe; and his position in the world is not controlled by any divine providence, but by physical laws governing all matter. Although human beings are distinguished from other animal forms by the possession of a soul, the soul also consists of atoms, more

---

[1] 'La Plainte de Théophile à son ami Tircis' (*Œuvres poétiques*, ed. cit., II, p. 87.) The poem is addressed to Théophile's fellow-*libertin*, Des Barreaux.

[2] 'There is no trace in his works of Lucretian materialism; his naturalism is pantheistic and mystical, not mechanistic and scientific'—J. S. Spink, *French Free Thought from Gassendi to Voltaire* (London, 1960), p. 44.

rarefied than those composing the body, and is therefore equally destructible and cannot survive after death.[1]

Thus (line 30) Liancour's father, once dead, 'n'est plus qu'os et que cendre': he has returned to the material elements of which human existence is composed, and it is as if he had never been. More than that (lines 33-40), the gods themselves, products of man's invention, are equally ephemeral, and the poet imaginatively sees them, after their brief spell of man-made existence, disintegrating to rejoin the 'petits flambeaux' of the physical heavens. But more far-reaching still is the theme of the remaining verses (lines 41-72). Not only is the individual human life, or ultimately that of the whole human race, seen as ephemeral, as the physical laws of cause and effect arbitrarily terminate what they had earlier brought into being: even the material existence of the world itself is subject to these same laws. At some future moment, rivers and seas will dry up, their component atoms being absorbed into the infinity from which they came together (lines 46-8), and the planets will likewise cease to be. The poet concludes with a powerful evocation of the dis-solution of the material universe as we know it: a concept expressed not in abstract philosophical language, yet with a sufficiently suggestive use of technical terms for the underlying philosophy to emerge in a challeng-ing way. The end of the world envisaged here is a far remove from the Christian conception of the Last Judgment, in spite of the prudent phrase with which the last stanza opens; nor is the vision merely a gratuitous flight of fancy on the poet's part, comparable to Prospero's

> . . . shall dissolve,
> And like this insubstantial pageant faded,
> Leave not a rack behind.

This poem was written, of course, before the intellectual revolution brought about by the general acceptance of the Copernican system; but it does reflect (as indeed Malherbe's choice of imagery in the ode 'Pour Alcandre'[2] may perhaps also be said to reflect) a certain interest in astronomy on the part of the educated public, to whom Descartes' theory of 'tourbillons' or vortices was to make its appeal some twenty years later.

---

[1] Cf. the conclusion of a modern editor of Théophile: 'S'il est permis de grouper les sentences et les saillies dispersées dans l'œuvre du poète, on le verra partisan de la théorie atomistique, d'un matérialisme vague et mitigé, se prêtant à un compromis avec un déisme fataliste, et s'imaginant un monde composé de forces aveugles, obstinées, hostiles'—*Pyrame et Thisbé*, ed. J. Hankiss (Strasbourg, 1933), p. 9.   [2] See passage no. I and commentary.

Théophile's distinctive quality as a poet can be seen to fit in with this philosophical naturalism. The love of concrete detail which makes him such a strikingly 'pictorial' writer, in sharp contrast to the tendency towards classical abstraction already represented by Malherbe, was not a mere literary idiosyncrasy, but part of a coherent attitude to life. In his *Fragments d'une histoire comique* he wrote: 'J'aime un beau jour, des fontaines claires, l'aspect des montagnes, l'étendue d'une grande plaine, de belles forêts; l'océan, ses vagues, son calme, ses rivages; j'aime encore tout ce qui touche plus particulièrement les sens: la musique, les fleurs, les beaux habits, la chasse, les beaux chevaux, les bonnes odeurs, la bonne chère'.[1] His love of vivid imagery, as well as his fondness for the pleasures of the flesh, are part of his intense awareness of the material world about him, a world of which man forms an organic part; M. Adam points to his 'souci de maintenir l'homme dans l'univers matériel où il se meut. Chez lui', he continues, 'dans son âme et dans son œuvre, la Nature demeure'.[2]

If the expression of this Epicurean philosophy had of necessity to be somewhat guarded in 1620, persecution of the *libertins*, and of Théophile in particular, was soon to succeed in repressing such ideas altogether. The poet's profession of religious orthodoxy in 1622 was of little avail, for the same year saw the publication of *Le Parnasse satirique*, a volume which opened with a blasphemous sonnet attributed to Théophile. Though he denied responsibility for the book, it was to be the cause of one of the most celebrated trials of the century. Denounced by the Jesuit Garasse in his *Doctrine curieuse des beaux esprits de ce temps* as 'le chef de la bande athéiste',[3] Théophile was sentenced in his absence by the Paris Parlement (August 1623) to make a public 'amende honorable' and then to be burnt. The sentence was carried out in effigy, and the poet went into hiding; but in September he was arrested on his way to the

[1] Quoted by A. Adam, op. cit., p. 326.

[2] Ibid.

[3] 'J'appelle libertins nos ivrognes, moucherons de tavernes, esprits insensibles à la piété, qui n'ont d'autre Dieu que leur ventre, qui sont enrôlés en cette maudite confrérie qui s'appelle la Confrérie des Bouteilles. . . . Il est vrai que ces gens . . . ne sont pas du tout abrutis dans le vice, s'imaginent qu'il y a un Enfer, mais au reste vivent licentieusement, . . . et pour cela sont bien nommés quand on les appelle libertins, car c'est comme qui dirait apprentis de l'athéisme.

'J'appelle impies et athéistes ceux qui sont plus avancés en malice, qui ont l'impudence de proférer d'horribles blasphèmes contre Dieu, qui commettent des brutalités abominables, qui publient par sonnets leurs exécrables forfaits, qui font de Paris une Gomorrhe, qui font imprimer le *Parnasse satirique*. . . .'—Garasse, *Doctrine curieuse*. . . quoted in Sorel, *Francion*, ed. cit., I, p. viii.

frontier, brought back to Paris and thrown into prison, where he was to remain untried for two years. After several preliminary hearings, the trial finally took place in September 1625; the charges were recognised as due to Jesuit intrigues, and Théophile was acquitted, though he was sentenced to formal banishment from Paris, as was Voisin, a Jesuit ally of Garasse. Although this was a victory for free thought, the poet's imprisonment was too clear a warning to be disregarded by other *libertins*: he was soon disowned by former associates among men of letters, and only noblemen with political power, such as Montmorency, were able to offer him open support; moreover, it was a hollow victory for the poet himself, for his health was broken by his harsh imprisonment, and he lived for only a year after his release.

The arrest and trial of Théophile, and with it the discomfiture and dispersion of the militant *libertins* of 1620, are a striking illustration of the movement towards intellectual and social conformism which is such a prominent feature of seventeenth-century French history. *Libertinage* was defeated not only by the forces of religious orthodoxy, by the Jesuits and other representatives of Christian thought, but also by those political forces which were already at work, imposing a stable central authority and suppressing all manifestations of independence. The powerful nobleman, embodying to some extent the social ideal of the *libertins*, with his own entourage of emancipated men of letters, was soon to be a thing of the past,[1] and the 'official' patronage of Richelieu, attempting to exercise control over the intellectual life of the nation, was to take its place. Friends and associates of Théophile's such as Balzac and Boisrobert lost no time in renouncing their dangerous ideas,[2] and the orthodox, conformist group of writers around Malherbe was consolidated.

For a time it had appeared that the way was open for a new social ethic, based on the nature-philosophy inherited from the ancients. This ethic would, it is true, have allowed complete sexual licence—Sorel's *Francion* advances a serious claim, amidst its 'Rabelaisian' anecdotes, for the practice of 'free' love based on the infallible impulses of human

[1] Théophile's friend and patron, Montmorency, was the most exalted victim of Richelieu's statesmanlike policy of curbing the power of the great nobles. He was executed in 1632 after an abortive revolt.
[2] Sorel, too, showed a similar prudence. The 'philosophical' passages of *Francion* (1623) were toned down or expurgated in the 1626 and 1633 editions. Cf. the passage beginning 'Je semais parmi eux le plus qu'il m'était possible les enseignements de la nouvelle philosophie ...'—ed. cit., I, p. 17, l. 3.

nature—but it would also have encouraged freedom from prejudice, hypocrisy and intolerance. Indeed, as M. Adam suggests,[1] the 'break-through' of liberal, humanitarian ideas based on non-Christian philosophy which was to happen in the eighteenth century had already taken place in the case of this small band of enlightened thinkers of Théophile's generation.

What happened to the current of free thought during the century and a half which separated these early *libertins* from the generation of Diderot and the Encyclopedists? *Libertinage* certainly did not disappear, but it ceased to offer a way of life that could be practised openly and with impunity. The dangers inherent in a too flagrant defiance of moral and religious convention are illustrated by the fate of Claude Le Petit, burnt at the stake in 1662 'pour avoir fait un livre intitulé *Le Bordel des Muses*,[2] écrit *Le Moine renié* et autres compositions de vers et de prose pleines d'impiétés et de blasphèmes, contre l'honneur de Dieu, de la Vierge et de l'État'. With such frightful penalties in store for the imprudent, it is small wonder that true *libertinage* either became respectable, or went underground. On the one hand, it became more erudite, the exchange of ideas between 'professional' philosophers such as Gassendi, the inter-preter and commentator of Epicurus, Gabriel Naudé or La Mothe Le Vayer: men whose reputation as scholars and whose blameless private lives preserved them from attack; elsewhere, less erudite but still essentially private, it characterised the intellectual life of *salons* such as those of Ninon de l'Enclos and Mme de la Sablière, which provided an important link with the free thought of the next century.[3] On the other hand, *libertinage de mœurs*, in a more pejorative sense of the term, seems to have become the prerogative of a certain kind of rich nobleman, whose unprincipled pursuit of pleasure was carried out under the immunity conferred by power and privilege, or under the cloak of a hypocritical *dévotion*:[4] the 'grand seigneur méchant homme' of whom Molière has given such a convincing portrait in his *Dom Juan*.[5]

---

[1] 'La génération de 1620 a failli orienter la pensée française dans un sens hardi et nouveau. La révolution qui s'est faite dans les esprits vers 1750 aurait pu se produire 130 ans plus tôt'—op. cit., p. 431.

[2] This work appeared in 1662 with the title *Le Bordel des Muses . . . Caprices satiriques de Théophile le jeune.*

[3] See the commentaries to passages nos. X and XIII.

[4] See the commentary to passage no. XV.

[5] See particularly Dom Juan's defence of hypocrisy in Act V, scene ii. Among the most notorious examples of this social type were the chevalier de Roquelaure and the prince de Conti.

Théophile and his friends, however, represent a different, and a more attractive, kind of *libertinage*. If their Epicureanism had not the solid philosophical basis of that of the *érudits* (Théophile has been classed by one authority on the seventeenth century among the 'demi-savants'),[1] on the other hand it never amounted to unprincipled self-indulgence. The *libertinage* of 1620 had its humane and idealistic side,[2] and among its adherents there is no more sympathetic figure than that of Théophile, whom Professor Boase has felicitously described as 'a kind of seventeenth-century Oscar Wilde'.[3]

[1] See A. M. Boase, *The Fortunes of Montaigne* (London, 1935), pp. 139 ff.
[2] Cf. *Francion*, ed. cit., II, p. 117.
[3] Op. cit., p. 143.

III

Guez de Balzac

(1597–1654)

Letter to Monseigneur le cardinal de Richelieu, 26th September 1622

Monseigneur,

Après avoir fermé ma lettre, il a passé ici un courrier, de qui j'ai appris que le Pape vous avait fait Cardinal. Je ne doute point que cette nouvelle n'ait été reçue de vous avec aussi peu d'émotion que si elle vous eût été indifférente, et qu'ayant élevé votre esprit au-dessus des choses du monde, vous ne les regardiez toutes d'un même visage. Néanmoins puisqu'en ceci le bien public se rencontre avec votre intérêt, et que pour l'amour de vous l'Église se réjouit jusque dans les prisons de l'Angleterre, il n'y a point d'apparence que vous vous priviez d'un contentement qui est aussi chaste que ceux qui se reçoivent au Ciel, et qui procède de la même cause. Les gens de bien,
10 Monseigneur, en une saison telle que celle-ci doivent désirer les grandes dignités comme des moyens nécessaires pour entreprendre de grandes choses. S'ils ne le font, outre que Dieu leur demandera compte de ses grâces, qui leur ont été inutiles, le monde a sujet de se plaindre qu'ils le laissent en proie aux méchants, et que le désir de leur repos leur fait abandonner la cause publique. C'est pour vous dire, Monseigneur, que vous devez réserver votre humilité aux actions qui se passent entre Dieu et vous, mais qu'au reste vous ne sauriez avoir trop de bien ni de crédit, puisqu'il faut que la prudence soit obéie, et qu'il y a des vertus qui ne peuvent être exercées par les pauvres. Je suis donc très-aise de vous voir
20 aujourd'hui en un lieu, d'où vous remplirez toute la terre de lumière, et où votre seul exemple aura tant d'autorité qu'il pourra faire revenir la face de l'Église à la pureté de son enfance. Certainement s'il y a apparence d'attendre ce bien, et de voir les esprits des rebelles persuadés, comme nous voyons leurs villes forcées, vous êtes celui de qui nous le devons espérer, et qui êtes capable d'achever les victoires des rois par la ruine de l'hérésie. Toute la chrétienté vous demande à cet effet vos ouvrages pour une dernière instruction, et la paix générale des consciences. Et moi qui cherche il y a si longtemps l'idée de l'éloquence, sans que j'en trouve parmi nous qui ne soit ou fausse ou imparfaite, je me promets que vous la

22

30 ramènerez telle qu'elle était, quand à Rome elle accusait les tyrans, et qu'elle défendait les provinces opprimées. Encore que la pourpre soit une chose fort éclatante, elle recevra du lustre de cette qualité, qui commande partout où elle est, et qui particulièrement est si propre au gouvernement des âmes, que c'est la seule puissance à qui elles veulent se soumettre. Si je puis espérer, Monseigneur, d'être connu d'un autre siècle que le nôtre, et que mon nom aille jusqu'à la postérité, elle saura que cette considération m'obligea premièrement de rechercher votre connaissance, et que vous ayant ouï parler, vous gagnâtes si absolument mon esprit et mon affection, que depuis ce temps-là je vous regardai toujours comme un homme
40 extraordinaire, et fus passionnément, Monseigneur,

Votre très-humble et très-

fidèle serviteur,

Balzac.

Les Premières Lettres de Guez de Balzac, ed. H. Bibas
and K. T. Butler (Paris, 1933-4), I, pp. 28-30

The most remarkable thing about Balzac's position in seventeenth-century literature is the tremendous prestige that he acquired at an early age through the medium of a genre which has normally conferred distinction only posthumously, if at all, on those who practise it. Although later in his life he was to publish more sustained treatises on political theory, administration and moral philosophy, he had made his reputation as a letter-writer by the time he was thirty (the first volume of his collected letters was published in 1624), and it was on his letters, and particularly on his epistolary style, that his fame continued to be based. He was known as 'l'Épistolier', 'l'unico eloquente', and the publication of each volume of his letters soon became an event of the greatest literary importance. Ménage tells of the impatience with which these publications were awaited:

> Rien n'est égal à l'empressement que témoignait le public, pour avoir des lettres de M. de Balzac, lorsqu'il s'en imprimait de nouvelles. C'était le présent le plus agréable que les galants pussent faire à leurs maîtresses. La galanterie, comme à présent, n'étouffait pas le goût de la littérature; c'était à qui en aurait des premiers, et les libraires savaient très bien profiter de cette impatience du public.[1]

---

[1] *Menagiana*, quoted by G. Guillaumie, *J.-L. Guez de Balzac et la prose française* (Paris, 1927), p. 3.

And this was no passing fashion: throughout his life, Balzac was over-whelmed with letters from correspondents, known and unknown, who hoped to elicit the favour of a reply from the celebrated master of the epistolary art. In 1636 he complained in a letter to Chapelain that his letter-writing was becoming 'une prostitution à tous les jours, à laquelle je n'ai garde de m'abandonner'; and he continues:

> Il faut seulement qu'à l'avenir mes compliments soient un peu plus rares. La plupart ne m'écrivent des lettres que pour montrer des réponses. Et ainsi je suis le martyr de leur vanité, et de cette fâcheuse réputation que vous et mes autres bons amis m'avez donnée.[1]

However, it should be emphasised that the kind of letter with which Balzac gained this remarkable reputation was not the spontaneous personal communication that we associate, for instance, with Mme de Sévigné, but a most carefully composed, highly polished piece of writing; Boileau, indeed, was to declare that Balzac's style, with its affect-ation and pomposity, was quite unsuitable for the genre: 'On s'est aperçu tout d'un coup que l'art où il s'est employé toute sa vie était l'art qu'il savait le moins; je veux dire l'art de faire une lettre'.[2] But there is no doubt at all that the epistolary form was deliberately chosen by the aspiring young writer as a means of assuring a widespread literary reputation among a discerning public. This distinction was drawn, indeed, by his friend Ogier, who had nothing but scorn for those authors who published volumes of purely private letters, 'croyant qu'il importait fort à la postérité de ne pas perdre une seule de leurs sottises et de savoir ce qui s'était passé entre leur femme et leurs domestiques'.[3] The positive aims of the letter-writer are set out more fully by the publicist Silhon, author of a dedication to Cardinal Richelieu which accompanied the 1627 edition of Balzac's letters:

> C'est un livre, Monseigneur, où vous ne trouverez rien de commun que le titre; où en entretenant un particulier, M. de Balzac fait des leçons à tout le monde; et où parmi la beauté des compliments, et les gentillesses de la raillerie, il traite souvent des matières les plus relevées, et des secrets les plus importants de la philosophie. Je n'entends pas de cette querelleuse, qui méprise les vérités nécessaires pour chercher les inutiles; qui ne

---

[1] Quoted by G. Mongrédien, *Les Grands Comédiens du XVIIe siècle* (Paris, 1927), p. 45.
[2] Quoted by F. E. Sutcliffe, *Guez de Balzac et son temps* (Paris, 1959), p. 16.
[3] Quoted by Guillaumie, op. cit., p. 62.

saurait exercer l'entendement sans irriter les passions, ni parler de la modération sans se troubler, et mettre l'âme en désordre; mais bien de celle-là par l'étude de laquelle Périclès s'est rendu autrefois le maître d'Athènes, et Épaminondas le premier homme de la Grèce; qui tempère les mœurs des particuliers, qui règle les devoirs des princes, et apporte nécessairement la félicité à tous les états où elle commande.[1]

Balzac had been initiated at an early age into political life, in the service first of the duc d'Épernon and then of the latter's son, the cardinal de la Valette, who had left him in Rome in order to obtain up-to-date information about current affairs. The Cardinal's instructions 'de ne rien laisser passer dans le monde sans lui en écrire son sentiment et de faire des sujets de lettres de toutes les affaires publiques'[2] serve as a reminder that in an age when the newspaper was still unknown—Théophraste Renaudot did not begin the publication of his *Gazette* until 1631—private or semi-private letters provided the only means of keeping in touch with the latest news. It was Balzac's letters to La Valette which laid the foundation of his literary reputation, and the eighteen months that he spent in Italy (January 1621 to August 1622) had a considerable effect on the formation of his prose style: he was able to meet and discuss with Italian humanists, and to develop his feeling for the simplicity and elegance of the best Latin and Italian authors. Years later he was to write to a relative of his, who had just returned from Rome: 'Vous vous êtes acquis de nouvelles grâces au pays de Cicéron, et l'air de Rome a purgé votre esprit de toutes les pensées du vulgaire'.[3] A purity of style worthy of the greatest classical prose-writers, and as regards subject-matter, the ideal wisdom of the ancients applied to contemporary issues: this is what earned for Balzac's letters the fulsome praise of his fellow-writers, and the eager following of a much wider public. 'Désormais', says M. Adam, speaking of the 1624 edition, 'une lettre de Balzac sera reçue dans les cercles de Paris avec la révérence qu'on accorde aux encycliques des souverains pontifes'.[4]

Nevertheless, flattering as this public acclaim must have been to the young writer, it is clear that Balzac was not satisfied with a purely literary success, and that he wanted to have a hand in shaping the affairs

[1] *Les Premières Lettres de Guez de Balzac* (1618-27), ed. H. Bibas and K. T. Butler (Paris, 1933-4), II, p. 11.
[2] Quoted by Guillaumie, op. cit., p. 63.
[3] Ibid., p. 67.
[4] *Histoire de la littérature française au XVIIe siècle* (Paris, 1949-56), I, p. 243.

of the world instead of merely commenting on them. Indeed, it is most
likely that at the time when the letter with which we are concerned was
written, he was already aspiring to play an influential part in political
life. The country was still far from settled in 1622, after the minority of
Louis XIII. The young King had asserted himself in 1619 with the
assassination of the unpopular favourite of the Queen Mother, Concini,
and had himself taken an active part in government since that date; but
the members of his Council were elderly and incompetent. Relations
with the Queen Mother remained strained, even after the Treaty of
Angoulême in 1619 and the Peace of Angers in 1620; Marie de Médicis
had the support of certain powerful nobles, as well as of the capable and
ambitious Bishop of Luçon, Richelieu. Richelieu had first achieved
prominence at the time of the States-General in 1614: Concini had
brought him into the Council, but on the latter's overthrow he had
been banished to a provincial exile at Avignon. After this temporary
eclipse, he had been recalled in 1619 in order to bring about the reconciliation between Louis and his mother, with the promise of a
Cardinal's hat as a reward; though owing to the King's lukewarm
support, this was not forthcoming until 1622. In spite of his ability,
Richelieu was distrusted by the King, and he was disliked by the other
ministers; it was not until 1624, after the death of Luynes and the
failure of La Vieuville, that he was again admitted to the Council.

The account of Richelieu's influence on men of letters, and on French
intellectual life generally in the 1630s, is familiar enough, particularly
his encouragement of the theatre and the role he played in the formation
and early activities of the Academy. By this time he was acknowledged
as the virtual ruler of the country, and was established in an impregnable
position, from which he was able to dispense patronage and disfavour.
Under the Cardinal's influence, a climate of political and intellectual
orthodoxy prevailed,[1] and this decade was to be if not the most glorious,
at least the most stable and settled decade of the century.

But in the early 1620s, the intellectual life of the country had not yet
developed along these lines, nor was Richelieu's own political position
at all assured. Later, the Cardinal could call on the services of a whole
team of writers faithful to his interests, under the orders of Boisrobert,
his secretary: men such as Silhon (Balzac's editor) or Hay du Chastelet,
who has been called the 'véritable chef d'un bureau de presse'.[2] But

[1] See the commentaries to passages nos. I and II.
[2] G. Mongrédien, *La Vie littéraire au XVIIe siècle* (Paris, 1947), p. 52.

Boisrobert came into contact with Richelieu only in 1623, and Silhon in 1624; and the Cardinal did not really become a magnet for venal pens until his political power was assured. Balzac's relations with Richelieu were of a rather different nature: if he sought him out in 1622, and made a bid to associate his own fortunes with those of the new Cardinal—for he was perceptive enough to see that the future lay with him—it is nevertheless probable that Balzac could never have become one of Richelieu's team of mercenary writers. His was a conventional and unadventurous mind compared to that of his contemporary Théophile, for instance, but he had a considerable pride and self-esteem— Théophile was to accuse him of trying to '[traiter] d'égal avec des cardinaux et des maréchaux de France'[1] and he was later to express a marked scorn for Richelieu's band of hack writers. He wrote of Silhon, for example: 'Il a l'âme d'un rebelle, et rend les soumissions d'un esclave'; and of Hay du Chastelet and Sirmond, another paid propagandist:

> J'aime mieux ruiner mes petites espérances que de renoncer entièrement à ma liberté et faire le Sirmond ou le Chastelet.[2]

Whatever the precise nature of Balzac's 'petites espérances' in 1622, it is most likely that his attempts to bring himself to the attention of the new Cardinal had a loftier end in view.

He was already known to Richelieu before his journey to Italy: the duc d'Épernon and the cardinal de la Valette were both of the Queen Mother's party. He had written him a flattering letter from Rome, and one of his first acts on returning to France was to pay court in another letter to the man whom he saw as certain, sooner or later, to regain a position of power and influence. He wrote on 4th September, probably from Balzac, his property in the Angoumois, where ill-health forced him to retire immediately on arriving back in France instead of going to pay his respect in person; and the tone of this letter leaves no doubt as to the author's hopes of benefiting from Richelieu's rise to power:

[1] Quoted by Sutcliffe, op. cit., p. 17.
[2] Ibid., pp. 37–8. An instance of the kind of services rendered by these writers is provided by the account of the trial of Marillac, one of the conspirators in the Journée des Dupes (1620) who was beheaded in 1632 and whose death was widely attributed by contemporaries to the personal animosity of Richelieu. Hay du Chastelet, appointed one of Marillac's judges, had so little respect for the independence of the judiciary that he published a defamatory libel against the accused during the course of the trial. This caused such an outcry that he was arrested and imprisoned; 'mais il n'y resta pas longtemps: le Cardinal avait besoin de lui'— B. Hauréau in *Nouvelle Biographie générale* (Paris, 1863), art. 'Chastelet'.

Les armées ayant été défaites, il s'en remet de nouvelles sur pied, et on peut équiper une seconde flotte après que la première s'est perdue. Mais s'il venait faute de vous, Monseigneur, le monde ne durerait assez pour réparer une telle perte, et il faudrait que le Roi le pleurât au milieu même de ses triomphes. Il a bien un royaume qui ne se saurait épuiser d'hommes; la guerre lui fait tous les jours des capitaines, le nombre des juges n'est guère moindre que celui des criminels. C'est seulement de gens sages, et capables de gouverner les états, que la stérilité est grande; et sans mentir, pour en voir un pareil à vous il est besoin que toute la nature travaille, et que Dieu le promette longtemps aux hommes avant que de le faire naître.[1]

This is the letter referred to in line 1 of the text with which we are more closely concerned; the apparent urgency and spontaneity of the opening sentence: 'Après avoir fermé ma lettre, il a passé ici un courrier, de qui j'ai appris . . .' does not necessarily indicate that the dates given to the two letters, 4th and 26th September, are misleading. Like Malherbe's 'occasional' odes, Balzac's letters are too carefully worked and polished to constitute a spontaneous comment on the events to which they relate; as his champion Ogier admits:

S'il ne voulait disputer de l'éloquence avec toute la Grèce et toute l'Italie, il ne vieillirait pas comme il fait sur un discours de trois feuilles, ni n'emploie-rait une semaine toute entière à achever une période.[2]

For his part, Richelieu was prepared to encourage the young writer, but it is highly unlikely that he ever thought of him in any other light than as a skilful polemist whose services he might hire. Balzac describes their first relations, in 1619, in a passage from the *Entretiens* (a work in which he regularly refers to himself in the third person: here he is 'votre voisin'):

Ce Monsieur de Luçon avait vu je ne sais quoi de votre voisin, qui lui avait, disait-il, chatouillé l'esprit, et qui l'obligea de rechercher son amitié. Ayant apporté d'Avignon un désir passionné de le connaître, il lui fit une infinité de caresses à Angoulême. Il le traita d' 'illustre', d' 'homme rare', de 'personne extraordinaire'. Et l'ayant un jour prié à dîner, il dit à force gens de qualité qui étaient à table avec lui: 'Voilà un homme' (cet homme n'avait alors que vingt et deux ans) 'à qui il faudra faire du bien, quand nous le pourrons, et il faudra commencer par une abbaye de dix mille livres de rente'.[3]

---

[1] *Premières Lettres* . . ., I, pp. 6–7.
[2] Quoted by Bibas and Butler, ed. cit., I, p. 36.
[3] *Premières Lettres* . . ., I, pp. 11–12.

Richelieu's reply to the two letters of September 1622 is in similar vein; thanking Balzac for his flattering message, he continues:

Si, en servant l'Église et ceux à qui je dois cette dignité, il se présente occasion de vous témoigner combien j'estime et la bonne volonté que vous avez en tout ce qui me touche, et votre mérite, vous avouerez que je suis plus d'effet que de paroles.[1]

But neither then nor at a later date was any rich benefice forthcoming. Perhaps Richelieu did not find it prudent to employ a writer who had taken sides so uncompromisingly in a conflict which he hoped was now past history; perhaps he thought less highly of Balzac's political judgment than of his epistolary style; perhaps he had detected the touch of proud independence in his character. In particular, there was the question of Balzac's independence with regard to religious matters. At the time of Théophile's trial, he was to define his own position on the one hand by letters deploring the aberrations of the poet, but on the other by a much more emphatic denunciation (in the *Lettre à Hydaspe*) of Théophile's principal enemy Garasse.[2] Professor Sutcliffe suggests that this attack on the Jesuit may well have earned Balzac Richelieu's support, for it agreed with the Gallican policy of the Cardinal's 'parti français', his desire to counter the political influence of Rome. But Garasse's reply (*Réponse du Sieur Hydaspe au Sieur Balzac*, 1624) and Goulu's attack (*Lettres de Phyllarque à Ariste*, 1627-8) were to raise again the question of Balzac's orthodoxy; and by 1627-8, as Professor Sutcliffe shows, the position was no longer the same; opposition to Richelieu's policy tied his hand, and forced him to make concessions to the Ultramontane interests represented in France by the Jesuits, the *dévots* and the 'parti espagnol'.[3] It is clear that Balzac was never a systematic freethinker, and the term 'libres propos' might perhaps more aptly be applied to his religious views than the term 'libre pensée'. His letters from Rome show him to have had few illusions about the Papacy, and he habitually treated religious matters with an air of levity. At the same time, he was too cautious to risk offending authority, and in the profession of orthodoxy which he made at the time of Théophile's arrest, he prudently describes himself as a man 'qui ne veut rien croire

---

[1] Letter of October 1622 in *Lettres . . . et papiers d'État du Cardinal Richelieu*, ed. M. Avenel (Paris, 1853), I, p. 735.
[2] See the commentary to passage no. II.
[3] Op. cit., p. 85.

de plus véritable que ce qu'il a appris de sa mère et de sa nourrice'.[1] But the stigma of early *libertin* associations remained: Garasse referred to 'un certain air de libertinage qui anime toutes vos épîtres';[2] and it is possible that this carried enough weight to shake the Cardinal's confidence in Balzac's dependability. At all events, whatever the reason for Richelieu's cautious response to his advances, Balzac was to spend virtually the rest of his life in semi-retirement in the provinces, with his political ambitions unfulfilled.

When we turn to the passage under discussion, however, it is easy to see to what extent it is inspired by hopes of personal advancement. After the misleading appearance of spontaneity in the opening sentence, the remainder of the letter is written in a measured, even a sententious style: Balzac is evidently bent on demonstrating his own statesmanlike views, as well as his devotion to the Cardinal's interests. It is worth noting that the passage from 'Les gens de bien . . . ' to ' . . . par les pauvres' (lines 9-19) appears again in a later letter: a proof of the contrived and self-conscious nature of Balzac's epistolary art.[3] It is the passage on the campaign against the Huguenots which particularly demonstrates his statesmanlike qualities; though the manner in which his views on religious matters are expressed suggests an aptitude for tact and diplomacy rather than sincerity of conviction.

Apart from conflict between the King's party and that of the Queen Mother, internal peace was disturbed round about 1620 by sedition and rebellion on the part of the Protestant minority; armed revolt broke out in 1621, and although the Huguenots' army was soon driven back into their strongholds of Montauban and La Rochelle, their strength in the kingdom as a whole constituted a serious threat to the unity of the State, for it was always possible that they would form an alliance with a foreign power, just as they had already taken sides with Marie de Médicis and the nobles. This was pre-eminently a political issue, and Richelieu's policy towards the Huguenots was dictated not by ideological ends but by political expediency: French Protestantism was not to be tolerated, because it set up a 'State within a State', but the Cardinal was ready enough to form an alliance with Protestants abroad when it suited his purpose; during the Valtelline affair of 1624-5, for instance, he supported the Protestant Grisons against Catholic Spain and the

---

[1] Letter of September 1623 to Bouthillier, Bishop of Aire (*Premières Lettres . . .*, I, p. 37).
[2] Quoted by Sutcliffe, op. cit., p. 82.
[3] See *Premières Lettres*, I, p. 29.

Vatican. There were plenty of faithful Catholics at this date, no doubt, who were working and praying for the extirpation of the Protestant heresy on orthodox religious grounds, because they sincerely wished for a reunited Christendom—this was after all the height of the Counter-Reformation—but to present Richelieu's campaign against the Huguenots as an attempt to 'faire revenir la face de l'Église à la pureté de son enfance', in answer to the prayers of 'toute la chrétienté', was to turn a deliberately blind eye to his real motives.

It is not a case, moreover, of Balzac's attributing to Richelieu his own religious zeal, for, as we have seen, he was at this time far from being a devout Catholic, and there is every reason to believe that in this matter he was just as much a pragmatist as the minister he hoped to serve. His prudent conservatism in religious matters can be seen in his letters to La Valette on the subject of the campaign against the Huguenots, and in any case he was realist enough in political affairs to see how the security of France was threatened by the existence of a powerful Huguenot minority. He wrote to La Valette, in a letter which bears the same date as the letter to Richelieu that we are considering:

> Quand je demande la paix, je la demande sous les conditions que je m'en vais dire. C'est à savoir, qu'on remette toutes choses en l'état où elles étaient du temps de Louis XII; que toutes les villes de ce royaume soient villes de sûreté pour les gens de bien; que tous les sujets du Roi s'appellent d'un même nom; qu'il n'y ait plus de ministres que ceux de l'État; que les nouveautés ne soient plus reçues que pour les couleurs, et la façon des habillements; que le peuple laisse entre les mains de ses supérieurs la liberté, la religion et le bien public; et que du gouvernement légitime et de la parfaite obéissance il naisse cette félicité que les politiques cherchent, et qui est la fin de la vie civile[1]

and again, on the rumour of a peace too favourable to the Huguenots:

> Je ne sais si le Roi ne se réserve point quelque pensée intérieure pour achever ses desseins par d'autres moyens que ceux qui sont connus du monde; mais je sais bien qu'il ne saurait faire changer de naturel à l'hérésie, et que quoiqu'il la flatte, elle sera toujours ennemie de son autorité, et rebelle à ses commandements. Tout le temps qui s'est passé depuis la naissance de cette nouvelle opinion jusqu'à cette heure a plutôt été un interrègne, et une suspension de la puissance légitime, que la véritable suite de l'ancien gouvernement de nos pères.[2]

---

[1] Ibid., I, p. 105.　　　　[2] Ibid., I, p. 165.

The thinking of Balzac's contemporaries was so conditioned by half
a century or more of civil strife, and by the very terms of the Edict of
Nantes itself, which made of the Huguenots a political power to be
reckoned with even in a time of peace, that any notion of genuine
co-existence was quite unacceptable. The majority of Frenchmen were
neither sympathetic to the Reformed religion, nor particularly fervent
in their devotion to Catholicism, but were willing to profess the religion
of their fathers, guided above all by a feeling for the political well-being
of their country. Richelieu in particular was known to support a Gallican,
nationalist policy (the Grâce d'Alais, which put an end to the war
against the Huguenots in 1629, was to show a generous measure of
religious tolerance, for, once their political power was broken, the
Protestants were allowed freedom of worship and full civil rights). Why,
then, should Balzac, in the passage under discussion, present a wholly
political issue as if it were a religious crusade, dressing it up in the
edifying phraseology of a pious idealism?

The answer is that already, at the time it was written, the letter was
destined for publication: hence the tendency to idealise and embellish
which characterises it throughout. Balzac is paying determined court to
the minister, of whose power and influence the news of the long-awaited
Cardinal's hat had just brought significant confirmation. His flattery is
not too blatant, however: it takes Richelieu's capabilities largely for
granted, and praises him, more subtly, for his disinterestedness, other-
worldliness and spirituality. Just as in the opening lines the Cardinal is
deemed to be above the honours and glories of this world, so also in his
campaign against the Huguenots he is given the exalted motives
appropriate to a Prince of the Church; he is presented as a defender of
the universal faith, not as an astute politician trying to unite a divided
France.

The last section of the letter contains a more conventionally fulsome
kind of flattery. It is true that Richelieu appears to have had a reputation
for eloquence: Tallemant writes that, at the States-General in 1614, 'il
fit quelques harangues qu'on trouva admirables; on ne s'y connaissait
guère alors';[1] but Balzac's assertion that he found his own inspiration in
the Cardinal's oratory, and that he would owe any reputation he
acquired to his example, is too obviously an empty compliment. It is
turned, however, with characteristic elegance: the balanced phrases,

---

[1] *Historiettes*, ed. cit., II, p. 234.

the abundance of abstractions, the discreet classical allusion, make this passage agreeably harmonious reading, like the rest of the letter.

We can appreciate what it was about Balzac's style which so impressed his contemporaries: with his ear for rhythms and cadences, his avoidance of pedantry and other forms of affectation, and his judicious use of the example of antiquity, he created a harmonious prose style which corresponded to the contemporary achievement of Malherbe in verse. Even Tallemant, elsewhere very critical of Balzac, says:

> Il est certain que nous n'avions rien vu d'approchant en France, et que tous ceux qui ont bien écrit en prose depuis, et qui écriront bien à l'avenir en notre langue, lui en auront l'obligation.[1]

But like Malherbe's, Balzac's was a style which was best suited to the elegant expression of commonplace ideas, and once the prestige of his style was no longer a novelty, there proved to be really little to sustain his reputation in the eyes of later generations. From a short-term point of view, his choice of the epistolary form was no doubt shrewd enough: he reached a wider public, and made a more immediate impact, than he would have done with the more sustained formal treatise. But there is the reverse of the medal to consider too: the slightness of the letter-form, and the deliberately impersonal flavour imparted by his search for eloquence and purity of style, meant that his appeal was relatively short-lived. In justice, it should be said that the renewed interest taken in recent years in the times whose events, ideas and attitudes of mind Balzac's letters reflect, has led to a reappraisal of the substance of these letters, which has not been unfavourable to their author.[2] But as regards his style, whatever his apologists may have said in their enthusiasm for the manner in which Balzac chose to use the epistolary form, it is the letter-writers who leave behind them a personal, idiosyncratic record who make a more lasting appeal to posterity.

[1] Ibid., I, p. 42.
[2] See Sutcliffe, op. cit., pp. 7, 257.

IV

Rotrou

(1609–50)

Le Véritable Saint-Genest, lines 1287–1372

GENEST
Et vous, chers compagnons de la basse fortune,
Qui m'a rendu la vie avecque vous commune,
Marcelle, et vous Sergeste, avec qui tant de fois
J'ai du Dieu des chrétiens scandalisé les lois,
Si je puis vous prescrire un avis salutaire,
Cruels, adorez-en jusqu'au moindre mystère,
Et cessez d'attacher avec de nouveaux clous
Un Dieu qui sur la croix daigne mourir pour vous;
Mon cœur, illuminé d'une grâce céleste . . .

MARCELLE
10 Il ne dit pas un mot du couplet qui lui reste.

SERGESTE
Comment, se préparant avecque tant de soin . . .

LENTULE, *regardant derrière la tapisserie*
Holà, qui tient la pièce?

GENEST
           Il n'en est plus besoin.
Dedans cette action, où le Ciel s'intéresse,
Un ange tient la pièce, un ange me redresse:
Un ange, par son ordre, a comblé mes souhaits,
Et de l'eau du baptême effacé mes forfaits.
Ce monde périssable et sa gloire frivole
Est une comédie où j'ignorais mon rôle.
J'ignorais de quel feu mon cœur devait brûler;
20 Le démon me dictait quand Dieu voulait parler;
Mais, depuis que le soin d'un esprit angélique
Me conduit, me redresse et m'apprend ma réplique,

34

J'ai corrigé mon rôle, et le démon confus,
M'en voyant mieux instruit, ne me suggère plus.
J'ai pleuré mes péchés, le Ciel a vu mes larmes ;
Dedans cette action il a trouvé des charmes,
M'a départi sa grâce, est mon approbateur,
Me propose des prix, et m'a fait son acteur.

LENTULE
Quoiqu'il manque au sujet, jamais il ne hésite.

GENEST
30 Dieu m'apprend sur-le-champ ce que je vous récite,
Et vous m'entendez mal, si dans cette action
Mon rôle passe encor pour une fiction.

DIOCLÉTIEN
Votre désordre enfin force ma patience :
Songez-vous que ce jeu se passe en ma présence ?
Et puis-je rien comprendre au trouble où je vous voi ?

GENEST
Excusez-les, Seigneur, la faute en est à moi ;
Mais mon salut dépend de cet illustre crime :
Ce n'est plus Adrien, c'est Genest qui s'exprime ;
Ce jeu n'est plus un jeu, mais une vérité
40 Où par mon action je suis représenté,
Où moi-même, l'objet et l'acteur de moi-même,
Purgé de mes forfaits par l'eau du saint baptême,
Qu'une céleste main m'a daigné conférer,
Je professe une loi que je dois déclarer.
Écoutez donc, Césars, et vous troupes romaines,
La gloire et la terreur des puissances humaines,
Mais faibles ennemis d'un pouvoir souverain
Qui foule aux pieds l'orgueil et le sceptre romain :
Aveuglé de l'erreur dont l'enfer vous infecte,
50 Comme vous des chrétiens j'ai détesté la secte,
Et si peu que mon art pouvait exécuter,
Tout mon heur consistait à les persécuter :
Pour les fuir et chez vous suivre l'idolâtrie,
J'ai laissé mes parents, j'ai quitté ma patrie,
Et fait choix à dessein d'un art peu glorieux
Pour mieux les diffamer et les rendre odieux :
Mais, par une bonté qui n'a point de pareille,
Et par une incroyable et soudaine merveille

Dont le pouvoir d'un Dieu peut seul être l'auteur,
60 Je deviens leur rival de leur persécuteur,
Et soumets à la loi que j'ai tant réprouvée
Une âme heureusement de tant d'écueils sauvée:
Au milieu de l'orage où m'exposait le sort,
Un ange par la main m'a conduit dans le port,
M'a fait sur un papier voir mes fautes passées
Par l'eau qu'il me versait à l'instant effacées;
Et cette salutaire et céleste liqueur,
Loin de me refroidir, m'a consumé le cœur.
Je renonce à la haine et déteste l'envie
70 Qui m'a fait des chrétiens persécuter la vie;
Leur créance est ma foi, leur espoir est le mien;
C'est leur Dieu que j'adore; enfin je suis chrétien.
Quelque effort qui s'oppose en l'ardeur qui m'enflamme,
Les intérêts du corps cèdent à ceux de l'âme.
Déployez vos rigueurs, brûlez, coupez, tranchez:
Mes maux seront encor moindres que mes péchés.
Je sais de quel repos cette peine est suivie,
Et ne crains point la mort qui conduit à la vie.
J'ai souhaité longtemps d'agréer à vos yeux;
80 Aujourd'hui je veux plaire à l'empereur des cieux;
Je vous ai divertis, j'ai chanté vos louanges;
Il est temps maintenant de réjouir les anges,
Il est temps de prétendre à des prix immortels,
Il est temps de passer du théâtre aux autels.
Si je l'ai mérité, qu'on me mène au martyre:
Mon rôle est achevé, je n'ai plus rien à dire.

Le Véritable Saint-Genest, ed. R. W. Ladborough
(Cambridge, 1954), pp. 48-50

This extract forms the climax to Rotrou's 'tragédie chrétienne', *Le Véritable Saint-Genest*, produced at the Hôtel de Bourgogne in 1645 and published two years later. Genest is the leader of a troupe of travelling players who are engaged by the Emperor Diocletian to give a performance of a play concerning the recent conversion and martyrdom of Adrien, one of the Emperor's officers formerly most zealous in the persecution of Christians. While he is rehearsing the role beforehand, Genest experiences a premonitory visitation of divine Grace; and during the actual performance, in the scene (Act IV, scene vii) from which this passage is taken, he departs from the text and begins to speak in his own voice, inspired, to the bewilderment of his fellow-actors and the Emperor's irritation. By a miraculous transformation his representation of Adrien's conversion has become the enactment and proclamation of his own. It remains for the play to close with the actor's martyrdom.

It is only in what we may call the 'Classical' period proper, from 1660 or so onwards, when dramatists were influenced by the inhibiting effect of the 'bienséances' as well as by the hardening of the Church's attitude against the theatre generally, that there is a virtual absence of plays on religious subjects. Racine's two Biblical plays (which in any case were written for private performance, not for the public theatre[1]) stand almost alone in the second half of the century, but the earlier brief flowering of distinguished religious drama in the years 1641-5 (which saw the performance of Corneille's *Polyeucte* and *Théodore* as well as Rotrou's play) had behind it an unbroken tradition of vigorous, if mediocre, plays. *Polyeucte* and *Saint-Genest* are examples of a genre nearly as old as the theatre in France itself, a genre whose history is intimately bound up with the role of the theatre in the life of the people throughout the Middle Ages. If *Polyeucte*, despite this, is one of the first masterpieces of the new neo-classical tragedy, *Saint-Genest* on the other hand still looks back in many ways to the popular tradition of the miracle play.

By the middle of the sixteenth century, the mystery and miracle plays had attracted the censure of both Catholics and Protestants. The excessive development of the familiar, popular element that they contained alongside the more edifying subject-matter explains their disrepute in the eyes of the Catholic Church; while they were condemned by the Protestants because the attention paid to the miracles of the Virgin and saints smacked of idolatry. After the production of sacred dramas of this type by the Confrérie de la Passion[2] had been banned in 1548, religious subjects still continued to be used by authors of the new form of serious 'tragedy'. While Protestant writers preferred Biblical subjects, Catholic playwrights continued the hagiological tradition of medieval drama; and the Counter-Reformation saw the production, in Paris and in the provinces, of a number of 'tragédies chrétiennes' on the lives of saints both well-known and obscure. And whereas 'la tragédie biblique'

[1] See the commentary to passage no. XVIII.
[2] See the commentary to passage no. V.

—which was in any case frequently bookish and erudite—lent itself more easily to a regular, Aristotelian form, 'la tragédie chrétienne' still inclined in part to the edification of a popular audience by means of spectacle, and thus tended to be episodic and irregular.

Thus, Baro's *Saint-Eustache*, an example of the genre probably performed in 1639 but not published until ten years later, is a most eventful and colourful treatment of the life and martyrdom of that saint. Its action covers many years, and among the incidents portrayed on stage are a storm, a shipwreck, children carried off by a lion and a wolf, a furnace in the form of a bronze bull for the sacrifice of Christians, and divine retribution on an unsympathetic character in the shape of a thunderbolt. With all this, there is an idyllic pastoral element, for Baro had been secretary to the novelist d'Urfé, and had himself completed *L'Astrée* after his master's death. Admittedly, the play is not called a tragedy, but a 'poème dramatique'. 'En réalité', says one historian of seventeenth-century religious drama, 'c'est une espèce d'opéra, moins la musique . . . une série de tableaux imparfaitement liés'.[1] This play, performed after *Le Cid* and published on the eve of the Fronde, is a good illustration of the way in which popular taste resisted the tendency towards simplicity, both of subject and of form, represented by the new psychological tragedy.

Rotrou's play does not make nearly as many concessions to popular taste for the spectacular: the hero's martyrdom is not shown on stage, but narrated by a messenger, and for the most part the events leading up to it are represented less by means of spectacle than by argument and discussion. Nevertheless, one has only to compare *Saint-Genest* with *Polyeucte* to see how much freer is the aesthetic governing it. Not only is Rotrou's imagery more vivid and colourful than Corneille's, his language more concrete, his style less polished, but his plot lacks the unity and concentration of that of *Polyeucte*, and the tone of *Saint-Genest* is altogether more varied. Rotrou's play has been seen, indeed, as marking the end of a period of creative writing more spontaneous and less disciplined than that of the generation which was to follow—a period to which it is now common among literary historians to attach the label 'baroque'. This term, borrowed from the fine arts, is notoriously difficult to use with any precision in a literary context, but if it is used with caution, the parallel between literature and the painting, sculpture

[1] K. Loukovitch, *L'Évolution de la tragédie religieuse classique en France* (Paris, 1933), p. 129.

and architecture of the time can be a fruitful one, and can help to illuminate the characteristic features of a period style.

As regards form, this style is distinguished by a delight in superficial embellishment, a proliferation of detail elaborated for its own sake, without regard for the exigencies of an overall unity: it is a style which appeals to the sensibility or the imagination rather than to the intellect. Similarly, as regards subject-matter, themes of instability, disguise, metamorphosis are everywhere to be found, while the treatment at great length of scenes of violence and suffering is again designed to have a direct impact on the sensibility of the reader or spectator. As analogous features in the fine arts, we may pick out the splendid baroque façade quite out of proportion to the requirements of the building behind it; the illusion of an extra dimension created by the painter of a *trompe-l'œil* ceiling; or the sensual disturbance expressed by a statue such as Bernini's St Teresa.[1]

In general, then, the term 'baroque' denotes a restless, even a febrile kind of literature, much freer and more subjective—and therefore of more unequal quality—by comparison both with what had preceded and with what was to follow. If we attempt to account for such a literary phenomenon by relating it to the historical and social background, the starting-point is to be found in the climate of violence and unrest, of passionate adherence to a faith side by side with treachery and self-seeking, that was produced by the Religious Wars; the same critic who sees in *Saint-Genest* the last baroque landmark dates the beginning of the baroque period from the Massacre of Saint Bartholomew in 1572.[2] In this turbulent age, which saw the assassination of Henri III followed by that of Henri IV, themes of violence and martyrdom, of impermanence and instability, abound in literature:[3] an outstanding masterpiece is d'Aubigné's *Les Tragiques*, in which the author's un-

---

[1] See J. Rousset, *La Littérature de l'âge baroque en France* (Paris, 1953); O. de Mourgues *Metaphysical, Baroque and Précieux poetry* (Oxford, 1953), especially chs. v. and vi; I. Buffum, *Studies in the Baroque from Montaigne to Rotrou* (New Haven, U.S.A., 1957), especially the Introduction and ch. vi.

[2] I. Buffum, op. cit., p. viii.

[3] It is interesting to note that even in 1649 Baro, dedicating *Saint-Eustache* to Henriette-Marie de France, widow of Charles I of England, makes an explicit, if misguided, comparison between the violence of his theme and that of contemporary events: '[Eustache] fut l'innocent et le misérable spectateur de l'enlèvement de sa femme, dont l'honneur faillit d'être la proie d'un ravisseur insolent; et Votre Majesté peut dire avoir vu la moitié de soi-même, ou plutôt son tout entre les mains des bourreaux, dont la rage criminelle a triomphé de son honneur et de sa vie'.

restrained invective against the Catholic cause is expressed in vivid imagery of blood and fire. In an age of individualism and anarchy, writers retreat into their own sensibility and write as individuals, even if they are writing 'littérature engagée'; so in place of the organised programme of the earlier Pléiade we find no literary 'school', but solitary writers such as Montaigne, d'Aubigné or La Ceppède.

In the opening decades of the seventeenth century, the country was hardly more settled; it is only with the coming to power of Richelieu that anarchy began to give way to order, as the individualism of the great nobles was checked. And it is at this point that the literary scene begins to reflect, alongside the vivid and idiosyncratic writings of a Théophile or a Saint-Amant, a more ordered and disciplined attitude to writing on the part of Malherbe or Balzac, for whom private sensibility was less important than responsiveness to collective influences. The consolidation of this attitude in the 1630s favoured Richelieu's project for the regimentation of literature by means of an Academy, as well as the development of regular tragedy in the hands of ambitious young dramatists.

Regular neo-classical tragedy was a type of theatre deliberately created by dramatists at the bidding of cultured patrons, in response to purely literary influences and in imitation of models from abroad; and its appeal, at any rate to begin with, was largely limited to a refined élite. Tragicomedy on the other hand, the baroque literary form *par excellence*, had its roots within the professional theatre, and had developed in response to a more popular taste at a time when audiences were relatively uncultured. The 1630s saw a considerable evolution of public taste: the influence of the *salons*, and the general increase of culture and refinement among theatre audiences, helped to establish the new form of regular tragedy, so that tragicomedy ceased, after 1640, to be the most flourishing genre; there are eighty tragicomedies extant from the period 1630-9—twice as many as the number of tragedies—but the 1640s produced only sixty-seven, against sixty-nine tragedies.[1] Rotrou, however, although he had experimented with regular tragedy along with Corneille and Mairet, did not abandon tragicomedy; his natural preference for a more robust and colourful kind of theatre was fortified by his independence of patronage and his retirement from the capital. He had returned to his home town of Dreux to take up an administrative

---

[1] See J. Scherer, *La Dramaturgie classique en France* (Paris, 1954), p. 459.

post in 1639, and continued to write in the freer vein of tragicomedy and irregular tragedy until his career was cut short at the early age of forty. The circumstances in which he died have been called, by one editor of *Saint-Genest*, 'worthy of the burning faith' that sustains the play itself:[1] for when Dreux was struck by plague in 1650 he refused to leave his post, and died an exemplary death.

Tragicomedy and plays of similar inspiration—it is not always possible to draw a clear-cut line between the genres—had exploited all the themes typical of baroque literature: violence and suffering; changeability of fortune; contradiction between appearance and reality; magic and miracle. *Saint-Genest*, like some of the other plays on the subject of martyrdom already mentioned, combines the theme of violence and suffering with that of the miraculous transformation achieved by divine Grace. In *Polyeucte*, on the other hand, we take the hero's conversion for granted: it has occurred before the play opens, and the climax is provided by the psychological conflict between faith and conjugal love. This difference between the two plays is not to be accounted for by any significant difference in didactic purpose: Corneille is just as much interested in the operation of Grace, and indeed explores its doctrinal implications more fully than Rotrou, in the discussion between Polyeucte and Néarque with which the play begins. It is partly, no doubt, a case of dramaturgical necessity: Corneille, concentrating on the psychological climax in keeping with the mature classical aesthetic, eliminates the events leading up to that climax, whereas Rotrou's dramatic formula is a more comprehensive one; but also, I think, it illustrates the sensibility of the baroque artist at work in the case of Rotrou. Whereas Corneille is content to treat the doctrine of Grace as a theological abstraction, Rotrou prefers to clothe it in visual form and to make Genest's conversion, rather than his martyrdom, the climax of his play.

In the manner in which he brings about the conversion, Rotrou follows the medieval legend of the saint's life, which had already inspired Lope de Vega's play, *Lo Fingido Verdadero*, in 1632, and *L'Illustre Comédien* by Desfontaines in the same year as Rotrou's own play. This enabled him to exploit the device of the 'play within a play', which had already been used by a handful of dramatists on the French stage, and which similarly recurs several times in Shakespeare and other English dramatists of the period we are discussing. It is this structural feature which more than anything else indicates the affinities of Rotrou's play

---

[1] *Le Véritable Saint-Genest*, ed. R. W. Ladborough (Cambridge, 1954), p. viii.

with the freer baroque aesthetic of tragicomedy. For the 'play within a play' allows an imaginative dramatist to exploit to the full the artistic possibilities inherent in the contrast between reality and illusion: the 'extra dimension' offered by a structure in which the 'framework', while completely fictitious in comparison with the real world in which the spectators live, itself represents the 'real' world by contrast with the doubly fictitious world of the inner play.[1]

One attraction for the playwright using this device of the 'play within a play' was the opportunity it offered for the portrayal of a troupe of actors at work. Thus Gougenot's *Comédie des comédiens* (1631) had shown the company of the Hôtel de Bourgogne, somewhat in the spirit in which Molière was later to portray his own troupe in his *Impromptu de Versailles* (though with a good deal less realism), and Scudéry's play of 1632, also called *La Comédie des comédiens*, had performed the same service for Mondory's company at the Marais. Direct portrayal of the contemporary theatre in this manner was obviously impossible in a play set in the ancient world, but Rotrou introduces discussions of technical matters connected with the theatre which are none the less topical for being expressed in general terms: we may compare the scene between Hamlet and the players in Act III, scene ii of Shakespeare's play. Thus we are shown fragments of rehearsal before Genest and his companions actually perform 'Le Martyre de Saint-Adrien'; and Genest discusses with his 'décorateur' questions of lighting and *mise en scène*.

The largely symbolic, two-dimensional 'multiple' stage of the medieval theatre had survived, in a modified form, until the 1630s, but the replacement of this outmoded *décor* by the perspective set with its greater realism offered the stage-designer much more scope. The following passage recalls the *trompe-l'œil* effects, as well as the rich detail, of baroque style in the fine arts:

> Il est beau; mais encore, avec peu de dépense,
> Vous pouviez ajouter à sa magnificence,
> N'y laisser rien d'aveugle, y mettre plus de jour,
> Donner plus de hauteur aux travaux d'alentour,
> En marbrer les dehors, en jasper les colonnes,
> Enrichir leurs tympans, leurs cimes, leurs couronnes,
> Mettre en vos coloris plus de diversité,
> En vos carnations plus de vivacité,
> Draper mieux ces habits, reculer ces paysages,

[1] See R. J. Nelson, *Play within a Play* (New Haven, U.S.A., 1958).

Y lancer des jets d'eau, renfondrer leurs ombrages,
Et surtout en la toile où vous peignez vos cieux
Faire un jour naturel au jugement des yeux,[1]
Au lieu que la couleur m'en semble un peu meurtrie,

while the *décorateur*'s reply invokes the technicalities of perspective design:

Le temps nous a manqué plutôt que l'industrie;
Joint qu'on voit mieux de loin ces raccourcissements,
Ces corps sortant du plan de ces renfondrements;
L'approche à ces desseins ôte leurs perspectives,
En confond les faux jours, rend leurs couleurs moins vives,
Et, comme à la nature, est nuisible à notre art
A qui l'éloignement semble apporter du fard.[2]

It has been suggested that this discussion of *mise en scène* was intended as a hint to contemporary managers: 'Les auteurs de l'époque se plaignent avec raison du fait que les comédiens négligent la question du décor', says one of the foremost authorities on the history of seventeenth-century staging, who points out that whereas actors' costumes are known often to have been very rich and ornate, there was probably little enough money available for the construction of stage-sets.[3] A design such as the one for Act V of Corneille's *Andromède* (reproduced in Plate II) may appear to achieve exactly the effect that Rotrou's character has in mind; but we must remember that the illustration represents the engraver's ideal of a stage-set, and that in practice the *décorateur*'s work may have fallen a long way short of this ideal.[4]

Implicit in the whole play there is the problem of the relationship of the actor to the role he is playing: a subject treated explicitly by Shakespeare in Hamlet's soliloquy at the end of Act II, and which was to form the subject of Diderot's celebrated study of the psychology of the actor in *Le Paradoxe du comédien* a century later. How far should the actor endeavour to identify himself with the character he is creating? Should he try genuinely to feel, as far as is possible, the passions he is called on to

---

[1] This couplet expresses in a nutshell the object of the painter creating *trompe-l'œil* effects on a ceiling, one of the most characteristic examples of baroque style.

[2] Lines 313-32.

[3] S. W. Deierkauf-Holsboer, *Histoire de la mise en scène dans le théâtre français à Paris de 1600 à 1673* (Paris, 1960,) p. 120.

[4] In any case, sets for a *pièce à grand spectacle* such as *Andromède*, inevitably much more elaborate, were not paid for by the actors themselves, but either from the royal purse or by a noble patron.

express, and be 'carried away' by his interpretation of the part; or should he, as Diderot was to claim, remain cold, detached and in complete intellectual control of his technique? Rotrou does not set out to provide an answer, of course; and we must bear in mind that Genest's assumption of the personality of the Christian Adrien is part of the miracle of divine Grace, so that when he confesses (lines 402-3):

> D'effet comme de nom je me trouve être un autre;
> Je feins moins Adrien que je ne le deviens,

it is not so much a matter of degree of identification as of complete transformation (indicated by the contrast between *feindre* and *être*). Nevertheless, the bearing of *Saint-Genest* on this question is undeniable, and one is tempted to agree with Sainte-Beuve that a lesson can be drawn from the play:

> Vaut-il mieux pour l'acteur être entraîné par son rôle que le dominer? Je répondrais, par l'exemple de Genest même, qu'il est plus sublime sans doute à mesure qu'il entre plus avant dans son personnage, mais cela jusqu'à un certain degré, et qu'au moment où il s'y abandonne trop sincèrement, il s'y perd, et qu'il en sort; qu'il brise le cadre, que la pièce manque et qu'il y a catastrophe. Donc l'acteur doit, jusqu'à un certain point, et sans en avoir l'air, se dominer, rester double et ne paraître qu'un.[1]

By the time we come to Act IV, scene vii, Genest, inspired by his new faith, has abandoned the role of Adrien, though the 'spectators' have not yet realised what is taking place:

> MAXIMIN
> Il feint comme animé des grâces du baptême.
>
> VALÉRIE
> Sa feinte passerait pour la vérité même.
>
> PLANCIEN
> Certes, ou ce spectacle est une vérité,
> Ou jamais rien de faux ne fut mieux imité,

and even Genest's fellow-actors still think that he has forgotten his lines and is being forced to extemporise: hence the naïve surprise expressed in lines 10-12 of the extract. Genest takes up Lentule's call to the prompter, and his speech beginning at line 12 is based on the ideas which will appeal most directly to his comrades: 'un ange tient la pièce, un ange me

---

[1] *Port-Royal*, ed. cit., I, pp. 158-9.

redresse', 'une comédie où j'ignorais mon rôle', 'le démon me dictait', 'le soin d'un esprit angélique me conduit, me redresse et m'apprend ma réplique', 'j'ai corrigé mon rôle', 'le démon . . . ne me suggère plus': a concentration of imagery very much in the baroque manner, which we may find verging on the superficial conceit, but which would certainly have a more immediate impact on a popular audience than the rarer, more intellectualised imagery of Corneille's theatre.[1]

There is another interruption from the wondering Lentule, and this time from the Emperor as well, whose impatience is caused, it would appear, by what he regards as the actor's incompetence, not by any suspicion of the truth. The language of Genest's next speech continues to draw on the terminology of the actor's profession, until the climax of the scene, at lines 38-44, when he ceases to speak metaphorically, and declares unequivocally that it is he, not Adrien, who is 'représenté' as the 'objet' of his 'action'. From line 45 onwards the tone changes: for Genest's fervent profession of faith Rotrou has chosen to use a more straightforward vocabulary in which abstractions abound. Imagery no longer provides the framework of the speech, but is incidental; and generally speaking, the passage from line 45 to line 78 is less colourful, and has more of the abstract, dialectical flavour of Corneille's alexandrines. The final short coda to the speech, while keeping to this rhetorical style, reverts in a more subdued and suggestive way to the imagery of the first part: the implied contrast between *jeu* and *vérité* underlies the opposition between 'vos yeux' (to the Emperor) and 'empereur des cieux',[2] between 'je vous ai divertis' and 'réjouir les anges', and between 'théâtre' and 'autels'; while the last line with its double reference, to Genest the actor, who has finished his curtain speech, and to Genest the Christian, about to be martyred, provides an effective, and a moving, conclusion to a powerful speech.

If it is not a masterpiece by absolute standards, *Saint-Genest* is the masterpiece of that irregular, imaginative theatre so similar in character to the English and the Spanish drama of the early seventeenth century,

---

[1] Cf. for instance *Polyeucte*, lines 1109-14.

[2] Sainte-Beuve comments (op. cit., I, p. 157) that 'Rotrou se gênait peu pour reproduire à satiété les mêmes rimes'. In fact, no fewer than thirty-three couplets reproduce either the rhyme *cieux/dieux* or else *cieux/glorieux, précieux, yeux*, etc. or *dieux/yeux, odieux*, etc.; but it would surely be wrong to conclude that this indicates carelessness or ineptitude on the author's part. *Cieux* and *dieux* represent respectively the Christian and the pagan worlds whose conflict forms the theme of the play; and Rotrou's use of 'significant' rhyme, though perhaps less subtle, can be compared with Corneille's use of the words 'Rome' and 'romain' in his Roman plays (see the commentary to passage no. VIII).

which had for a time succeeded in satisfying French popular taste to an extent that the later classical drama never pretended to do. Rotrou had not the genius of the young Corneille, nor had he Corneille's ambition; he was not an aspiring member of a literary élite, but he was more completely a man of the theatre than Corneille. *Saint-Genest* is the work of a dramatist whose inspiration comes from the living theatre with all its naïvety and lack of polish; if it has not the intellectual force and the harmonious style of *Polyeucte*, it has more human warmth and colour. Genest himself, though a less impressive figure than Corneille's hero, is a humbler and more sympathetic representative of Christianity. In a century whose religious history is dominated by theological controversy and intolerance, Rotrou's play is a reminder of the simple, uncomplicated faith of the ordinary believer.

V

Scarron

(1610-60)

From *Le Roman comique*, Part I, chapter viii

La troupe comique était composée de Destin, de l'Olive et de la Rancune, qui avaient chacun un valet prétendant à devenir un jour comédien en chef. Parmi ces valets, il y en avait quelques-uns qui récitaient déjà sans rougir et sans se défaire. Celui de Destin, entre autres, faisait assez bien, entendait assez ce qu'il disait et avait de l'esprit. Mlle de l'Étoile et la fille de Mlle de la Caverne récitaient les premiers rôles; la Caverne représentait les reines et les mères et jouait à la farce. Ils avaient de plus un poète, ou plutôt un auteur, car toutes les boutiques d'épiciers du royaume étaient pleines de ses œuvres, tant en vers qu'en prose. Ce bel esprit s'était donné
10 à la troupe quasi malgré elle, et, parce qu'il ne partageait point et mangeait quelque argent avec les comédiens, on lui donnait les derniers rôles, dont il s'acquittait très mal. On voyait bien qu'il était amoureux de l'une des deux comédiennes; mais il était si discret, quoiqu'un peu fou, qu'on n'avait pu découvrir encore laquelle des deux il devait suborner sous espérance de l'immortalité. Il menaçait les comédiens de quantité de pièces, mais il leur avait fait grâce jusqu'à l'heure; on savait seulement par conjecture qu'il en faisait une intitulée *Martin Luther*, dont on avait trouvé un cahier, qu'il avait pourtant désavoué, quoiqu'il fût de son écriture.

Quand nos comédiens arrivèrent, la chambre des comédiennes était
20 déjà pleine des plus échauffés godelureaux de la ville, dont quelques-uns étaient déjà refroidis du maigre accueil qu'on leur avait fait. Ils parlaient tous ensemble de la comédie, des bons vers, des auteurs et des romans: jamais on n'ouït plus de bruit en une chambre, à moins que de s'y quereller. Le poète, sur tous les autres, environné de deux ou trois qui devaient être les beaux esprits de la ville, se tuait de leur dire qu'il avait vu Corneille, qu'il avait fait la débauche avec Saint-Amant et Beys, et qu'il avait perdu un bon ami en feu Rotrou. Mlle de la Caverne et Mlle Angélique, sa fille, arrangeaient leurs hardes avec une aussi grande tranquillité que s'il n'y eût eu personne dans la chambre. Les mains d'Angélique étaient
30 quelquefois serrées ou baisées, car les provinciaux sont fort endémenés[1]

[1] *endémené :* 'qui se démène, excité' (Littré).

47

et patineurs,[1] mais un coup de pied dans l'os des jambes, un soufflet ou un coup de dent, selon qu'il était à propos, la délivraient bientôt de ces galants à toute outrance. Ce n'est pas qu'elle fût dévergondée, mais son humeur enjouée et libre l'empêchait d'observer beaucoup de cérémonies; d'ailleurs elle avait de l'esprit et était très honnête fille. Mlle de l'Étoile était d'une humeur toute contraire: il n'y avait pas au monde une fille plus modeste et d'une humeur plus douce; et elle fut lors si complaisante qu'elle n'eut pas la force de chasser tous ces gracieuseux[2] hors de sa chambre, quoiqu'elle souffrît beaucoup au pied qu'elle s'était démis, et qu'elle eût grand besoin
40 d'être en repos. Elle était tout habillée sur un lit, environnée de quatre ou cinq des plus doucereux, étourdie de quantité d'équivoques qu'on appelle pointes dans les provinces, et souriant bien souvent à des choses qui ne lui plaisaient guère. Mais c'est une des grandes incommodités du métier, laquelle, jointe à celle d'être obligé de pleurer et de rire lorsque l'on a envie de faire toute autre chose, diminue beaucoup le plaisir qu'ont les comédiens d'être quelquefois empereurs et impératrices, et être appelés beaux comme le jour quand il s'en faut plus de la moitié, et jeune beauté, bien qu'ils aient vieilli sur le théâtre et que leurs cheveux et leurs dents fassent une partie de leurs hardes. Il y a bien d'autres choses à dire sur ce
50 sujet; mais il faut les ménager et les placer en divers endroits de mon livre pour diversifier. Revenons à la pauvre mademoiselle de l'Étoile, obsédée de provinciaux, la plus incommode nation du monde, tous grands parleurs, quelques-uns très impertinents, et entre lesquels il s'en trouvait de nouvellement sortis du collège. Il y avait entre autres un petit homme veuf, avocat de profession, qui avait une petite charge dans une petite juridiction voisine. Depuis la mort de sa petite femme, il avait menacé les femmes de la ville de se remarier et le clergé de la province de se faire prêtre, et même de se faire prélat à beaux sermons comptants. C'était le plus grand petit fou qui ait couru les champs depuis Roland. Il avait étudié toute sa vie; et,
60 quoique l'étude aille à la connaissance de la vérité, il était menteur comme un valet, présomptueux et opiniâtre comme un pédant et assez mauvais poète pour être étouffé s'il y avait de la police dans le royaume. Quand Le Destin et ses compagnons entrèrent dans la chambre, il s'offrit de leur lire, sans leur donner le temps de se reconnaître, une pièce de sa façon, intitulée *Les Faits et Gestes de Charlemagne, en vingt-quatre journées.* Cela fit dresser les cheveux en la tête à tous les assistants; et Le Destin, qui conserva un peu de jugement dans l'épouvante générale où la proposition avait mis la compagnie, lui dit, en souriant, qu'il n'y avait pas apparence de lui donner audience devant le souper.

ed. E. Magne (Paris; Garnier, n.d.), pp. 23-5

[1] *patineur :* 'celui qui patine, manie indiscrètement, attouche avec trop de liberté' (Littré).
[2] *gracieuseux :* 'cajoleurs' (notes to *Le Roman comique,* ed. Magne).

By the time *Le Roman comique* appeared—the first part was published in 1651, the second in 1657—its author had already acquired a considerable reputation in the fields of comedy and burlesque; a reputation based on the comedies written for the actor Jodelet at the Hôtel de Bourgogne, on his *Virgile travesti*, a burlesque version of the *Aeneid*, and his *Mazarinade*, a scathing attack on the Cardinal written at the time of the Fronde, as well as on his occasional verse and his talent as a conversationalist.

In *Le Roman comique*, Scarron was breaking fresh ground. His aim was to acclimatise in France the type of novel, already familiar to French readers through translations from the Spanish, which offered, alongside its romanesque plot and its abundance of incident, a lifelike picture of contemporary manners. It is debatable whether the label 'realist' can properly be applied at all to the novel in the seventeenth century, though if it is used with due caution it seems reasonable enough to adopt it as the logical antithesis of 'idealist', which serves to designate those romanesque works, from *L'Astrée* to the novels of Mlle de Scudéry and her contemporaries, in which the conception of historical setting is completely fanciful. It is not possible, of course, to speak of realism in the nineteenth-century sense: instead of the scrupulous 'photographic' reproduction of externals practised by Courbet and his followers, which served as a model for those nineteenth-century novelists who called themselves Realists, an appropriate analogy from the fine arts would be something more like the humorous genre painting of the Flemish school. If we are looking for a parallel to the limited realism of Scarron or of Sorel—whose *Francion* (1623) was to some extent a precursor of *Le Roman comique* in this respect—among contemporary French painters, it is perhaps to be found in Callot's engravings rather than in the 'straight' naturalism of a Louis Le Nain[1]. That is to say, though the portrayal of certain aspects of society is lifelike, the principle of selection is consciously at work—it must always be at work, of course, in any novel, but its importance is reduced to a minimum in the case of pure nineteenth-century realism—and it operates in the interests of satire and caricature, so as to emphasise the comic elements of low life and present a critical view of the society studied.

The title of the novel should perhaps be explained at this point: 'le roman comique' does not mean 'an amusing novel', but 'a novel about actors, or the theatre' (cf. the title of Corneille's early comedy *L'Illusion*

[1] See Plates IIIa and IIIb.

comique, which is concerned with *theatrical* illusion). In *Le Roman comique* we are shown an itinerant troupe of actors, and the provincial society with which they come into contact; we are made to look at the provinces through the patronising eye of the Parisian, and at the strolling players through the critical eye of one used to the standards of the Marais and the Hôtel de Bourgogne.[1]

Scarron was born in Paris, and was forced into an ecclesiastical career without any vocation at all, because of the possibility of obtaining a lucrative benefice: a possibility which led to his leaving Paris at the age of twenty-three in order to be near the well-disposed Bishop of Le Mans. He assumed the 'petit collet' of the *abbé*, but never proceeded to take priest's Orders, even when, in 1636, he became a canon of Le Mans. His clerical functions—or rather, his clerical status, for he seems never to have been very regular in the discharge of his duties as a canon—did not prevent him from enjoying to the full a life of pleasure; though by the time he returned to Paris in 1641 he was already the victim of the illness —it is uncertain whether or not this was a result of his earlier excesses— which reduced him to the condition of a helpless, hunchbacked cripple. It was in that state that he resigned his clerical Orders at the age of forty-two in order to marry the young girl of seventeen who was to look after him for the remainder of his life, the future Mme de Maintenon.

In a novel which accumulates so many farcical episodes of the slapstick variety, the passage under consideration is possibly not entirely representative: it is an example of Scarron's more sober and restrained writing, in which the treatment of the subject is not distorted by the author's extravagant invention. It has, therefore, a definite documentary value, and we may accept Scarron's picture of the troupe of actors on tour in the provinces as evidence of the conditions in which the members of this colourful profession in fact lived and worked round about the date of the author's arrival in Le Mans.

Theatrical activity flourished in the provinces in the early decades of the century, one of the contributory causes being the restrictions imposed on companies wishing to establish themselves in Paris. The Confrérie de la Passion, sole survivor of the medieval guilds of players and proprietor of the only permanent theatre, the Hôtel de Bourgogne, exercised a legal monopoly over all dramatic performances in the capital. Premises available were makeshift—usually a converted *jeu de paume*

[1] Cf. Part I, ch. xii of the novel: ' . . . le théâtre de l'Hôtel de Bourgogne ou du Marais, qui sont l'un et l'autre le non plus ultra des comédiens'.

—and the agreements drawn up by the Confrérie were usually unsatisfactory, so that most troupes stayed in Paris for only a short time, and then went off to tour the provinces. At the turn of the century, for instance, Valleran Leconte and his 'Comédiens du Roi', who were the first French troupe to employ a professional dramatist, in the person of Alexandre Hardy, performed only intermittently at the Hôtel de Bourgogne or at other Paris theatres, between long spells in the provinces or in the Low Countries; and not until the 1630s did the theatrical scene in the capital become settled, with Mondory's troupe established at the Théâtre du Marais as the rivals of the 'Comédiens du Roi' at the Hôtel de Bourgogne. It was on his way back to Paris from his last tour in the provinces that Mondory was approached at Rouen by a young lawyer who had just written his first play; he agreed to put it on in Paris, and the production of Corneille's *Mélite* (probably in 1629) was the beginning of a most fruitful partnership between the dramatist and the actor-manager.

The organisation of these early troupes was already, in a rudimentary form, the same as was to characterise the Comédie-Française on its foundation in 1680 and which has been preserved, with modifications, down to the present day. Each full member of the company (like the *sociétaires* of the Comédie-Française) received an equal share of the profits remaining after all expenses had been paid: in the early days the takings were shared out immediately after each performance, if we are to believe the evidence of Corneille's *L'Illusion comique*.[1] Beginners (the 'valets' of Scarron's passage) received a half, or smaller fraction, of a share, or else were paid a daily wage; while the manager of the troupe commonly took a double share. Relations between actor and dramatist were very much to the advantage of the former; although Hardy and, a generation later, Rotrou, did manage to make a living as 'poète à gages' to a particular troupe, it was a somewhat precarious living, and Scarron tells us that his poet Roquebrune 'ne partageait pas' (in other words, did not receive a 'share'). Such profits as the author drew from performances of his play ceased once the takings fell below a certain level, when the play became the property of the company; and copyright was in any case non-existent: as soon as a play was published, it could be performed by any troupe without acknowledgment—and even before

---

[1] Act V, scene vi. Cf. S. Chappuzeau, *Le Théâtre français* (Lyons, 1674), pp. 174 ff.; and S. W. Deierkauf-Holsboer, 'Le Partage de la recette par les comédiens du Roi au début du XVIIᵉ siècle' in *Revue d'histoire littéraire de la France* (1947), pp. 348-54.

publication if the text could somehow be procured.[1] The following passage written by a contemporary, quoting an actress in Mondory's troupe, bears witness to the dependent position normally occupied by the playwright, as well as to the exceptional prestige which Corneille had so quickly acquired:

> M. Corneille nous a fait un grand tort. Nous avions ci-devant des pièces de théâtre pour trois écus, que l'on nous faisait en une nuit, on y était accoutumé, et nous gagnions beaucoup; présentement, les pièces de M. de Corneille nous coûtent beaucoup d'argent et nous gagnons peu de chose.[2]

As regards the size of the troupe, the figure given by Scarron may at first sight seem inadequate, but the normal establishment, at any rate of an itinerant troupe, does not appear to have exceeded ten,[3] which is the total number of Scarron's troupe if we include Roquebrune. Versatility was an essential requirement, of course: if La Caverne 'représentait les reines et les mères et jouait à la farce', this was inevitable, if the provincial taste for farce was to be satisfied. In the capital, under Bellerose at the Hôtel de Bourgogne and Mondory at the Marais, the public were educated to the works of Corneille, Mairet, Rotrou and Tristan, and farce fell into disrepute; but in the provinces the cruder taste for farce remained, as Molière was to find when he took to the road with the Béjarts' company, l'Illustre Théâtre, in 1644.[4]

It was suggested in the nineteenth century by the Molière scholar Paul Lacroix that l'Illustre Théâtre formed the model for Scarron's

---

[1] It was only in the second half of the eighteenth century that playwrights obtained really satisfactory conditions regarding copyright, etc., largely owing to the efforts of Beaumarchais, who founded a 'Société des auteurs dramatiques'.

[2] Segrais, *Œuvres diverses*, quoted by E. Cottier, *Le Comédien auvergnat Mondory* (Clermont-Ferrand, 1937), p. 140. The actress in question was Mlle de Beaupré.

[3] 'From eight to twelve'—W. L. Wiley, *The Early Public Theatre in France* (Cambridge, U.S.A., 1960), p. 91.

[4] Fléchier's account of a performance by some 'comédiens de campagne' at Clermont-Ferrand in 1665 makes it clear that farce was their strongest suit: 'Ils disaient tout rôle du mieux qu'ils pouvaient, changeant l'ordre des vers et des scènes, et implorant de temps en temps le secours d'un des leurs qui leur suggérait des vers entiers, et tâchait de soulager leur mémoire. Je vous avoue que j'avais pitié de Corneille, et que j'eusse mieux aimé, pour son honneur, que M. d'Aubignac eût fait des dissertations critiques contre ses tragédies, que de les voir citer par des acteurs de cette façon. Il y avait une de leurs femmes qui récitait assez bien, et il leur faut donner cette louange qu'ils représentaient assez bien le burlesque, parce qu'ils étaient meilleurs farceurs que comédiens. Comme ils sont seuls dans la province, il faut bien se contenter d'eux'—*Mémoires de Fléchier sur les Grands-Jours d'Auvergne*, ed. P.-A. Chéruel (Paris, 1856), p. 125.

troupe, and that Le Destin had an original in Molière himself. While this has long been rejected by Molière scholars, it is nevertheless possible that Scarron did have an actual theatrical troupe in mind as a model when writing *Le Roman comique*, just as it is certain that he used the novel to settle old scores with acquaintances from Le Mans, by portraying in an unfavourable light some readily-identifiable characters among the provincials. In fact, the identification of the originals of the actors in *Le Roman comique* must remain highly speculative, though it has been suggested that Léandre (here referred to as Le Destin's 'valet') and Angélique correspond to one Filandre and his wife Angélique.[1] Both Le Destin and Léandre prove in the course of the novel to be 'fils de famille' who have abandoned a life of comfort and prosperity in order to take up the rough, nomadic life of an itinerant actor: this was not merely a fanciful romanesque embellishment on the author's part, for there are examples enough of this happening in real life throughout the century: Filandre himself, for instance, Mondory, or the much more illustrious case of Molière.

But the great majority of the profession were born to a way of life in which elegance and refinement were lacking, and it was this lack of refinement, together with the Church's condemnation of the profession,[2] which caused conventional bourgeois families to be scandalised at the thought of their sons taking to the stage. The question of the morals of the acting profession at this time is a somewhat controversial one. Even if we regard Tallemant's account of the early years of the century as gossipy and inaccurate:

> Il y avait deux troupes alors à Paris; c'étaient presque tous filous, et leurs femmes vivaient dans la plus grande licence du monde; c'étaient des femmes communes, et même aux comédiens de l'autre troupe dont elles n'étaient pas,[3]

it is clear from more reliable sources that there was over the years a considerable increase in order and decorum among actors, and a consequent improvement in their social status. Corneille, for instance, makes Pridamant, the bourgeois in *L'Illusion comique* whose son Clindor has become an actor, confess:

[1] See H. Chardon, *Scarron inconnu, et les Types des personnages dans le Roman comique* (Paris, 1904), II, pp.228 ff.
[2] See the commentary to passage no. XX.
[3] *Historiettes*, ed. cit., II, p. 773.

Je n'ose plus m'en plaindre: on voit trop de combien
Le métier qu'il a pris est meilleur que le mien.
Il est vrai que d'abord mon âme s'est émue:
J'ai cru la comédie au point où je l'ai vue;
J'en ignorais l'éclat, l'utilité, l'appas,
Et la blâmais ainsi, ne la connaissant pas.[1]

Scarron himself, in the passage under consideration and in the novel generally, presents his actors as models of decorum. The only exception is La Rancune, whose behaviour is often coarse and unprincipled; for the rest, though the quality of their theatrical performances may leave something to be desired, the behaviour of the actors is extremely genteel, and on the whole, they seem a little colourless by the side of the provincial society with which they come into contact. Indeed, as emerges quite clearly from this passage, Scarron tends to identify himself with the actors, to look at the provincials through their eyes, and to use their judgment, explicit or implicit, as a means of expressing his own.

Thus Angélique (line 35) 'avait de l'esprit et était très honnête fille', and of Mlle de l'Etoile we are told (lines 36-7) that 'il n'y avait pas au monde une fille plus modeste et d'une humeur plus douce'. The passage about the 'incommodités du métier' (lines 43 ff.) shows an obvious sympathy for the profession, and even the irony of lines 45-9 is gentle rather than malicious. The irony remains quite restrained in the case of the poet Roquebrune, though his portrait is much more of a caricature, and he is clearly distinguished from the other members of the company ('Il menaçait les comédiens de quantité de pièces, mais il leur avait fait grâce jusqu'à l'heure'). In fact, with the copies of his unsold works providing grocers' wrapping-paper, his incompetence as an actor, and the rather patronising attitude of his companions, the poor poet cuts a sorry figure, though not a wholly unsympathetic one. It is difficult to see why Scarron should adopt such a condescending attitude towards the profession of hack dramatist as a whole, by contrast with that of itinerant actor, and it may well be that the portrait of Roquebrune was intended as

[1] Lines 1807-12. Cf. Scarron's own tribute to the improved moral tone of the theatre (Part II, ch. viii): '[La comédie] est aujourd'hui purgée, au moins à Paris, de tout ce qu'elle avait de licentieux. Il serait à souhaiter qu'elle le fût aussi des filous, des pages et des laquais et autres ordures du genre humain que la facilité de prendre des manteaux y attire encore plus que ne faisaient les mauvaises plaisanteries des farceurs; mais aujourd'hui la farce est comme abolie et j'ose dire qu'il y a des compagnies particulières où l'on rit de bon cœur des équivoques basses et sales qu'on y débite, desquelles on se scandaliserait dans les premières loges de l'Hôtel de Bourgogne'.

a caricature of an individual acquaintance. Chardon has suggested, indeed,[1] that the original of this character may have been one Desfontaines, actor and playwright, who is known to have been with the troupe of Charles Dufresne in 1643, and with l'Illustre Théâtre in the following year; though there is no proof that he was in the region of Le Mans at the time of Scarron's residence there.

Whereas the rest of the troupe either ignore or else rebuff the provincials, the poet responds to their advances by boasting of his literary acquaintances (it is interesting to observe, in passing, the distance that contemporary repute, in 1651, already placed between Corneille and the other authors mentioned: while Roquebrune claims to have been a boon companion of Beys and Saint-Amant, and a friend of Rotrou, it is sufficient for him to claim that he had 'seen' Corneille). But this final touch to the portrait of the poet is incidental to the main purpose of the second paragraph: having paused in his narrative, in order to review the members of Le Destin's troupe, Scarron goes on to use the arrival of the troupe in Le Mans as an opportunity for a satirical attack on provincial culture. It is a direct, and not very subtle, attack, though it is spiced by Scarron's own peculiar wit: thus the 'échauffés godelureaux' of line 20 have been 'refroidis' by their reception at the hands of the female members of the company, and alongside the more straightforward descriptive terms 'endémenés' and 'patineurs' we have the inventive 'galants à toute outrance' and the neologism 'gracieuseux'. After the confidential aside to the reader—a familiar feature of this kind of 'realist' novel, from Scarron's Spanish models down to Fielding or Smollett—the unfavourable picture of provincial society reaches its height, with the unequivocal reference to '(les) provinciaux, la plus incommode nation du monde'.

'Provincial', says Furetière's *Dictionnaire* (1690), 'se dit presque toujours en mauvaise part. Un *provincial*, c'est un homme qui n'a pas l'air et les manières de la cour; qui n'est pas poli; qui ne sait pas vivre; qui n'a point vu le monde'; and the picture of the provincial given by writers of the time is a generally unflattering one. From Scarron's novel; from Gillet de la Tessonnerie's *Le Campagnard* (1657) with its central character, the 'Baron de la campagne, peu fait à la cour, affectant le proverbe et la pointe' and from *Les Précieuses ridicules* (1659) with its 'pecques provinciales'; from Molière's later sketches of the provincial gentry in *Monsieur de Pourceaugnac* (1669) and *La Comtesse d'Escarbagnas*

[1] Op. cit., II, pp. 253 ff.

(1671) and from the occasional references in La Bruyère's *Caractères* (1689)[1]—from such sources as these we can build up a composite picture of the provincial seen through Parisian eyes. He is a character lacking in polish and in taste, behind the times in his ideas, inclined to be vain—cf. Scarron's description of M. de la Garouffière, who appears later in the novel:

> Il avait de l'esprit . . . et ne se croyait point homme de province en nulle manière, venant d'ordinaire, hors de son semestre, manger quelque argent dans les auberges de Paris et prenant le deuil quand la cour le prenait: ce qui, bien vérifié et enregistré, devrait être une lettre, non pas de noblesse tout à fait, mais de non-bourgeoisie, si j'ose ainsi parler[2]

—and over-susceptible to criticism, if we are to believe La Bruyère's scathing comment:

> Les provinciaux et les sots sont toujours prêts à se fâcher, et à croire qu'on se moque d'eux ou qu'on les méprise.[3]

In modern times, provincial society has always been regarded as fair game for the writers of the capital and their more sophisticated readers, but the contrast between Paris and the provinces has never been as striking as in the seventeenth century. In the sixteenth century a vigorous intellectual, artistic and social life had flourished in such centres as Lyons or the Loire valley; and the eighteenth century was to see a notable revival of provincial culture. But throughout the seventeenth century, and particularly during the second half of the century, the domination of the provinces by the capital was almost complete. The provinces were economically crippled by the long series of wars and the burden of taxation, and this naturally affected social and intellectual life. Persons appointed to administrative posts in a remote province were commonly anxious to spend as little time there as possible; while provincials with enough wealth and leisure to be able to leave their province were unwilling to remain isolated from the social and cultural advantages of Paris and the court. In Louis XIV's reign, of course, the

[1] Cf. also *Le Théophraste moderne, ou Nouveaux Caractères sur les mœurs* (1700) by an imitator of La Bruyère, P.-J. Brillon. This very mediocre work contains a chapter devoted to 'La Province', in which the prejudices of half a century are complacently crystallised into a series of dogmatic clichés, e.g.: 'On peut parler de la province, mais il n'y a guère de bien à en dire: les climats éloignés de Paris et de la Cour ne produisent ni la justesse de l'esprit, ni la politesse des mœurs' (p. 204).
[2] Part II, ch. xii.
[3] *Caractères*, V, para. 51.

nobility were irresistibly attracted by the powerful magnet of Versailles, while writers and artists saw possibilities of patronage in Paris, at Versailles or at other princely courts in the Île-de-France. But this was merely the culmination of a process that can be traced back to Richelieu's time; and by the time the passage we are considering was written, the social consequences of the Cardinal's political policy (as well as of the impoverishment of the provinces during the costly Thirty Years' War) were already plain to see. The centralisation of the intellectual life of the nation on the capital came to match that of its social life; and very few indeed of the major works of art and letters during the remainder of the century were to be produced outside the environment of Paris and Versailles. It is not difficult, in these circumstances, to understand the talismanic force of the phrase 'la cour et la ville'.[1]

Having lampooned the provincials in general—and, as we have seen, highly conventional—terms, Scarron chooses this point in his narrative to introduce as an example of the type a character (subsequently given the name of Ragotin), who is to become one of the most important in the novel. The tone of the passage changes, and Ragotin's portrait provides a colourful set-piece. It is a caricature, we are told, of a colleague in the service of the Bishop of Le Mans. Ambroïs Denisot, the Bishop's secretary, was, like Ragotin, a lawyer, and actually took Orders (cf. line 57) on the death of his wife; also like Ragotin, he was a pedant with literary pretentions. It is not known, however, what he had done to earn Scarron's enmity, or at least to justify his portrayal, in Ragotin, as the butt of so many practical jokes and the object of general ridicule.[2]

In place of the straightforward pejorative description of the provincial society in general, Scarron builds up his portrait of Ragotin by a variety of stylistic devices, beginning with the amusing repetition of the epithet

---

[1] This is not to say, of course, that cultural life in the provinces was non-existent: the educated *bourgeoisie*, particularly the magistracy, of the large provincial towns contained many men with literary and scientific interests. It is a field largely unexplored by historians: A. Jacquet, in *La Vie littéraire dans une ville de province sous Louis XIV* (Paris, 1886), endeavours with some success to define the intellectual atmosphere of Dijon in the second half of the century, and something is known of the cultural situation of Rouen and Clermont-Ferrand at the beginning of the century because of the connection with Corneille and Pascal respectively. It is impossible to generalise from the evidence concerning one or two particular towns; though it is perhaps significant that in the cases referred to, the Pascal family left Clermont-Ferrand because of the cultural advantages of Paris, just as Corneille was to leave Rouen, attracted by the theatres of the capital. One cannot imagine Bordeaux satisfying the intellectual interests of a major seventeenth-century writer, as it had done in the case of Montaigne and was to do again with Montesquieu.

[2] See Chardon, op. cit., II, pp. 30 ff.

petit ('un petit homme veuf..., une petite charge..., une petite juridiction..., sa petite femme...' and finally, after a break, 'le plus grand
petit fou', coupled with a literary allusion to the still-popular *Orlando
furioso*). Like the poet with his plays, Ragotin is said to 'threaten' both
the womenfolk of the town and the clergy; and Scarron rounds off the
sentence by the extravagant addition 'et même de se faire prélat à beaux
sermons comptants'. The following sentence likewise ends pleasingly
with a ternary grouping of phrases, the last phrase again contributing an
amusing extravagance ('menteur comme un valet', 'présomptueux et
opiniâtre comme un pédant', 'assez mauvais poète pour être étouffé...').
Finally, the passage closes with a brief piece of action, in which the
comic flavour is once more provided by exaggeration and the incon-
gruous: even Hardy's long-winded marathon *Théagène et Chariclée* had
consisted of only eight 'journées' (i.e. eight separate five-act plays), but
Ragotin proposes, without more ado, to read to the company a work
three times as long—to which Le Destin, keeping his head amid the
general alarm (extravagantly rendered by 'cela fit dresser les cheveux
...', 'l'épouvante générale...') calmly replies that it would be difficult
to fit it in before supper! Beneath the comic fantasy there is the satirical
implication that provincial taste is a long way behind the times.

If on the whole it is more subdued, less racy and boisterous than some
of the more distinctive episodes in the novel, this extract nevertheless
illustrates the author's comic inventiveness, as well as the 'documentary'
quality of his descriptive passages. Scarron's novel has a unique place in
the literature of the century as an authentic record of small-town
provincial life: a record which is of course selective, the episodes being
chosen with an eye to satire as well as slapstick. But the satire, if sometimes pointed, is never cruel or bitter, and *Le Roman comique* stands out
as one of the most good-humoured works of its age.

VI

La Rochefoucauld

(1613-80)

From *Portrait du duc de La Rochefoucauld, fait par lui-même*

J'ai les sentiments vertueux, les inclinations belles, et une si forte envie d'être tout à fait honnête homme que mes amis ne me sauraient faire un plus grand plaisir que de m'avertir sincèrement de mes défauts. Ceux qu me connaissent un peu particulièrement et qui ont eu la bonté de me donner quelquefois des avis là-dessus, savent que je les ai toujours reçus avec toute la joie imaginable et toute la soumission d'esprit que l'on saurait désirer. J'ai toutes les passions assez douces et assez réglées: on ne m'a presque jamais vu en colère et je n'ai jamais eu de haine pour personne. Je ne suis pas pourtant incapable de me venger, si l'on m'avait offensé et qu'il y allât
10 de mon honneur à me ressentir de l'injure qu'on m'aurait faite. Au contraire, je suis assuré que le devoir ferait si bien en moi l'office de la haine, que je poursuivrais ma vengeance avec encore plus de vigueur qu'un autre. L'ambition ne me travaille point. Je ne crains guère de choses, et ne crains aucunement la mort. Je suis peu sensible à la pitié, et voudrais ne l'y être point du tout. Cependant, il n'est rien que je ne fisse pour le soulagement d'une personne affligée; et je crois effectivement que l'on doit tout faire, jusqu'à lui témoigner même beaucoup de compassion de son mal; car les misérables sont si sots que cela leur fait le plus grand bien du monde. Mais je tiens aussi qu'il faut se contenter d'en témoigner et se garder soigneuse-
20 ment d'en avoir. C'est une passion qui n'est bonne à rien au dedans d'une âme bien faite, qui ne sert qu'à affaiblir le cœur et qu'on doit laisser au peuple, qui, n'exécutant jamais rien par raison, a besoin de passions pour le porter à faire les choses. J'aime mes amis, et je les aime d'une façon que je ne balancerais pas un moment à sacrifier mes intérêts aux leurs. J'ai de la condescendance pour eux; je souffre patiemment leurs mauvaises humeurs et j'en excuse facilement toutes choses; seulement je ne leur fais pas beaucoup de caresses, et je n'ai pas non plus de grandes inquiétudes en leur absence. J'ai naturellement fort peu de curiosité pour la plus grande partie de tout ce qui en donne aux autres gens. Je suis fort secret et j'ai
30 moins de difficulté que personne à taire ce qu'on m'a dit en confidence. Je

59

suis extrêmement régulier à ma parole; je n'y manque jamais, de quelque conséquence que puisse être ce que j'ai promis et je m'en suis fait toute ma vie une obligation indispensable. J'ai une civilité fort exacte parmi les femmes et je ne crois pas avoir jamais rien dit devant elles qui leur ait pu faire de la peine. Quand elles ont l'esprit bien fait, j'aime mieux leur conversation que celle des hommes: on y trouve une certaine douceur qui ne se rencontre point parmi nous; et il me semble outre cela qu'elles s'expliquent avec plus de netteté et qu'elles donnent un tour plus agréable aux choses qu'elles disent. Pour galant, je l'ai été un peu autrefois;
40 présentement je ne le suis plus, quelque jeune que je sois. J'ai renoncé aux fleurettes et je m'étonne seulement de ce qu'il y a encore tant d'honnêtes gens qui s'occupent à en débiter. J'approuve extrêmement les belles passions; elles marquent la grandeur de l'âme, et quoique, dans les inquiétudes qu'elles donnent, il y ait quelque chose de contraire à la sévère sagesse, elles s'accommodent si bien d'ailleurs avec la plus austère vertu que je crois qu'on ne les saurait condamner avec justice. Moi qui connais tout ce qu'il y a de délicat et de fort dans les grands sentiments de l'amour, si jamais je viens à aimer, ce sera assurément de cette sorte; mais, de la façon dont je suis, je ne crois pas que cette connaissance que j'ai me
50 passe jamais de l'esprit au cœur.

Œuvres complètes, ed. L. Martin-Chauffier

(Paris, 1950), pp. 29-31

This self-portrait, the first piece of writing by La Rochefoucauld to be published, was included by the publisher Sercy in his *Recueil des portraits et éloges en vers et en prose* of 1659. Written half-way between the end of the Fronde, in which the author had played an active and indeed a prominent part, and the publication of the first edition of the *Maximes* in 1665, it is interesting as a reflection of the drastic change which his career had undergone, from the intrigues and ambitions of his early life to the cultured leisure in which his literary activities took shape. There was a considerable vogue for literary 'portraits' round about 1660, and the habitués of the *salons* greatly appreciated these physical and moral descriptions of acquaintances, whether in the transparent disguise of characters in Mlle de Scudéry's novels 'à l'antique', or direct and undisguised, as in the *Recueil de Sercy*. A certain degree of idealisation was inevitable in most of these literary exercises, owing to the need to flatter the great (cf. Mlle de Scudéry's portrait of Condé quoted on p. 159) or the desire to gloss over the shortcomings of a friend.

One might imagine, however, that a self-portrait would be an exception to this general rule, and indeed La Rochefoucauld writes:

Voilà naïvement comme je pense que je suis fait au dehors, et l'on trouvera, je crois, que ce que je pense de moi là-dessus n'est pas fort éloigné de ce qui en est. J'en userai avec la même fidélité dans ce qui me reste à faire de mon portrait; car je me suis assez étudié pour me bien connaître, et je ne manquerai ni d'assurance pour dire librement ce que je puis avoir de bonnes qualités, ni de sincérité pour avouer franchement ce que j'ai de défauts.

But in the event, his 'assurance' is more in evidence than his 'sincérité', and the portrait is very much an ideal picture of the author as he would like to be, the perfect example of an 'honnête homme'. In all fairness, there is every reason to believe that he endeavoured to live up to this ideal after his retirement to a more contemplative life: his biographer, Émile Magne, suggests that 'ce portrait, innocent en apparence, était, en réalité, une sorte de manifeste, car La Rochefoucauld y donnait assurance de sa sagesse future'[1]; on the other hand, the portrait hardly corresponds to the picture we have of La Rochefoucauld from other sources during the turbulent years of the Fronde.

The author of the *Maximes* belongs, roughly speaking, to the same generation as Condé and Retz, in whom was typified the heroic spirit of the Fronde, and of Corneille, whose theatre mirrors that same spirit. Descartes was ten years older than Corneille, and twenty-five years older than Condé, but the slow maturing of the philosopher's ideas, together with the precocious military genius of the great general, meant that the latter's victory at Rocroi preceded the publication of the *Traité des passions* by six years; and it is in this treatise that the psychology of these self-centred heroes, with their will-power and ambition, is most fully explored.

The *Traité des passions de l'âme*, written in 1646 and published in 1649, analyses the complex interactions between those bodily functions which man shares with the rest of the animal kingdom[2] and his 'soul', the seat of his intellect and the source of his will, by which his moral and intellectual life is controlled. Descartes distinguishes between the 'actions de l'âme' and the 'passions de l'âme': the latter are the perceptions or impressions we receive through our senses from the world

[1] *Le Vrai Visage de la Rochefoucauld* (Paris, 1923), p. 127.
[2] See the commentary to passage no. XIII.

around us, while the former are the effects of 'la volonté', by which the mind imposes itself on the external world. Whilst the 'passions'constitute an influence of the body on the mind—

> le principal effet de toutes les passions dans les hommes est qu'elles incitent et disposent leur âme à vouloir les choses auxquelles elles préparent leur corps; en sorte que le sentiment de la peur l'incite à vouloir fuir . . .[1]

—the mind is under no mechanical compulsion to respond to these influences in a given way:

> la volonté est tellement libre de sa nature, qu'elle ne peut jamais être contrainte; et des deux sortes de pensées que j'ai distinguées dans l'âme, dont les unes sont ses actions, à savoir, ses volontés, les autres ses passions,... les premières sont absolument en son pouvoir et ne peuvent qu'indirectement être changées par le corps, comme au contraire les dernières dépendent absolument des actions qui les conduisent, et elles ne peuvent qu'indirectement être changeés par l'âme.[2]

The *Traité des passions* examines methodically the various 'passions', and endeavours to teach the mastery over them which comes from the proper exercise of the will: 'Il n'y a point d'âme si faible,' declares the often-quoted article 50, 'qu'elle ne puisse, étant bien conduite, acquérir un pouvoir absolu sur ses passions'.

The other literary phenomenon to which reference has been made, Corneille's 'éthique de la gloire' (as it is generally known, particularly since the publication of M. Nadal's authoritative study of that author's theatre [3]) was of course quite independent of Descartes' theoretical approach to the psychology of the passions—it was embodied, for one thing, in plays which appeared several years earlier than the *Traité*— but it was a product of the same intellectual climate. Even if modern scholarship has shown that the parallel drawn by Lanson in his article 'Le Héros cornélien et le généreux selon Descartes'[4] is too rigid and schematic,[5] the affinity holds good in a more general sense. The same moral atmosphere produced not only the *Traité des passions* and such plays as *Horace*, *Rodogune* or *Nicomède*, but also the real-life heroics of the Fronde; and however different their birth and background as well

---

[1] Article 40.
[2] Article 41.
[3] *Le Sentiment de l'amour dans l'œuvre de Pierre Corneille* (Paris, 1948).
[4] *Revue d'histoire littéraire de la France* (1894), pp. 397-411.
[5] See especially Nadal, op. cit., and P. Bénichou, *Morales du Grand Siècle* (Paris, 1948).

as the careers they followed, the scholar living in exile and seclusion and the dramatist of bourgeois origins illustrate the same heroic, aristocratic ethic as the ecclesiastical intriguer Retz, Condé the brilliant and impetuous general, and La Rochefoucauld the ambitious nobleman so conscious of the obligations imposed on him by his rank and breeding. It is an ethic which owes a good deal to the traditions of neo-stoicism which the seventeenth century had inherited from the humanist thinkers of the sixteenth.

Birth, temperament and force of circumstances all made it inevitable that the prince de Marcillac (as La Rochefoucauld was called until the death of his father in 1650) should take sides with the rebels in the 'Fronde des Princes'. Involved from an early age in the intrigues against Richelieu under the influence of the duchesse de Chevreuse, he had been disappointed, after the death of the Cardinal and of Louis XIII, at not receiving an important post as a mark of gratitude from the new Regent, Anne of Austria. His opposition to Mazarin made him the natural ally of the Condé family, of whom Condé's sister, Mme de Longueville, and his younger brother, the prince de Conti, were the most active plotters. He became the lover of Mme de Longueville, and when in 1650, after the first Fronde, Mazarin arrested Condé, Conti and the duc de Longueville, it was Mme de Longueville and Marcillac who were chiefly responsible for organising the resistance to Mazarin which led to the resumption of civil war.

But La Rochefoucauld emerged from the Fronde years a disillusioned man. His political ambitions had been frustrated, he had been deceived by Mme de Longueville, and he had been badly wounded in the battle of the Faubourg Saint-Antoine. He exchanged the life of the Court, with its ambitions and its intrigues, for the more tranquil life of the *salon*, where he could take pleasure in the company of Mme de Sablé and, later, of Mme de Lafayette, and devoted himself to the writing of his *Mémoires* and his *Maximes*. Even his family pride, the powerful motive force of his turbulent years, he was now content to gratify vicariously, and as early as 1671, nine years before his death, he renounced his title of *duc et pair* in favour of his eldest son. In a large measure, then, he can be said to have abandoned the pursuit of the self-centred 'éthique de la gloire', and adopted the more disciplined, and socially more responsible, code of the *honnête homme* to which he subscribes in the self-portrait; and when towards the end of his life he had cause to express his disappointment in his son, and his disapproval of his way of life, it is by the same standard of *honnêteté* that he implicitly judges him:

> Vous avez beaucoup de bonnes qualités; personne n'a plus de probité, de fidélité et de noblesse dans le cœur que vous; vous avez de l'esprit et du bon sens dans votre conduite à la cour; vous aimez tous vos proches, vous leur faites beaucoup de bien et tous ont sujet de s'en louer; vous avez une reconnaissance parfaite des grâces que vous avez reçues du roi; vous aimez véritablement vos amis tant qu'ils suivent votre goût, mais vous vous en rebutez aisément et vous avez de la sécheresse et de l'aigreur dans l'humeur et dans l'esprit quand leurs sentiments ne sont pas soumis aux vôtres. L'âge et la prospérité augmenteront encore ces défauts. Vous n'êtes pas avare, mais on n'est pas aussi véritablement libéral quand on donne sans choix, quand on dissipe sans mesure et sans règle, plus par vanité que par bonté pour ceux à qui on fait du bien . . . . Vous avez un air un peu trop rude et impérieux dans votre maison, plus sur des bagatelles que sur des choses sérieuses, qui blesse tous ceux qui y ont intérêt. . . . Ils trouvent que vous sortez des mesures qui vous conviennent et que, par vanité, vous vous faites un plaisir caché de copier de grands exemples et de donner comme eux un pouvoir absolu et indépendant à chacun de ceux qui vous servent. . . .[1]

But if by the end of his life La Rochefoucauld was able to practise the restraint and self-effacement that were recognised as the mark of the *honnête homme*,[2] it was not an easy matter for him to overcome the imperious dictates of his aristocratic pride, and the portrait which Retz gives of him is probably fairer than the idealised self-portrait in showing how strong was the pull of ambition:

> Il y a toujours eu du *je ne sais quoi* en tout M. de La Rochefoucauld. Il a voulu se mêler d'intrigue, dès son enfance, et en un temps où il ne sentait pas les petits intérêts, qui n'ont jamais été son faible, et où il ne connaissait pas les grands, qui, d'un autre sens, n'ont pas été son fort. Il n'a jamais été capable d'aucune affaire, et je ne sais pourquoi; car il avait des qualités qui eussent suppléé, en tout autre, celles qu'il n'avait pas. . . . Il n'a jamais été guerrier, quoiqu'il fût très-soldat. Il n'a jamais été par lui-même bon courtisan, quoiqu'il ait eu toujours bonne intention de l'être. Il n'a jamais été bon homme de parti, quoique toute sa vie il y ait été engagé. Cet air de honte et de timidité que vous lui voyez dans la vie civile s'était tourné dans les affaires en air d'apologie. Il croyait toujours en avoir besoin; ce qui, joint à ses *Maximes*, qui ne marquent pas assez de foi en la vertu, et à sa

---

[1] Quoted by E. Magne, op. cit., pp. 162-3.
[2] See passage no. VII and commentary, and also the commentary to passage no. X.

pratique, qui a toujours été de chercher à sortir des affaires avec autant d'impatience qu'il y était entré, me fait conclure qu'il eût beaucoup mieux fait de se connaître et de se réduire à passer, comme il l'eût pu, pour le courtisan le plus poli, et le plus honnête homme, à l'égard de la vie commune, qui eût paru dans son siècle.[1]

Even the self-portrait we are considering, though it purports to show La Rochefoucauld, having renounced the claims of ambition, in single-minded pursuit of the more modest goal of perfect *honnêteté*, betrays clearly enough the self-centred aristocratic outlook that we associate with the 'éthique de la gloire', and it would be wrong to take the portrait of the would-be *honnête homme* entirely at its face value. Or perhaps more accurately, it would be wrong to assume that there is a complete incompatibility between *honnêteté* and the 'éthique de la gloire'; and if we look at it in this light it is a particular interest of La Rochefoucauld's self-portrait that it illustrates the similarities, as well as the differences, between the two ideals.

There is no doubt about the sincerity of La Rochefoucauld's admiration for the social ideal of the *honnête homme* expressed in the opening lines of the passage under consideration: in the *Maximes* it is this ideal which provides the only positive standard to set against the predominantly cynical tone of the rest of the work. Even the author's professed willingness to listen to criticism of his shortcomings is in line with maxim no. 202:

> Les faux honnêtes gens sont ceux qui déguisent leurs défauts aux autres et à eux-mêmes; les vrais honnêtes gens sont ceux qui les connaissent parfaitement et les confessent.

It is a mark of the *honnête homme*, as of the Cartesian *généreux*, that the 'passions' should be responsive to the control of the will; but what La Rochefoucauld says about vengeance reminds us more of the intransigent Cornelian hero than of the socially adaptable *honnête homme*. In particular, the notion of 'devoir' invoked in lines 9 ff. has a recognisably Cornelian ring, and it is surely correct to interpret it principally, if not exclusively, in the sense of 'duty to oneself'. As M. Nadal says, commenting on Corneille's vocabulary:

> Dans ce théâtre, le devoir ne consiste pas en définitive à être juste, bon, honnête, mais à satisfaire la gloire, principe même de l'obligation ou du devoir.[2]

[1] Quoted in La Rochefoucauld, *Œuvres complètes*, ed. cit., pp.588-9.   [2] Op. cit., p. 294.

It is the passage about 'la pitié' in lines 14 ff. which seems to bring out most fully the affinity between the ideas underlying the self-portrait and the self-centred aristocratic ethic which the heroes of the Fronde shared with those of Corneille's plays; for Christian compassion is as foreign to the make-up of the Cornelian hero (even in the case of Polyeucte) as it evidently was to the utterly self-absorbed supermen of the 1650s.[1] The antithesis between 'passion' and 'raison' in line 22 is thoroughly Cartesian, as is the notion of the 'âme bien faite' which can control and regulate the effects of the undesirable passions. However, whereas Descartes had suggested that this self-control was largely a matter of discipline and training ('Il n'y a point d'âme si faible qu'elle ne puisse, étant bien conduite . . .'), Corneille seems to insist on the importance of noble birth in the formation of the *généreux*:

> Les princes ont cela de leur haute naissance:
> Leur âme dans leur sang prend des impressions
> Qui dessous leur vertu rangent leurs passions.
> Leur générosité soumet tout à leur gloire [2]

and the disparaging contrast that La Rochefoucauld draws between the mass of the people and the aristocratic élite is everywhere implicit in Corneille's conception of the hero.

Even friendship, though he approves of it, like 'les belles passions', as one of the nobler things in life, is for La Rochefoucauld a controlled, not a spontaneous, passion. It should evidently not be over-demonstrative, yet it must not be half-hearted; and the self-sacrificing devotion to a friend's interests that he claims should be the mark of the *honnête homme* seems at least partly to have its source in that same notion of *gloire* that has been analysed above. It is interesting in this respect to compare the action of Molière's Dom Juan who, disregarding his own safety, goes to the rescue of a stranger attacked by three bandits, with the comment: 'Notre propre honneur est intéressé dans de pareilles aventures'.[3] Dom Juan can hardly be reckoned the ideal *honnête homme*, of course, but that is immaterial: his comment provides a useful clue

---

[1] M. Jacques Vier in *Histoire de la littérature française*, XVIe et XVIIe siècles (Paris, 1959), p. 277, makes this comment on the hero of *Cinna*: 'Octave, devenu Auguste, relève le malheureux Cinna, non par compassion, mais par surabondance de vitalité'; and goes on to quote Nietzsche's formula: 'L'homme noble relève les malheureux non par compassion mais par surabondance'.

[2] *Pompée*, lines 373-6.

[3] Act III, scene iii.

to the motivation of the zealous self-sacrifice recommended by La Rochefoucauld. The Cornelian hero, the *frondeur* and the *honnête homme* have in common a worldly ethic, according to which their actions are judged, and justified, by the opinion of others. La Rochefoucauld, it is true, recognises the existence of a higher, more absolute criterion in maxim no. 216:

> La parfaite valeur consiste à faire sans témoins ce qu'on serait capable de faire devant tout le monde

—but in general all these worldly heroes are conscious that the eyes of the world are upon them and that their reputation stands to gain or lose as a result of their actions.

In the closing sentences, the self-portrait comes nearer to the conventional picture of the *honnête homme*, enjoying the pleasures of conversation and at home in the society of women;[1] while the homage to 'les belles passions' (lines 42 ff.) reminds one of the distinction that the author was to draw in the *Maximes*:

> Un honnête homme peut être amoureux comme un fou, mais non pas comme un sot.[2]

But even here, the picture of the *honnête homme* that La Rochefoucauld would like to be bears the imprint of the self-sufficient, aloof aristocrat who had always been accustomed to insist on his rank and who liked to distinguish himself from the common run of men (lines 45-7).

Altogether, the self-portrait presents a singular mixture of aspiration towards an ideal and unconscious self-revelation. It is not difficult to reconcile it with the picture given by Retz of an irresolute, dissatisfied man attempting to accommodate two ethical systems which, whatever features they may have had in common, represented two very different ways of life. Disappointed in his political ambitions, having failed to realise the heroic ideal after which he still hankered, he seems at this stage of his life at any rate not yet to have been prepared to resign himself contentedly to the more restricted and less lofty ideal of *honnêteté*.

---

[1] See the commentary to passage no. VII.
[2] No. 353.

VII
Pascal

(1623-62)

Pensées (Lafuma edition, nos. 984-7)

(984) On ne passe point dans le monde pour se connaître en vers, si l'on n'a mis l'enseigne de poète, de mathématicien, etc. Mais les gens universels ne veulent point d'enseigne, et ne mettent guère de différence entre le métier de poète et celui de brodeur.

Les gens universels ne sont appelés ni poètes, ni géomètres, etc.; mais ils sont tout cela, et juges de tous ceux-là. On ne les devine point. Et parleront[1] de ce qu'on parlait quand ils sont entrés. On ne s'aperçoit point en eux d'une qualité plutôt que d'une autre, hors de la nécessité de la mettre en usage; mais alors on s'en souvient, car il est également de ce
10 caractère qu'on ne dise point d'eux qu'ils parlent bien, quand il n'est point question du langage, et qu'on dise d'eux, qu'ils parlent bien, quand il en est question.

C'est donc une fausse louange qu'on donne à un homme quand on dit de lui, lorsqu'il entre, qu'il est fort habile en poésie et c'est une mauvaise marque, quand on n'a pas recours à un homme quand il s'agit de juger de quelques vers.

(985) L'homme est plein de besoins: il n'aime que ceux qui peuvent les remplir tous. «C'est un bon mathématicien», dira-t-on.—Mais je n'ai que faire de mathématiques; il me prendrait pour une proposition.—«C'est un
20 bon guerrier».—Il me prendrait pour une place assiégée. Il faut donc un honnête homme qui puisse s'accommoder à tous mes besoins généralement.

(986) Sa règle[2] est l'honnêteté.

Poète et non honnête homme.

Beautés d'omission, de jugement.

(987) *Honnête homme*—Il faut qu'on n'en puisse dire, ni: il est mathématicien, ni prédicateur, ni éloquent, mais il est honnête homme. Cette qualité universelle me plaît seule. Quand en voyant un homme on se souvient de son livre, c'est mauvais signe; je voudrais qu'on ne s'aperçût

---

[1] Variant: Ils parleront . . .(Brunschvicg edition).
[2] Variant: La règle . . . (Brunschvicg edition).

30 d'aucune qualité que par la rencontre et l'occasion d'en user (*Ne quid nimis*), de peur qu'une qualité ne l'emporte, et ne fasse baptiser; qu'on ne songe point qu'il parle bien, sinon quand il s'agit de bien parler, mais qu'on y songe alors.

Pensées, ed. L. Lafuma
(Paris, 1951), pp. 419-20

This sequence of fragments from the *Pensées*, Pascal's notes for an 'Apologia for the Christian Religion', may appear to be of doubtful relevance to his main theme, the apologetic based on a sustained contrast between 'la misère de l'homme sans Dieu' and 'la grandeur de l'homme avec Dieu'. In Lafuma's edition, now fairly generally regarded as the best guide to the order of the *Pensées*, this impression is strengthened by the editor's relegating these particular fragments to the 'Notes diverses' which form a sort of appendix to the main groupings.[1] It is clear, nevertheless, that this delineation of the contemporary social ideal of the *honnête homme* would have had its appointed place in the argument of the completed apologia, and we shall suggest presently what that place might have been.

Leaving out of account the cryptic paragraph 986 (an instance of the highly-condensed formulae which provide some of the most difficult cruxes in the *Pensées*), the fragments presented here offer a good example of Pascal's direct and vigorous prose style. Many of his contemporaries and near-contemporaries write in a French heavy with Latinisms, particularly the long period with a very complicated structure of subordinate clauses. This is particularly true of Descartes; and even in the case of Balzac, whose reputation for harmony and elegance in the writing of French prose matched that of Malherbe in verse, the sentence-structure is based on that of Latin.[2] Pascal on the contrary eschews the

---

[1] As an incomplete work left in manuscript form on Pascal's death, the *Pensées* have always presented a serious editorial problem. Lafuma's edition attempts to reproduce the text as nearly as possible in the order in which the manuscript material seems to have been left by Pascal himself. Other modern editors have preferred to impose a coherent logical order on the unfinished material, in an attempt to arrive at the plan which the author himself had in mind for the completed work; thus, for example, these fragments form paragraphs 30,34, 35, 36 and 38 of the edition by L. Brunschvicg (Paris, 1897).

[2] Cf. a modern editor's remark about Faret, whose *L'Honnête Homme, ou l'Art de plaire à la cour* (1633) deals with very much the same subject-matter as this passage from the *Pensées*: 'En général, la phrase de Faret, un peu longue et lourde, et d'allure périodique, est toute latine. Son caractère principal semble être l'accentuation des jointures logiques, la prédilection pour les tournures qui soulignent et mettent en lumière le raisonnement'— *L'Honnête Homme*, ed. M. Magendie (Paris, 1925), p. 1.

long, involved sentence, and it is his characteristic brevity and clarity which make him seem such a relatively modern writer to the reader of today. His style owes much to the rhythms of spoken French (and also, no doubt, to the example of Montaigne, whose terse, concrete, vigorous style, 'tel sur le papier qu'à la bouche', Pascal very much admired). An extreme case is the highly elliptical sentence 'Et parleront . . .' which, even if one accepts the variant reading 'Ils parleront . . .', is still forceful and expressive at the expense of strict grammatical accuracy; we may also note the use of the image 'mettre l'enseigne' ('to put up one's sign'), and the striking absolute use of the verb *baptiser*. Above all, Pascal's is a spontaneous style of writing; it is equally free from the ponderous pedantry of the technical treatise and from the self-conscious striving after effect of the 'professional' man of letters.[1] He wants any book he reads to be written by a man, as he says, and not by an author; and this is how he himself writes. In this respect, of course, his style could not be more in keeping with the subject-matter of the above passage, for a natural, unforced, undemonstrative manner is the hallmark of the *honnête homme*.

Pascal was not writing about the ideal of *honnêteté* without first-hand knowledge. During what is customarily referred to as his 'période mondaine', from about 1651 to 1654, he emerged from his rather sheltered life of study, and mixed in a fashionable and animated social milieu. In particular, he made the acquaintance of the chevalier de Méré, the future author of the *Discours de la vraie honnêteté* and of other writings in which the social ideal of the *honnête homme* is set out; he undertook a journey into Poitou in Méré's company in 1652, and frequented the same society in Paris. In view of the reference at the beginning of this extract to the 'mathématicien' as an example of the 'professional' type of man, and the further reference in paragraph 985, it is interesting to read Méré's account of the Poitou journey in which he describes the first meeting with Pascal, already a celebrated mathematician, but hardly (on this evidence) an *honnête homme* :

Le Duc de Roannez a l'esprit mathématique et, pour ne pas s'ennuyer sur le chemin, il avait fait provision d'un homme entre deux âges, qui n'était alors que fort peu connu, mais qui depuis a bien fait parler de lui. C'était un grand mathématicien, qui ne savait que cela. Ces sciences ne donnent pas les agréments du monde; et cet homme, qui n'avait ni goût ni sentiment, ne

[1] This is a characteristic feature of Balzac's writing: see passage no. III and commentary.

laissait pas de se mêler en tout ce que nous disions, mais il nous surprenait toujours et nous faisait toujours rire.[1]

The social ideal of the *honnête homme* which Pascal characterises in the fragments under consideration, and of which Méré was one of the principal theoretical exponents, may be said essentially to be the Renaissance ideal of the 'universal man' acclimatised in France by such intermediaries as translations of Castiglione's *Il Corteggiano* and Montaigne's *Essais*. Although in bourgeois circles the term *honnête homme* retains some of the moral connotations which long usage had given it (as the equivalent of 'homme d'honneur'), one can distinguish quite early in the century a new use of the word in predominantly aristocratic society, whereby it approximates in meaning to 'galant homme'. Thus *honnêteté*, in the aristocratic scale of values, is without moral connotations; it is determined by reference to such things as birth, breeding, exterior manner and social graces. Malherbe, for instance, translating an account of a battle given by Livy, writes:

> [Antiochus] fit là une très grande perte, non seulement . . . de simples soldats, mais encore d'honnêtes hommes et de personnes dont il faisait cas.[2]

and at the end of the century the following dictionary definitions again show that the term commonly implied no moral considerations:

> *Honnête :* on le dit premièrement de l'homme de bien, du galant homme, qui a pris l'air du monde, qui sait vivre.[3]
> On appelle aussi *honnête homme* un homme en qui on ne considère alors que les qualités agréables et les manières du monde. Et en ce sens, *honnête homme* ne veut dire autre chose que galant homme, homme de bonne conversation, de bonne compagnie.[4]

Generally speaking, the terms *honnête homme* and *honnêteté* provide something of a problem for the reader of seventeenth-century texts, and their meaning has to be carefully evaluated according to context. In the mouth of one of Molière's typical *raisonneurs*, for instance, the terms have more of a bourgeois flavour, and Molière's conception of *honnêteté* would appear to carry with it more conventional moral

---

[1] Quoted in Pascal, *Pensées et opuscules*, ed. Brunschvicg (Paris, n.d.), p. 115.
[2] Translation of Livy, Book XXXIII (1616) in *Œuvres*, ed. Lalanne (Paris, 1862-9), I, p. 450.
[3] Furetière, *Dictionnaire universel* (1690).
[4] *Dictionnaire de l'Académie française* (1694).

implications; on the other hand, when Alceste says to Oronte:

> ... N'allez point quitter, de quoi que l'on vous somme,
> Le nom que dans la Cour vous avez d'honnête homme,
> Pour prendre, de la main d'un avide imprimeur,
> Celui de ridicule et misérable auteur[1]

he is using the word in its aristocratic sense, for the action of *Le Misanthrope* takes place in the social milieu in which the ideal of *honnêteté* flourished.

Faret's manual *L'Honnête Homme, ou l'Art de plaire à la cour* (1633) shows too much of Castiglione's influence to be fully representative of the seventeenth-century French ideal: the author sets too much store by success, and his aim would appear to be to turn out almost the 'professional' courtier. What Pascal has in mind here has more affinity with *honnêteté* as delineated by Méré in his *Conversations* and in his *Discours de la vraie honnêteté*; an ideal that it is easier to illustrate than to define, and which tends to be defined by an accumulation of negatives: the *honnête homme* does not parade his knowledge, he does not monopolise conversation, he is not a pedant... or, as La Rochefoucauld expresses it: 'Le vrai honnête homme est celui qui ne se pique de rien'.[2] Its appeal is to the aesthetic rather than to the ethical sense, as is shown by this remark of Méré's:

> C'est la quintessence de toutes les vertus; et ceux qui ne l'ont point, sont mal reçus parmi les personnes de bon goût, et même quand ils parlent des choses du monde, c'est pour l'ordinaire de si mauvaise grâce, qu'on ne les peut souffrir. Cette science est proprement celle de l'homme, parce qu'elle consiste à vivre et à se communiquer d'une manière humaine et raisonnable.[3]

Another difficulty of terminology is provided by the word *monde* in line 1. In Méré's phrase, above, 'quand ils parlent des choses du monde', or in 'les manières du monde' or 'l'air du monde' (both of which occur in the dictionary definitions quoted above), it is clear that 'le monde' means 'high society', the exclusive, predominantly aristocratic milieu where the ideal of *honnêteté* prevails; but Pascal, paradoxically enough, seems to use the word to indicate not this particular social milieu but rather the world at large with the exception of this restricted, exclusive society. In any case, there is an apparent contradiction between

---

[1] *Le Misanthrope* (1666), lines 369-72.
[2] *Maximes* (1665), no. 203.
[3] *Œuvres* (Paris, 1930), III, pp. 71-2.

what Pascal says in this extract and paragraph 386 of the *Pensées* (according to Lafuma's numbering; Brunschvicg groups it with part of the material reproduced here, as no. 37):

> . . . il est bien plus beau de savoir quelque chose de tout que de savoir tout d'une chose; cette universalité est la plus belle. Si on pouvait avoir les deux, encore mieux, mais s'il faut choisir, il faut choisir celle-là, et le monde le sait et le fait, car le monde est un bon juge souvent.

Here, 'le monde' is Méré's aristocratic élite, whose judgment can be relied on; in the passage under discussion, the popular judgment of 'le monde' (in its less restricted sense) is shown to be fallible, for it fails to recognise the superiority of the 'gens universels'.

It is the 'universality' of the *honnête homme*, his 'qualité universelle' (line 28), which provides the closest link with the Renaissance ideal, the Italian 'uomo universale'. All professional specialisation is abhorrent; to quote Méré:

> C'est un malheur aux honnêtes gens d'être pris à leur mine pour des gens de métier, et quand on a cette disgrâce, il s'en faut défaire à quelque prix que ce soit.[1]

The man of culture and breeding must have an unobtrusive all-round competence without affecting any single expertise in particular: even the military profession, by general consent the most fitting for a gentleman, is subject to the same reservation:

> La guerre est le plus beau métier du monde, il en faut demeurer d'accord; mais, à le bien prendre, un honnête homme n'a point de métier. Quoiqu'il sache parfaitement une chose, et que même il soit obligé d'y passer sa vie, il me semble que sa manière d'agir ni son entretien ne le font point re-marquer.[2]

Faret, too, emphasises the 'universality' of the *honnête homme*:

> Je l'aime mieux passablement imbu de plusieurs sciences, que solidement profond en une seule; puisqu'il est vrai que notre vie est trop courte pour parvenir à la perfection des moindres de toutes celles que l'on nous propose, et que qui ne peut parler que d'une chose, est obligé de se taire trop souvent.[3]

[1] Ibid., p. 142.
[2] Méré, *Œuvres*, I, p. 11.
[3] *L'Honnête Homme, ou l'Art de plaire à la cour*, ed. cit., p. 26.

Thus we find Pascal expressing here the scorn felt by the 'amateur' man of letters—and I think we can be confident that he is at this point speaking in his own person—for the 'métier de poète'; a view which is very different from that of writers such as Boileau or La Bruyère, who were very insistent on the status due to their profession.

The second paragraph particularises, and characterises the *honnête homme* by his behaviour in society. The art of conversation had an especial importance in the theory of *honnêteté* and in practice in seventeenth-century polite society. Here, one can point to the particular influence of Montaigne's essay 'De l'art de conférer' as well as of manuals such as Faret's *L'Honnête Homme*. The following passage from Méré's *Discours de la conversation* shows how seriously this accomplishment was regarded:

> Encore qu'on soit né fort heureusement, il y a peu de choses qu'on puisse bien faire sans les avoir apprises. . . . Mais s'il y a quelque chose, où le soin de s'instruire sous les meilleurs maîtres soit nécessaire, c'est la conversation; et quand on y veut réussir, on doit principalement s'étudier à devenir honnête homme, et pour cela comment faut-il faire?

What one must not do, Méré suggests, is to spend one's time at court:

> Ce n'est pas qu'on n'y puisse apprendre à bien vivre et à bien parler. Mais pour ne s'y pas tromper, il est bon de se souvenir que cette Cour qu'on prend pour modèle, est une affluence de toute sorte de gens; que les uns ne font que passer, que les autres n'en sont que depuis peu, et que la plupart quoiqu'ils y sont nés ne sont pas à imiter.[1]

We must beware, therefore, of attributing the ideal and practice of *honnêteté* exclusively, or even mainly, to court circles: 'le monde', used in this special sense, was at once something wider and more exclusive.

The conversational ideal, then, is one which avoids all trace of affectation and jargon; the speaker must show good sense and judgment, not learning and prejudice. The 'specialist' is not only caricatured in the extravagant portraits of Molière's pedants, but is also criticised, more soberly, by such different writers as La Bruyère in his picture of the narrow-minded musician:

[1] *Œuvres*, II, pp. 110-11.

Appellerai-je homme d'esprit celui qui, borné et renfermé dans quelque art, ... ne montre hors de là ni jugement, ni mémoire, ni vivacité, ni mœurs, ni conduite? ... un musicien, par exemple, qui après m'avoir comme enchanté par ses accords, semble s'être remis avec son luth dans un même étui [1]

or Saint-Évremond, writing of the limitations of the mathematician:

Il n'y a point de louanges que je ne donne aux grands mathématiciens, pourvu que je ne le sois pas. J'admire leurs inventions, et les ouvrages qu'ils produisent; mais je pense que c'est assez aux personnes de bon sens de les savoir bien employer; car, à parler sagement, nous avons plus d'intérêt à jouir du monde qu'à le connaître. [2]

The strongly marked Epicurean flavour of this last text, incidentally, points to the close relationship between the social ideal of *honnêteté* and the moral ideas of the *libertins*, the free-thinkers to whom Pascal intended to address his *Apologie*, and in whose beliefs and habits he was therefore keenly interested. [3]

It remains perhaps to suggest that the theoretical picture of the *honnête homme* did not always correspond to reality, and that the aristocratic ideal was not maintained for very long. La Bruyère's portrait of Arrias[4] gives a satirical sketch of the would-be 'homme universel', and in the chapter 'Des Jugements' the same author paints a thoroughly disillusioned picture of the *honnête homme*:

L'honnête homme tient le milieu entre l'habile homme et l'homme de bien, quoique dans une distance inégale de ces deux extrêmes. La distance qu'il y a de l'honnête homme à l'habile homme s'affaiblit de jour à autre, et est sur le point de disparaître. ... L'honnête homme est celui qui ne vole pas sur les grands chemins, et qui ne tue personne, dont les vices enfin ne sont pas scandaleux. [5]

At the time when Pascal was writing, however, *honnêteté* was a clearly formulated and influential ideal; but an ideal social rather than moral, and one which, in the final analysis, the author of the *Pensées* was writing about as an outsider, however well informed and interested. The

---

[1] *Caractères*, XII, para. 56.
[2] 'Jugement sur les sciences où peut s'appliquer un honnête homme' (1662) in *Œuvres*, ed. Planhol (Paris, 1927), I, p. 86.
[3] See the commentaries to passages nos. II and X.
[4] *Caractères*, V, para. 9.
[5] Ibid., XII, para. 55.

portrait of the *honnête homme* given in this passage is a sympathetic one, but allowance must be made for the dialectical pattern of the *Pensées*: it is virtually certain that the only justification such a portrait could have had in the final structure of the work would have been to introduce the theme of the inadequacy of such a wholly worldly ideal. This hypothesis appears to be corroborated beyond any reasonable doubt by what Pascal says in another passage:

> Il n'y a que la religion chrétienne qui rende l'homme *aimable et heureux* ensemble. Dans l'honnêteté, on ne peut être aimable et heureux ensemble.[1]

For however well obedience to the code of *honnêteté* might equip a man for the day-to-day requirements of social intercourse, this was for Pascal merely a trivial consideration; and a life lived exclusively according to this code must necessarily be judged by the author of the *Pensées* to be lacking in an essential dimension.

[1] *Pensées*, ed. Lafuma, para. 726.

VIII
Corneille
(1606-84)
Sertorius, lines 749-816

SERTORIUS

Seigneur, qui des mortels eût jamais osé croire
Que la trêve à tel point dût rehausser ma gloire ?
Qu'un nom à qui la guerre a fait trop applaudir
Dans l'ombre de la paix trouvât à s'agrandir ?
Certes je doute encor si ma vue est trompée,
Alors que dans ces murs je vois le grand Pompée,
Et quand il lui plaira je saurai quel bonheur
Comble Sertorius d'un tel excès d'honneur.

POMPÉE

Deux raisons, mais Seigneur, faites qu'on se retire,
10 Afin qu'en liberté je puisse vous les dire.
    L'inimitié qui règne entre nos deux partis
N'y rend pas de l'honneur tous les droits amortis.[1]
Comme le vrai mérite a ses prérogatives
Qui prennent le dessus des haines les plus vives,
L'estime et le respect sont de justes tributs
Qu'aux plus fiers ennemis arrachent les vertus ;
Et c'est ce que vient rendre à la haute vaillance,
Dont je ne fais ici que trop d'expérience,
L'ardeur de voir de près un si fameux héros,
20 Sans lui voir à la main piques ni javelots,
Et le front désarmé de ce regard terrible,
Qui dans nos escadrons guide un bras invincible.
    Je suis jeune et guerrier, et tant de fois vainqueur,
Que mon trop de fortune a pu m'enfler le cœur ;
Mais (et ce franc aveu sied bien aux grands courages)
J'apprends plus contre vous par mes désavantages
Que les plus beaux succès qu'ailleurs j'aie emportés
Ne m'ont encore appris par mes prospérités.
Je vois ce qu'il faut faire, à voir ce que vous faites :

---

[1] 'n'amortit pas entre ces deux partis tous les droits de l'honneur'.

30 Les sièges, les assauts, les savantes retraites,
Bien camper, bien choisir à chacun son emploi,
Votre exemple est partout une étude pour moi.
Ah! si je vous pouvais rendre à la République,
Que je croirais lui faire un présent magnifique!
Et que j'irais, Seigneur, à Rome avec plaisir,
Puisque la trêve enfin m'en donne le loisir,
Si j'y pouvais porter quelque faible espérance
D'y conclure un accord d'une telle importance!
Près de l'heureux Sylla ne puis-je rien pour vous?
40 Et près de vous, Seigneur, ne puis-je rien pour tous?

SERTORIUS
Vous me pourriez sans doute épargner quelque peine,
Si vous vouliez avoir l'âme toute romaine;
Mais avant que d'entrer en ces difficultés,
Souffrez que je réponde à vos civilités.
   Vous ne me donnez rien par cette haute estime
Que vous n'ayez déjà dans le degré sublime.
La victoire attachée à vos premiers exploits,
Un triomphe avant l'âge où le souffrent nos lois,
Avant la dignité qui permet d'y prétendre,
50 Font trop voir quels respects l'univers vous doit rendre
Si dans l'occasion je ménage un peu mieux
L'assiette du pays, et la faveur des lieux,
Si mon expérience en prend quelque avantage,
Le grand art de la guerre attend quelquefois l'âge;
Le temps y fait beaucoup, et de mes actions
S'il vous a plu tirer quelques instructions,
Mes exemples un jour ayant fait place aux vôtres,
Ce que je vous apprends, vous l'apprendrez à d'autres,
Et ceux qu'aura ma mort saisis de mon emploi
60 S'instruiront contre vous, comme vous contre moi.
   Quant à l'heureux Sylla, je n'ai rien à vous dire.
Je vous ai montré l'art d'affaiblir son empire,
Et si je puis jamais y joindre des leçons
Dignes de vous apprendre à repasser les monts,
Je suivrai d'assez près votre illustre retraite,
Pour traiter avec lui sans besoin d'interprète,
Et sur les bords du Tibre une pique à la main
Lui demander raison pour le peuple romain.

Théâtre complet, ed. P. Lièvre
(Paris, 1950), II, pp. 728-9

After the failure of *Pertharite* (1651), Corneille retired from the theatre for eight years; *Sertorius*, the third play produced after his return to dramatic writing, was performed in February 1662 and published in the same year. The action is set in Spain in the first century B.C. and concerns the struggle of the exiled general Sertorius against the troops of the dictator Sulla. Sertorius has been fighting at the head of an army of exiles, with a formally constituted copy of the Roman Senate, and as the ally of the Queen of Lusitania, Viriate; he has successfully driven back Sulla's troops, commanded by the young Pompée, who has asked for a truce. He faces a threat, however, from a dissident faction within his own ranks, led by his lieutenant Perpenna, who is advised by his evil counsellor Aufide to assassinate Sertorius, assume the leadership and marry Viriate. Sertorius has himself aspired to the hand of Viriate, and not only does Viriate desire to marry him—for political reasons, since she does not love the ageing warrior—but Aristie, the former wife of Pompée, recently arrived in Spain in order to stir up vengeance against Sulla, who had forced Pompée to repudiate her, is also ready to use marriage with Sertorius as a means of increasing her political strength. This initial situation, which is typical of the whole series of Corneille's later tragedies, with its complicated personal relationships depending on political and matrimonial ambitions, is finally resolved when Perpenna gives in to the promptings of Aufide and has Sertorius assassinated. The troops refuse to accept Perpenna as leader, however, and surrender to Pompée, who hands the traitor over to them for summary vengeance.

The play was a great success, both on the stage (it was played by Molière's company at the Palais-Royal, and also at the Hôtel de Bourgogne) and in print. By general agreement, the *pièce de résistance* was a scene which forms something of an *hors-d'œuvre*, dramatically speaking: a long interview (Act III, scene i; lines 749-992) between Sertorius and Pompée: 'Cette conférence,' says Corneille in his *Au Lecteur*, 'que quelques-uns des premiers dans la Cour, et pour la naissance, et pour l'esprit, ont estimé [*sic*] autant qu'une pièce entière'. The passage given here forms the opening part of this scene, and presents the exchange of compliments between the two heroes, followed by the opening exchanges in the debate which ensues.

Pompée has taken advantage of the suspension of hostilities to come into Sertorius's camp; the meeting between them has obviously been somewhat artificially contrived by Corneille in order to provide a kind of 'set piece' at the centre of the play. The scene is said to have been criticised by Boileau on the grounds that although it is 'pleine d'esprit', it is neither 'dans la raison ni dans la nature'.[1] It offends against reason because it does not fit logically into the structure of the play as a whole: the previous action does not lead up to it, nor does the subsequent action depend on it; and it offends against nature because it is 'invraisemblable'. Corneille admits the force of the latter charge:

> Pompée semble s'écarter un peu de la prudence d'un général d'armée, lorsque sur la foi de Sertorius il vient conférer avec lui. . . . Ce n'est pas que je ne veuille bien accorder aux critiques qu'il n'a pas assez pourvu à sa propre sûreté, mais il m'était impossible de garder l'unité de lieu sans lui faire faire cette échappée, qu'il faut imputer à l'incommodité de la règle plus qu'à moi qui l'ai bien vue.[2]

Nevertheless, such a criticism betrays a certain uncharitable prejudice, and a sympathetic study of the scene by Lanson shows how its place in the play can be fully justified. Analysing the spirit of the interview, Lanson concludes:

> Quant au ton de cette scène, il est d'une vérité historique, non de la vérité historique de l'époque où l'entrevue est censée avoir eu lieu, mais de celle de 1650 à 1652, au moment des guerres civiles, de la Fronde. Et cela n'a rien qui doive nous étonner: le XVII siècle conçoit l'histoire comme une matière à raisonnements politiques.[3]

The scene was *vraisemblable*, that is, if such an interview between leaders of opposing armies seemed convincing and plausible to the generation for whom Corneille wrote the play. Evidence that it did seem plausible is to be found in the *Mémoires* of the cardinal de Retz, in the account of a similar interview during the Fronde between Retz himself and Condé. 'Les deux adversaires se tâtent, s'observent, raisonnent comme Pompée et Sertorius,' says Lanson;[4] and a more recent Corneille scholar, M. G. Couton, adds weight to the analogy by referring to another passage in the *Mémoires* in which Retz himself, writing of Condé's difficulties in preserving a united front among the leaders of the 'Fronde des Princes', makes an explicit comparison with the situation of Sertorius:

[1] According to a collection of his miscellaneous critical remarks published posthumously under the title of *Bolæana*.

[2] *Au Lecteur*, published together with *Sertorius*.

[3] 'L'Entrevue de Pompée et de Sertorius' in *Revue des cours et conférences* (1900-1), pp. 736-41.   [4] Ibid., p. 741.

Cette constitution des esprits auxquels M. le Prince avait affaire eût embarrassé Sertorius. Jugez, s'il vous plaît, quel effet elle pouvait faire dans l'esprit d'un prince du sang couvert de lauriers innocents et qui ne regardait la qualité de chef de parti que comme un malheur.[1]

Elsewhere,[2] M. Couton has shown how the plays which Corneille wrote at the time of the Fronde troubles (*Don Sanche d'Aragon*, *Nicomède* and *Pertharite*) all reflect the political preoccupations of his contemporaries. By the time of *Sertorius* the country was in a more settled political state, and Louis XIV had assumed effective control on the death of Mazarin in 1661 : but Condé, whose opposition to Mazarin and Anne of Austria at the time of the Fronde had driven him into an alliance with Spain, was still a prominent figure, as were others among the principal protagonists of the Fronde; Retz, for instance, had continued his intrigues in pursuit of his own ambitions throughout the 1650s, and did not retire from the political scene until 1662. The questions of the ethics of civil war, and the loyalty of a patriot under a dictatorship, which constitute the central political themes in *Sertorius*, still retained considerable topicality, therefore; and it is in the light of these preoccupations that Corneille's intentions in writing the scene of the interview between Sertorius and Pompée, and its effect on contemporary playgoers, are best judged. Not the least interesting aspect of the scene is the skill with which the dramatist has managed to present both protagonists in a sympathetic light. It may seem at first that Sertorius has the greater claim on our admiration, for he has preserved his independence and stands as a champion of liberty, whereas Pompée not only fights under the orders of the dictator, but has suffered the personal humiliation of giving up his wife at Sulla's command. Sertorius, moreover, has the better of the first exchanges: cf. his proud rejection (lines 61 ff. of the above passage) of Pompée's suggestion that he should come to terms with Sulla. But as the argument progresses, Pompée shows that he too is fighting in his own way for a Rome which will be free and independent in the future:

> Je lui prête mon bras sans engager mon âme.
> Je m'abandonne au cours de sa félicité,
> Tandis que tous mes vœux sont pour la liberté;
> Et c'est ce qui me force à garder une place

[1] *La Vieillesse de Corneille* (Paris, 1949), p. 77.
[2] *Corneille et la Fronde* (Clermont-Ferrand, 1951).

Qu'usurperaient sans moi l'injustice et l'audace,
Afin que, Sylla mort, ce dangereux pouvoir
Ne tombe qu'en des mains qui sachent leur devoir.[1]

The 'message' of the whole scene seems to be that in times of civil war, both sides have their measure of right, and neither is wholly in the right. The emphasis is on the dilemma of the individual, and the conclusion seems to be clearly drawn that at such times loyalty to the State, to one's own conception of the best way of serving the State, comes before everything else. Applying this to contemporary events, it would follow that the cause of the legitimate monarchy in France must stand above both the evils of Mazarin's oppressive rule and the too-individualistic aims and ideals of the Frondeurs.

Essential to the full understanding of the play as this analogy with seventeenth-century political preoccupations undoubtedly is, one must guard against the temptation to interpret tragedies like *Sertorius* in too literal a sense as *pièces à clef*. M. Couton emphasises quite rightly that Corneille's is 'un art non réaliste mais allégorique':[2] it is not so much the characters and events in the play that correspond to particular characters and events in contemporary life, as the situations and the ideas discussed, which in a more general way reproduce the sort of situation and idea that had a contemporary relevance. Any more directly representational purpose would have conflicted with Corneille's object, as a writer of heroic tragedy, to portray idealised, exemplary characters capable of arousing in the spectator that admiration on which his conception of tragedy was largely based. Thus, Corneille's hero is not a portrait of Condé in the guise of Sertorius; nor is he, by the same token, the Sertorius of history, whom the historian Appian paints as brutal and debauched: he owes his origin, as does Pompée, to the largely unhistorical, literary conception of ideal Roman virtue derived principally from Plutarch's *Lives*.[3]

Very much the stock-in-trade of French Renaissance thinkers, this dealised picture of Rome had been revived by seventeenth-century

[1] Lines 862-8.
[2] *La Vieillesse de Corneille*, p. 79.
[3] It should be remembered that this idealised view of Rome existed side by side with a much more serious and solid interest in Roman history on the part of the educated publie. Many Roman historians were translated into French between the years 1610 and 1650 or so, by such men as Jean Baudoin and Perrot d'Ablancourt, and the lessons drawn from this reading played an influential part in the shaping of seventeenth-century political thought, as well as perpetuating the tradition of late sixteenth-century neo-stoicism in the field of ethics.

moralists and publicists as a basis for a new aristocratic ethic.[1] In his *Discours* called 'Le Romain', addressed to Mme de Rambouillet, Balzac, who was one of the most influential of these moralists, writes:

> [Le Romain] ne sait pas moins obéir aux lois, qu'il sait commander aux hommes; et dans une élévation d'esprit, qui voit les couronnes des souverains au-dessous de lui, il a une âme tout à fait soumise à la puissance du peuple. Il révère la sainteté de cette puissance entre les mains d'un tribun, ou furieux ou ennemi, ou peut-être l'un et l'autre. Croyant que faillir est le seul mal qui puisse arriver à l'homme de bien, il croit qu'il n'y a point de petites fautes; et se faisant une religion de la moindre partie de son devoir, il pense qu'on ne peut pas même être négligent sans impiété. Il estime plus un jour employé à la vertu, qu'une longue vie délicieuse; un moment de gloire, qu'un siècle de volupté. Il mesure le temps par les succès, et non pas par la durée.[2]

Corneille's characters move in this same ideal world. The most immediate appeal to the spectator's or the reader's admiration in the passage under consideration is through the mutual admiration of the two heroes themselves. Both generals are already endowed with such immense prestige by their past exploits that Sertorius can claim that a visit from the younger man will enhance his own repute ('rehausser ma gloire': a phrase which owes its resonance to the ethical system that animates all Corneille's theatre, with *la gloire*, a combination of reputation and self-esteem, as the mainspring of all his heroes' actions);[3] while Pompée in his turn welcomes the chance to pay personal tribute to the hero of an older generation. The fact that the two heroes are enemies lends force to their admiration for each other, and helps the spectator to evoke an ideal civilisation in which not even civil war can suppress the claims of honour and chivalry (line 12). Effective play is made throughout the tragedy, as elsewhere in Corneille's theatre, with the terms *Rome* and *romain*, rich with a wealth of ideal characteristics. In Sertorius's speech beginning at line 41, the adjective occurs twice in the emphatic

---

[1] See the commentary to passage no. VI.

[2] *Œuvres* (Paris, 1665), II, pp. 420-1. Cf. F. E. Sutcliffe: 'Certes, la Rome de Balzac est en grande partie mythique, et il n'est pas question de déterminer dans quelle mesure elle traduit une réalité quelconque. L'essentiel du problème n'est pas là. Ce qui importe, c'est le contenu du mythe même qui, lui, est à double profondeur: on trouve dans l'idéologie romaine des éléments qui répondent à un besoin senti par l'époque; et on prête aux Romains des qualités qui sont proprement l'apanage de la société contemporaine française'—*Guez de Balzac et son temps* (Paris, 1959), p. 205.

[3] See the commentary to passage no. VI.

rhyming position;[1] and this is a prelude to the vigorous exchange which forms, perhaps, the climax of the scene:

> POMPÉE
> Il est doux de revoir les murs de la patrie.
> C'est elle par ma voix, Seigneur, qui vous en prie,
> C'est Rome . . .
>
> SERTORIUS
>   Le séjour de votre potentat,
> Qui n'a que ses fureurs pour maximes d'état ?
> Je n'appelle plus Rome un enclos de murailles
> Que ses proscriptions comblent de funérailles;
> Ces murs, dont le destin fut autrefois si beau,
> N'en sont que la prison, ou plutôt le tombeau.
> Mais pour revivre ailleurs dans sa première force,
> Avec les faux Romains elle a fait plein divorce,
> Et comme autour de moi j'ai tous ses vrais appuis,
> Rome n'est plus dans Rome, elle est là où je suis.[2]

The effect of this heroic magnanimity, this self-confident pride, on the part of both speakers, is enhanced by the elevated language of the passage. Although it is less markedly rhetorical than most passages of sustained Cornelian dialectic, the scene is written in the refined abstract language which is typical of the author's heroic style. Abstractions predominate: in Pompée's speech, for instance, the framework is provided by 'l'inimitié', 'les droits de l'honneur', 'le vrai mérite', 'les haines les plus vives', 'l'estime et le respect', 'les vertus', 'la haute vaillance', 'mon trop de fortune', 'mes désavantages', 'les plus beaux succès,' 'mes prospérités', 'votre exemple'. Epithets are sparingly used, colourless and conventional: 'le *vrai* mérite', 'de *justes* tributs', '*fiers* ennemis', 'la *haute* vaillance', 'un si *fameux* héros', 'ce regard *terrible*', '*grands* courages'. Where concrete terms are used, they are generally in weak, conventional figures of speech: 'l'ombre de la paix', 'sans lui voir à la main piques ni javelots' (discreetly echoed in 'une pique à la main', line 67), 'le front désarmé', 'un bras invincible'. When Sertorius remarks that Pompée had been granted a triumphal procession at an exceptionally early age, the allusion is phrased in a concentrated, abstract manner;

---

[1] In each case, moreover, in the second line of the couplet, so that its force is increased by a certain discreet 'anticipation'. Cf. lines 5-6, where the anticipated rhyme-word 'Pompée' is much too obvious, producing a rather banal effect; see also p. 45, note 1.

[2] Lines 925-36.

and even when technical aspects of generalship are envisaged, in lines 51-3, the language does not lose its abstract character. Nevertheless, the language is not so highly intellectualised as to be lacking in human warmth and vitality, and the grandiloquent evocation of heroic achievements in the past and *grandeur d'âme* in the present combines with the regular rhythm of the alexandrine line to produce that intangible quality of the 'sublime' in which Corneille's contemporaries recognised his principal appeal. Saint-Évremond, writing a few years later on the subject of Racine's tragedy *Alexandre*, regrets that the younger author has not taken the opportunity to create a similar interview between his two heroes:

> J'aurais souhaité que ... dans une scène digne de la magnificence du sujet on eût fait aller la grandeur de leurs âmes jusqu'où elle pourrait aller. Si la conversation de Sertorius et de Pompée a tellement rempli nos esprits, que ne devait-on espérer de celle de Porus et d'Alexandre sur un sujet si peu commun ?[1]

But Racine appealed to his public by other means than by 'combats de générosité' between idealised embodiments of Roman virtue. His career was to begin in 1664, and tastes were already changing. *Sertorius* was to be one of Corneille's last great successes.

[1] In his *Dissertation sur la tragédie de Racine intitulée Alexandre le Grand, Œuvres choisies* (Paris, 1866), p. 171.

IX

Molière

(1622-73)

From *La Critique de l'École des femmes*, scene iii

URANIE
Quel est donc votre mal ? et depuis quand vous a-t-il pris ?

CLIMÈNE
Il y a plus de trois heures, et je l'ai rapporté du **Palais-Royal.**

URANIE
Comment ?

CLIMÈNE
Je viens de voir, pour mes péchés, cette méchante rapsodie de *l'École des femmes.* Je suis encore en défaillance du mal de cœur que cela m'a donné, et je pense que je n'en reviendrai de plus de quinze jours.

ÉLISE
Voyez un peu comme les maladies arrivent sans qu'on y songe.

URANIE
Je ne sais pas de quel tempérament nous sommes, ma cousine et moi; mais nous fûmes avant-hier à la même pièce, et nous en revînmes toutes deux
10 saines et gaillardes.

CLIMÈNE
Quoi ? Vous l'avez vue ?

URANIE
Oui, et écoutée d'un bout à l'autre.

CLIMÈNE
Et vous n'en avez pas été jusqu'aux convulsions, ma chère ?

URANIE
Je ne suis pas si délicate, Dieu merci; et je trouve, pour moi, que cette comédie serait plutôt capable de guérir les gens, que de les rendre malades.

CLIMÈNE
Ah mon Dieu! que dites-vous là ? Cette proposition peut-elle être avancée par une personne qui ait du revenu en sens commun ? Peut-on impuné-

ment, comme vous faites, rompre en visière à la raison ? Et dans le vrai de la chose, est-il un esprit si affamé de plaisanterie, qu'il puisse tâter des
20 fadaises dont cette comédie est assaisonnée ? Pour moi, je vous avoue que je n'ai pas trouvé le moindre grain de sel dans tout cela. Les «enfants par l'oreille» m'ont paru d'un goût détestable; la «tarte à la crème» m'a affadi le cœur, et j'ai pensé vomir au « potage ».[1]

ÉLISE

Mon Dieu! que tout cela est dit élégamment! J'aurais cru que cette pièce était bonne; mais Madame a une éloquence si persuasive, elle tourne les choses d'une manière si agréable, qu'il faut être de son sentiment, malgré qu'on en ait.

URANIE

Pour moi, je n'ai pas tant de complaisance; et, pour dire ma pensée, je tiens cette comédie une des plus plaisantes que l'auteur ait produites.

CLIMÈNE

30 Ah! vous me faites pitié de parler ainsi, et je ne saurais vous souffrir cette obscurité de discernement. Peut-on, ayant de la vertu, trouver de l'agrément dans une pièce qui tient sans cesse la pudeur en alarme, et salit à tous moments l'imagination ?

ÉLISE

Les jolies façons de parler que voilà! Que vous êtes, Madame, une rude joueuse en critique, et que je plains le pauvre Molière de vous avoir pour ennemie!

CLIMÈNE

Croyez-moi, ma chère, corrigez de bonne foi votre jugement; et pour votre honneur, n'allez point dire par le monde que cette comédie vous ait plu.

URANIE

40 Moi, je ne sais pas ce que vous y avez trouvé qui blesse la pudeur.

CLIMÈNE

Hélas! tout; et je mets en fait qu'une honnête femme ne saurait la voir sans confusion, tant j'y ai trouvé d'ordures et de saletés.

URANIE

Il faut donc que pour les ordures vous ayez des lumières que les autres n'ont pas; car, pour moi, je n'y en ai point vu.

---

[1] The references are to *L'École des femmes*, lines 159-64, 95-100 and 430-9.

CLIMÈNE

C'est que vous ne voulez pas y en avoir vu, assurément; car enfin toutes ces ordures, Dieu merci, y sont à visage découvert. Elles n'ont point la moindre enveloppe qui les couvre, et les yeux les plus hardis sont effrayés de leur nudité.

L'École des femmes and *La Critique de l'École des femmes*, ed. W. D. Howarth (Oxford, 1963), pp. 86-8

L'École des femmes, first performed in December 1662, was the first of Molière's plays to provoke a widespread critical controversy. Throughout 1663 and into the following year, a series of hostile plays and pamphlets appeared, their authors for the most part connected with the Hôtel de Bourgogne, which housed the rival troupe of players to Molière's own company established at the Palais-Royal. As was not uncommon in literary polemic at the time, serious criticism on genuine aesthetic grounds was mixed in these writings with scurrilous personal attacks on the playwright's private life, and the general tone remained petty and narrow-minded. Molière's own contribution to the 'guerre comique', as it came to be called, took the form of two one-act plays, the *Critique de l'École des femmes* (produced in June 1663) and the *Impromptu de Versailles* (performed before the King in October of the same year). The interest of both plays far exceeds the narrow limits of the controversy: the latter gives us valuable information about Molière's technique as an actor and producer, while the interest of the *Critique* is more varied. On the one hand, it provides the fullest and most coherent statement of Molière's own aesthetic; and in addition to this the author shows a gift for the recording of natural dialogue which makes it a genuine work of art in the genre of the 'conversation piece', so that it is still performed very successfully as a play in its own right at the Comédie-Française.

The scene is set in a fashionable *salon*. Molière entrusts the defence of *L'École des femmes* to two sympathetic characters, Uranie (the hostess) and the chevalier Dorante; while criticism—of the sort that had already found expression in the course of the controversy—is put into the mouths of an extravagant marquis,[1] the pedantic poet Lysidas and the *précieuse* Climène. The latter is the first to arrive, and scene iii is devoted to

[1] This fashionable and empty-headed character represented a common social type, whom Molière had already ridiculed in *Les Précieuses ridicules* and his *Remercîment au Roi*. One of the most offensive of the attacks on Molière at this time was called *La Vengeance des marquis*.

establishing her affectation and prudery. Her unreliability as a judge of literature is shown up by serious argument on the part of Uranie, and by mocking approval on the part of Uranie's vivacious cousin, Élise, who has already before Climène's arrival expressed her real opinion:

ÉLISE
Est-ce qu'il y a une personne qui soit plus véritablement qu'elle ce qu'on appelle précieuse, à prendre le mot dans sa plus mauvaise signification?

URANIE
Elle se défend bien de ce nom pourtant.

ÉLISE
Il est vrai; elle se défend du nom, mais non pas de la chose; car enfin elle l'est depuis les pieds jusqu'à la tête, et la plus grande façonnière du monde.[1]

The study of the seventeenth-century historical phenomenon known as preciosity is complicated by the widely-differing views held by modern scholars, especially with regard to chronology: compare, for instance, the definition: 'a social and literary movement, taking place in France, say between 1588 and 1665'[2] with the categorical statement: 'La préciosité est née très exactement en 1654'.[3] Moreover, there is the additional difficulty that the term 'précieux' is widely used in literary criticism to denote a style of writing by no means limited to the seventeenth century. There is, of course, a close connection between the two senses of the word, and in a sense Bray was justified in claiming that 'on a eu tort d'isoler dans l'histoire une portion assez courte du mouvement précieux. . . . Une grande histoire critique de la préciosité . . . traverserait toute notre littérature du XIIᵉ au XXᵉ siècle'.[4] But such an approach, however well founded, runs the risk of over-emphasising aesthetic considerations at the expense of the historical and social factors which were essential in determining the character of seventeenth-century preciosity, in its better as well as in its worse forms, social as well as literary. For A. Adam, preciosity is essentially 'non pas une attitude en face de l'art et des lettres, mais une position prise devant les problèmes de la vie sentimentale'. It is a declaration of feminist principles on the part of women of culture and intelligence, rebelling against ce tain features of the social order of the time:

[1] Scene ii.
[2] O. de Mourgues, *Metaphysical, Baroque and Précieux Poetry* (Oxford, 1953), p. 103.
[3] A. Adam, 'Baroque et préciosité' in *Revue des sciences humaines* (1949), p. 208.
[4] R. Bray, *La Préciosité et les précieux* (Paris, 1948), p. 8.

Elles affirment le droit de la femme à disposer librement d'elle-même, à choisir le compagnon de sa vie, à cultiver, s'il lui plaît, avant et durant le mariage, l'art et les belles-lettres, à connaître les plaisirs de l'esprit.[1]

Seen in this light, preciosity in the 1650s is far from being a self-contained phenomenon; it forms part of a more general social activity throughout the century, the development of polite society round the fashionable *salons* which brought together men and women of quality and representatives of the world of letters. In these regular gatherings the art of conversation and other social graces were cultivated, the ideal of *honnêteté* was elaborated, and men of taste and discernment took an active interest in literature.

The most celebrated of these meeting-places was the 'chambre bleue' (the term *salon* is strictly an anachronism when we are dealing with the early years of the century) of the marquise de Rambouillet. An inaccurate tradition maintains that this lady was the first to hold a *salon*, and that she began to do this when she ceased to frequent the Court in disgust at the uncouth manners displayed there; in fact, other hostesses had already begun to receive company in the same way, and her retirement from court life seems to have been largely due to ill-health. The pre-eminence of the Hôtel de Rambouillet is, however, well established: Tallemant des Réaux calls it 'le rendez-vous de ce qu'il y avait de plus galant à la Cour, et de plus poli parmi les beaux-esprits du siècle'.[2] The prestige and influence of this *salon* were at their height from about 1625 until about 1650. Such great men as Richelieu and Condé were to be seen there, and noblemen and men of letters mixed on terms of easy equality; there were few of the leading writers of the time who did not come to read their works or to join in the discussion of literary or linguistic topics. Conversation at the Hôtel de Rambouillet might be light-hearted or serious, but was never pedantic.

Other hostesses who served their apprenticeship, as it were, at the Hôtel de Rambouillet included Mlle de Scudéry, whose *salon* is most representative of the social-literary climate of the 1650s. The gatherings here were less aristocratic and *mondaines*, and the activities were more exclusively literary in character.[3] Mlle de Scudéry was herself an authoress, and her novels *Le Grand Cyrus* (1649-53) and *Clélie* (1654-60) catered for the fashion for literary 'portraits' by depicting the *habitués* of her *salon* or other contemporary notabilities in the guise of characters

---

[1] A. Adam, op. cit., p. 200.   [2] *Historiettes*, ed. cit., I, p. 443.   [3] See Plate IV.

from antiquity. Another extremely popular feature of the latter novel was the allegorical 'Carte de Tendre', which charted the way from Nouvelle Amitié to the cities of Tendre sur Estime, Tendre sur Reconnaissance and Tendre sur Inclination, an indication of the preoccupations which reigned in Mlle de Scudéry's circle.

It is in connection with this and similar *salons* which flourished about the middle of the century that it becomes proper to speak of preciosity in the more restricted sense. We are dealing now not only with the civilising influence of cultured women in society in a general sense, but with a veritable cult of feminism. The *précieuses* were seeking to emancipate themselves from the social disabilities from which women still suffered in all classes of society except the very lowest: an inferior education, marriages of convenience which were often little more than business transactions, and a repressive attitude to marriage itself, which insisted on the wife's duty of complete submission to her husband.[1] The earlier *salons* had of course represented a reaction against this state of affairs, but in the 1650s we witness a shift of emphasis: from the free exchange of ideas between men and women of culture, we move to the *précieux* conception of an intellectual society ruled by women of taste, and whose principal preoccupation is the discussion and analysis of the affairs of the heart. In place of—or at least outside—the conventional social obligations of marriage, the *précieuses* set up their ideal of love according to a code, not unlike the courtly code of the Middle Ages: the lover was to defer in all things to his mistress, proving his devotion if necessary by years of unrewarded service, while some *précieuses* idealised the relationship still further by insisting on the virtues of platonic love, and the solid merit of 'honnête amitié' between the sexes. (Thus Julie d'Angennes, Mme de Rambouillet's daughter, married the duc de Montausier only after keeping him waiting for thirteen years, and Mlle de Scudéry had a long and celebrated platonic relationship with the much younger writer Pellisson.) The searching discussion of the detailed psychology of love, the 'questions d'amour' which were continually debated in these *salons*,[2] brought with them the need for a precise analytical language; hence the exploitation by the *précieuses* of fine nuances of meaning, hence their recourse to neologism and to figurative ways of expression which, taken to extremes, soon became extravagant jargon.

[1] See the commentary to passage no. XII.
[2] Ibid.

For with all their serious culture and their laudable aspirations towards social emancipation for women,[1] there was a certain exhibitionism about the *précieuses*. Some sought to distinguish themselves as bluestockings, by the range of their intellectual interests; others to prove feminine supremacy by refinement of taste and judgment; while others invented more superficial affectations of speech, behaviour or dress. It was not long, therefore, before the new fashion became the subject of satire; and inevitably the satirical portraits of the extravagant excesses of preciosity have tended to colour the historical view of the original phenomenon.

The name 'précieuse' was first applied to the new movement in the early 1650s;[2] to begin with it is used with a pejorative intention, though it seems to have been accepted by the *précieuses* themselves. By 1660 it was in common use to describe not only Mlle de Scudéry's circle, but a widespread social fashion. A verse *Épître* by Scarron, d'Aubignac's *Nouvelle Histoire du temps ou Relation véritable du royaume de Coquetterie*, a lost one-act farce by the abbé de Pure, and a verse satire, *Le Cercle*, by Saint-Évremond: these provide the first critical comment on the new fashion, which is ridiculed for its affectation and its jargon, and also for its over-subtle analysis of the psychology of love:

> Dans un lieu plus secret on tient la précieuse,
> Occupée aux leçons de morale amoureuse.
> Là se font distinguer les fiertés des rigueurs,
> Les dédains des mépris, les tourments des langueurs;
> On y sait démêler la crainte et les alarmes,
> Discerner les attraits, les appas et les charmes;
> On y parle du temps qu'on forme le désir,
> Mouvement incertain de peine et de plaisir.
> Des premiers maux d'amour on connaît la naissance,
> On a de leurs progrès une entière science,
> Et toujours on ajuste à l'ordre des douleurs
> Et le temps de la plainte et la saison des pleurs.[3]

These, however, were slight and ephemeral writings, and satire of preciosity was expressed with much greater effect not only in Molière's *Les Précieuses ridicules* (1659), but also in two substantial works, a novel

---

[1] For a less praiseworthy development of seventeenth-century feminism in an extreme form, see the commentary to passage no. XIV.

[2] It is already found in some medieval texts, however, with the pejorative meaning of 'affected' (cf. Littré).

[3] Saint-Évremond, *Le Cercle*, quoted in Bray, op. cit., p. 131.

by the abbé de Pure with the same title as his lost play, *La Précieuse* (1656-8) and Somaize's *Grand Dictionnaire des précieuses* (1660). The latter contains an interesting lexicon of *précieux* jargon, as well as a copious portrait-gallery; the tone is gossipy rather than malicious, and the work possibly has more documentary value from the linguistic than from the biographical point of view.[1] The abbé de Pure's novel has a good deal of documentary value as an account of the ideas behind the *précieux* movement, and his criticism is not lacking in sympathy.[2] But no other satire had anything like the impact of Molière's play; and when *Les Précieuses ridicules* is considered together with *Les Femmes savantes* (1672), it is easy to understand why it is generally accepted that Molière, as the champion of common-sense against affectation and extravagance, saw the *précieux* movement on the whole as an object of ridicule.

In fact, however, the question of Molière's relations with the *précieuses*, and his attitude to the ideas underlying preciosity, is not nearly as simple as this. On the one hand, Magdelon and Cathos, the 'précieuses ridicules', are presented as ignorant provincials, aping the manners of the capital; but they speak the authentic jargon, and their second-hand notions, extravagant though they are, come from a reading of Mlle de Scudéry herself. Molière, it is true, drew the distinction between true and false preciosity in his Preface:

> Ces vicieuses imitations de ce qu'il y a de plus parfait ont été de tout temps la matière de la comédie; et... par la même raison que les véritables savants et les vrais braves ne se sont point encore avisés de s'offenser du Docteur de la comédie et du Capitan,... aussi les véritables précieuses auraient tort de se piquer lorsqu'on joue les ridicules qui les imitent mal

—but this is at best a very conventional sort of disclaimer, of no more value as a clue to the real aim of his satire than the tradition that both Mme de Rambouillet and Mlle de Scudéry were present at the first performance of the play, and watched it with approval. It is hardly enough to outweigh the evidence of a passage such as the following:

> L'air précieux n'a pas seulement infecté Paris, il s'est aussi répandu dans les provinces, et nos donzelles ridicules en ont humé leur bonne part. En un mot, c'est un ambigu de précieuse et de coquette que leur personne.[3]

[1] See the edition by C. Livet (Paris, 1856).
[2] See the Introduction to the edition by E. Magne (Paris, 1938-9).
[3] Scene i.

and *Les Précieuses ridicules* offers little indication that Molière saw anything to admire in preciosity.

It is when we come to *L'École des maris* and *L'École des femmes* that we are led to revise such an extreme view. In these two plays Molière treats the theme of the upbringing of young women: both the question of the moral and social liberty of the grown woman before marriage, and that of formal education at an earlier stage, which is dealt with more specifically in *L'École des femmes*. The central character of each play represents the traditional view of marriage: each has had the legal guardianship of the young girl he has elected to marry, and in both cases the tutelage has been harsh and repressive. Sganarelle explains what he looks for in a wife as follows:

> J'entends que la mienne
> Vive à ma fantaisie, et non pas à la sienne;
> ... Qu'enfermée au logis, en personne bien sage,
> Elle s'applique toute aux choses du ménage,
> A recoudre mon linge aux heures de loisir,
> Ou bien à tricoter quelques bas par plaisir;
> Qu'aux discours des muguets elle ferme l'oreille,
> Et ne sorte jamais sans avoir qui la veille[1]

and Arnolphe takes the same sort of view still further:

> Bien qu'on soit deux moitiés de la société,
> Ces deux moitiés pourtant n'ont point d'égalité:
> L'une est moitié suprême et l'autre subalterne;
> L'une en tout est soumise à l'autre qui gouverne;
> Et ce que le soldat, dans son devoir instruit,
> Montre d'obéissance au chef qui le conduit,
> Le valet à son maître, un enfant à son père,
> A son supérieur le moindre petit frère,
> N'approche point encor de la docilité,
> Et de l'obéissance, et de l'humilité,
> Et du profond respect où la femme doit être
> Pour son mari, son chef, son seigneur et son maître.[2]

In showing these two suitors in a comic light, and in suggesting by dramatic means that a marriage based on such principles is doomed to failure, for it drives the oppressed wife to look elsewhere than to her husband for understanding and respect, Molière is making common

---

[1] *L'École des maris*, lines 115-24.   [2] *L'École des femmes*, lines 701-12.

cause with the *précieuses*, in their feminist campaign at least. Indeed, Arnolphe makes specific reference to the *précieuses* and their ways when he scornfully rejects the arguments in favour of intelligence in a wife:

> Une femme habile est un mauvais présage;
> Et je sais ce qu'il coûte à de certaines gens
> Pour avoir pris les leurs avec trop de talents.
> Moi, j'irais me charger d'une spirituelle
> Qui ne parlerait rien que cercle et que ruelle,
> Qui de prose et de vers ferait de doux écrits,
> Et que visiteraient marquis et beaux esprits,
> Tandis que, sous le nom de mari de Madame,
> Je serais comme un saint que pas un ne réclame? [1]

In his view, the proper sort of partner is a wife with limited intelligence and a minimum of education:

> Épouser une sotte est pour n'être point sot.[2]

It may seem strange in view of Molière's sympathy with the *précieux* views on marriage that among the critics of his play introduced into the *Critique* there should appear the *précieuse* Climène. It is a fact, however, that some contemporaries did manage so to misunderstand the play that Arnolphe's strictures against women's education and social emancipation were credited to Molière himself, and Climène's complaint of 'les satires désobligeantes qu'on y voit contre les femmes'[3] can be matched from actual criticisms of the play.[4]

If a distinction can be drawn between 'true' and 'false' preciosity—and I think the distinction is a genuine one, though it is doubtful how far Molière himself would have been prepared to take it—Climène obviously represents the latter variety. Her criticism of *L'École des femmes* is based on the type of affectation denounced by Uranie in a later passage from the same scene:

> L'honnêteté d'une femme n'est pas dans les grimaces. Il sied mal de vouloir être plus sage que celles qui sont sages. L'affectation en cette matière est pire qu'en toute autre; et je ne vois rien de si ridicule que cette délicatesse d'honneur qui prend tout en mauvaise part, donne un sens criminel aux plus innocentes paroles, et s'offense de l'ombre des choses.

---

[1] Ibid., lines 84-92.   [2] Ibid., line 82.   [3] Scene vi.
[4] Robinet's *Panégyrique de l'École des femmes* (1664) offers some particularly interesting examples of this.

Women who behave like this, warns the sensible Uranie, run the risk of appearing 'plus chastes des oreilles que de tout le reste du corps'.[1] In fact, this sort of criticism is not really criticism at all; it is no more than the arbitrary attempt by a coterie to determine literary fashion, an activity which Molière was to satirise in *Les Femmes savantes* :

> Nous serons par nos lois les juges des ouvrages;
> Par nos lois, prose et vers, tout nous sera soumis;
> Nul n'aura de l'esprit hors nous et nos amis;
> Nous chercherons partout à trouver à redire,
> Et ne verrons que nous qui sache bien écrire[2]

and which has little in common with the more high-minded aspirations of the *précieuses*, with which he seems to have had considerable sympathy.

The passage under consideration is principally interesting for the way in which Molière has brought the *précieuse* Climène to life, and in particular for the authentic flavour of *précieux* speech, with its typical features of exaggeration, hyperbole and outlandish imagery. The tendency is continually to substitute the concrete and the vivid for the abstract and the prosaic. Thus the commonplace experience of a visit to the theatre conjures up the most startling physical effects: 'Je suis encore en défaillance du mal de cœur . . .', 'vous n'en avez pas été jusqu'aux convulsions . . .?' with the hyperbole 'je n'en reviendrai de plus de quinze jours' thrown in for good measure; while the consideration of the shortcomings of Molière's play gives rise to a picturesque series of metaphors: 'affamé . . . , tâter de . . . , assaisonnée . . . , le moindre grain de sel . . . , d'un goût détestable . . . , affadir le cœur . . . , vomir . . .'. ('Un grain de sel' has of course survived in general currency, as have the *précieux* neologism 'obscénité' and the figurative use of 'épouvantable',

---

[1] Cf. the absurd 'project' of the 'femmes savantes' (also referred to in scene vi of the *Critique*):

> Mais le plus beau projet de notre académie,
> Une entreprise noble, et dont je suis ravie,
> Un dessein plein de gloire, et qui sera vanté
> Chez tous les beaux esprits de la postérité,
> C'est le retranchement de ces syllabes sales
> Qui dans les plus beaux mots produisent des scandales,
> Ces jouets éternels des sots de tous les temps,
> Ces fades lieux communs de nos méchants plaisants,
> Ces sources d'un amas d'équivoques infâmes,
> Dont on vient faire insulte à la pudeur des femmes.
>   (*Les Femmes savantes*, lines 909-18.)

[2] Ibid., lines 922-6.

which occur later in the scene.) Other characteristic examples of figurative speech are 'une personne qui ait du revenu en sens commun', 'rompre en visière à la raison', 'tenir la pudeur en alarme', 'salir l'imagination'; and in place of 'ce manque de jugement' we have 'cette obscurité de discernement'. The passage closes with another example of sustained imagery: 'à visage découvert . . . , la moindre enveloppe qui les couvre . . . , leur nudité'. Contemporary texts bear witness to affectations just as extravagant as these; and where the fashion itself was so fanciful, it is hardly possible to speak of caricature. It can be said, however, that there is a consistency about Climène's speech which makes it seem like a genuine copy of the real thing beside the somewhat cruder satire of *Les Précieuses ridicules*.

The vogue of preciosity in its most extreme form was not very long-lived. La Bruyère writes of it as a thing of the past:

> L'on a vu, il n'y a pas longtemps, un cercle de personnes des deux sexes, liées ensemble par la conversation et par un commerce d'esprit. Ils laissaient au vulgaire l'art de parler d'une manière intelligible; une chose dite entre eux peu clairement en entraînait une autre encore plus obscure, sur laquelle on enchérissait par de vraies énigmes, toujours suivies de longs applaudissements; par tout ce qu'ils appelaient délicatesse, sentiments, tour et finesse d'expression, ils étaient enfin parvenus à n'être plus entendus et à ne s'entendre pas eux-mêmes[1]

and Boileau credits Molière with having hastened its end:

> une précieuse,
> Reste de ces esprits jadis si renommés
> Que d'un coup de son art Molière a diffamés.[2]

Boileau himself was opposed to more than the superficial affectations of the movement, if his 'Satire contre les femmes' is to be taken as evidence, for his attitude there is hardly any more liberal than that of Arnolphe. But in Molière's case, as we have seen, it is necessary to distinguish the superficial absurdities of *précieux* behaviour from the important social aspirations which the more intelligent *précieuses* put forward. If the 'femmes savantes' are held up to ridicule in the play of that name, so once again is the representative of the traditional bourgeois attitude to marriage in the person of Chrysale. Molière was himself on excellent terms with Mme de la Sablière, in whose *salon*, as in Philaminte's,

---

[1] *Caractères*, V, para. 65.
[2] *Satire* X, lines 438-40.

serious scientific and philosophical interests were pursued;[1] but whereas in the case of Mme de la Sablière learning was accompanied by intelligence and common-sense, Philaminte's intellectual activities obscure her judgment and cause her to make a mess of her private affairs. Clitandre's well-known speech points the moral:

> Je consens qu'une femme ait des clartés de tout;
> Mais je ne lui veux point la passion choquante
> De se rendre savante afin d'être savante;
> Et j'aime que souvent, aux questions qu'on fait,
> Elle sache ignorer les choses qu'elle sait;
> De son étude enfin je veux qu'elle se cache,
> Et qu'elle ait du savoir sans vouloir qu'on le sache[2]

—and we need only compare these lines with the following passage written by Mlle de Scudéry:

> Encore que je voulusse que les femmes sussent plus de choses qu'elles n'en savent pour l'ordinaire, je ne veux pourtant jamais qu'elles agissent ni qu'elles parlent en savantes. Je veux donc bien qu'on puisse dire d'une personne de mon sexe qu'elle sait cent choses dont elle ne se vante pas, qu'elle a l'esprit fort éclairé, qu'elle connaît finement les beaux ouvrages, qu'elle parle bien, qu'elle écrit juste et qu'elle sait le monde; mais je ne veux pas qu'on puisse dire d'elle: c'est une femme savante. Ce n'est pas que celle qu'on n'appellera point savante ne puisse savoir autant et plus de choses que celles à qui on donnera ce terrible nom; mais c'est qu'elle se sait mieux servir de son esprit, et qu'elle sait cacher adroitement ce que l'autre montre mal à propos[3]

to see how remarkably close Molière's ideas on the subject were to those of the high-priestess of preciosity herself.

[1] See the commentary to passage no. XIII.
[2] *Les Femmes savantes*, lines 218-24.
[3] From *Le Grand Cyrus*, quoted by C. Livet in his edition of Somaize: *Le Grand Diction-naire...*, II, p. 373. It is interesting to compare this passage with some of those quoted in the commentary to passage no. VII, and to reflect on the affinity between the social ideal of *honnêteté* and the aspirations of the less extravagant *précieuses*.

X

Saint-Evremond

(1614-1703)

From *Lettre à monsieur le maréchal de Créqui*

J'ai passé d'une étude de métaphysique à l'examen des religions; et retournant à cette antiquité qui m'est si chère, je n'ai vu chez les Grecs et chez les Romains qu'un culte superstitieux d'idolâtres, ou une invention humaine politiquement établie pour bien gouverner les hommes. Il ne m'a pas été difficile de reconnaître l'avantage de la religion chrétienne sur les autres; et tirant de moi tout ce que je puis pour me soumettre respectueusement à la foi de ses mystères, j'ai laissé goûter à ma raison, avec plaisir, la plus pure et la plus parfaite morale qui fût jamais.

Dans la diversité des croyances qui partagent le christianisme, la vraie
10 catholicité me tient à elle autant par mon élection, si j'avais encore à choisir, que par habitude et par les impressions que j'en ai reçues. Mais cet attachement à ma croyance ne m'anime point contre celle des autres, et je n'eus jamais ce zèle indiscret qui nous fait haïr les personnes, parce qu'elles ne conviennent pas de sentiment avec nous. L'amour-propre forme ce faux zèle, et une séduction secrète nous fait voir de la charité pour le prochain où il n'y a rien qu'un excès de complaisance pour notre opinion.

Ce que nous appelons aujourd'hui *les religions*, n'est, à le bien prendre, que *différence dans la religion*, et non pas *religion différente*. Je me réjouis de croire plus sainement qu'un huguenot; cependant, au lieu de le haïr
20 pour sa différence d'opinion, il m'est cher de ce qu'il convient de mon principe. Le moyen de convenir à la fin en tout, c'est de se communiquer toujours par quelque chose. Vous n'inspirerez jamais l'amour de la réunion, si vous n'ôtez la haine de la division auparavant. On peut se rechercher comme sociables, mais on ne revient point à des ennemis. La feinte, l'hypocrisie dans la religion, sont les seules choses qui doivent être odieuses; car qui croit de bonne foi, quand il croirait mal, se rend digne d'être plaint, au lieu de mériter qu'on le persécute. L'aveuglement du corps attire la compassion: que peut avoir celui de l'esprit pour exciter de la haine? Dans la plus grande tyrannie des anciens, on laissait à l'entendement une pleine
30 liberté de ses lumières; et il y a des nations aujourd'hui, parmi les chrétiens,

où l'on impose la loi de se persuader ce qu'on ne peut croire! Selon mon sentiment, chacun doit être libre dans sa croyance, pourvu qu'elle n'aille pas à exciter des factions qui puissent troubler la tranquillité publique. Les temples sont du droit des souverains; ils s'ouvrent et se ferment comme il leur plaît; mais notre cœur en est un secret, où il nous est permis d'adorer leur maître.

Œuvres, ed. R. de Planhol
(Paris, 1927), I, pp. 160-1

Although as a man of letters he belongs to the period of Louis XIV, Saint-Évremond's intellectual formation took place in the closing years of Louis XIII's reign, and his career as soldier and courtier spans the middle years of the century. He was born, most probably, in 1614, entered the army at an early age, and saw active service under Condé, being wounded at the battle of Nordlingen (1645). He subsequently fell into disfavour with Condé and left his service in 1649; and during the Fronde, although he played an active part in the political intrigue, he was able to take a critical view of the motives and conduct of the leaders of both parties. Though he was later employed by Mazarin, he seems always to have been suspect to him—he spent a short period in the Bastille for expressing his opinions too freely—and it was in fact a letter attacking the Cardinal's absolutist policy which brought Saint-Évremond's career as a courtier to a sudden end. Although this letter came to light only after Mazarin's death, its contents, together with Saint-Évremond's connection with the disgraced Fouquet,[1] made it prudent for him to flee the country, and in spite of his pleas for a political pardon, he was never again to set foot on French soil after 1661.

In the enforced leisure of the next phase of his life, Saint-Évremond set out to cultivate those intellectual pursuits in which he had already shown an active interest before his exile. Amongst his acquaintances in France he had been admired as a typical representative of *honnêteté*—one of the first works written in exile was the *Jugement sur les sciences où peut s'appliquer un honnête homme*, of 1662[2]—and if his reputation as a cultured sage was by the end of his life out of all proportion to the volume

---

[1] Nicolas Fouquet, who had reached a position of great wealth and power under Mazarin's administration, was arrested in 1661 and tried in 1664, charged with misappropriation of public money. Sentenced to imprisonment for life, he remained in prison until his death in 1680.

[2] See the commentary to passage no. VII.

of his published work, this was at least partly due to the example of his life of Epicurean tranquillity, and to the flavour of his conversation and letters to his friends. The most important influences on his intellectual development were those of Montaigne and Gassendi: he was critical of the traditional systems of thought based on the authority of the ancients, but he had no taste for the speculative rationalism of Descartes. For Saint-Évremond, the dogmatic side of religion was subordinated to the ethical, and while in France he had practised the prudent conformism common to the *libertins* of the middle of the century.[1] Whatever the extent of his own scepticism with regard to Christian dogma, however, he retained a genuine admiration for the Christian ethic, and a respect for the ritual and traditions of the Catholic Church as a framework within which that ethic could most effectively be practised. Theological controversy, on the other hand, he deplored, and in the entertaining *Conversation du maréchal d'Hocquincourt avec le père Canaye* (1654) he reduces the quarrel between Jansenists and Jesuits to intrigue and self-interest:

> Ce n'est ni la Grâce, ni les cinq Propositions qui nous ont mis mal ensemble. La jalousie de gouverner les consciences a tout fait. Les jansénistes nous ont trouvés en possession du gouvernement, et ils ont voulu nous en tirer. Pour parvenir à leurs fins, ils se sont servis de moyens tout contraires aux nôtres. Nous employons la douceur et l'indulgence; ils affectent l'austérité et la rigueur; nous consolons les âmes par des exemples de la miséricorde de Dieu; ils les effrayent par ceux de sa justice. Ils portent la crainte où nous portons l'espérance, et veulent s'assujettir ceux que nous voulons nous attirer. Ce n'est pas que les uns et les autres n'aient dessein de sauver les hommes, mais chacun se veut donner du crédit en les sauvant; et à vous parler franchement, l'intérêt du directeur va presque toujours devant le salut de celui qui est sous sa direction.[2]

The early years of his exile reinforced his interest in the sociological or utilitarian aspects of religious belief, and in particular led him to develop enlightened views on the subject of religious toleration. After a brief stay in Holland, the first years of exile (1662-5) were spent in England; from 1665 until 1670, however, Saint-Évremond lived in Holland, and the letter to Créqui, from which the passage under discussion is taken, was written shortly after his return to England, in

[1] See the commentary to passage no. II.

[2] *Œuvres*, ed. R. de Planhol (Paris, 1927), I, p. 114. Sainte-Beuve refers to the *Conversation* as 'la dix-neuvième Provinciale'—*Port-Royal*, ed. cit., III, p. 48.

1671. At this time Holland occupied in the eyes of liberal-minded Frenchmen the position which England was to fill a generation or so later: for the time being the memory of the civil war and of Cromwell's rule was still too fresh, and England, in French eyes, was the home of regicide and fanaticism rather than of toleration and liberty of conscience. Holland, on the other hand, was 'le pays des sectes et des refuges';[1] the Dutch printing-presses enjoyed a freedom unknown in France, and many a French fugitive found a welcome there. On the subject of religious toleration in Holland, Saint-Évremond writes in 1664:

> La différence de religion, qui excite ailleurs tant de troubles, ne cause pas ici la moindre altération dans les esprits. Chacun cherche le Ciel par ses voies;[2] et ceux qu'on croit égarés, plus plaints que haïs, s'attirent une charité pure et dégagée de l'indiscrétion du faux zèle.[3]

In addition to being able to witness at first hand this freedom from religious strife, Saint-Évremond made contact through Dutch scholars with the tradition of Christian humanism deriving from Erasmus, and his frequenting of liberal theologians led him to approach the study of the different Christian sects from a relativist point of view, as the products of particular historical circumstances. At this particular moment in France, the long-standing controversy between Jesuits and Jansenists had given way to the rather uneasy truce known as the 'Paix de l'Église' (1668), and public attention was focussed on the debate between the Jansenists Nicole and Arnauld and the Protestant pastor Claude on the question of the value of historical tradition in determining points of doctrine. The following poem by Saint-Évremond is not merely a superficial satire on the protagonists in the debate, it is the sincere protest of a humanist at the way in which the spirit of Christianity is travestied by theological controversy:

> Claude le protestant allègue l'Écriture,
> Dont le sens par Nicole est toujours contesté:
> Dans la tradition, que Nicole tient sure,
> Claude ne reconnaît aucune vérité.

[1] Sainte-Beuve, *Port-Royal*, ed. cit., V, p. 311.
[2] It is interesting to note the striking resemblance to Voltaire's celebrated phrase: 'Un Anglais, comme homme libre, va au Ciel par le chemin qui lui plaît'—*Lettres philosophiques*, ed. G. Lanson (Paris, 1924), I, p. 61.
[3] *Œuvres*, ed. cit., I, p. 90.

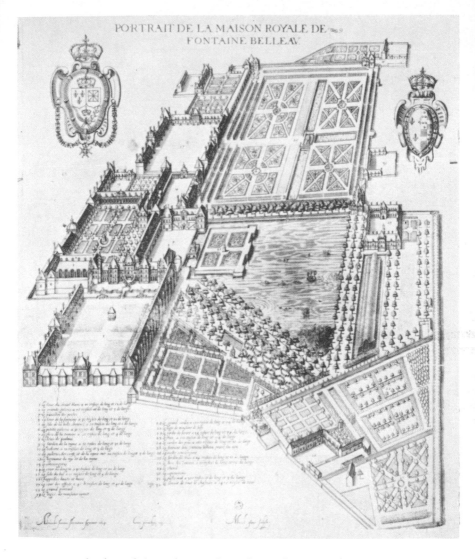

PLATE I   A plan of the palace and gardens of Fontainebleau,
from an engraving of *c*. 1614

PLATE II The stage-set for Act V of Corneille's *Andromède*

Toutes ces belles controverses
Sur les religions diverses
N'ont jamais produit aucun bien:
Chacun s'anime pour la sienne;
Et que fait-on pour la chrétienne?
On dispute, et l'on ne fait rien.

Comment! on ne fait rien pour elle?
On condamne les *juifs* au feu!
On extermine l'*infidèle!*
Si vous jugez que c'est trop peu,
On fera pendre l'*hérétique;*
Et quelquefois le *catholique*
Aura même peine à son tour.
Où pourrait-on trouver plus de zèle et d'amour?

Non, non, tu travailles contre elle;
Tout supplice, gêne, tourment,
Tient d'un noir et funeste zèle,
Que ton humanité dément:

Tu combats sa propre nature,
Sous prétexte de l'honorer,
Quand pour elle tu fais l'injure
Qu'elle t'ordonne d'endurer![1]

Before his exile, Saint-Évremond had found in the maréchal de Créqui a man of like tastes and interests: 'un esprit universel qui s'étend à tout. . . . Il pourrait se donner de la réputation par les lettres s'il ne la voulait par les armes....Il joint à l'avantage de savoir beaucoup le mérite de cacher discrètement ses connaissances'.[2] The letter of 1671 takes the form of a lengthy autobiographical essay giving an account of Saint-Évremond's intellectual activities, and the development of his ideas, over the previous decade. In a sense, it may be considered to be a development of the *Jugement sur les sciences où peut s'appliquer un honnête homme,* in which he had confessed: 'Je ne trouve point de sciences qui touchent plus particulièrement les honnêtes gens que *la morale, la politique* et la connaissance des *belles-lettres*'. In the present

---

[1] *Œuvres mêlées* (Amsterdam, 1706), III, pp. 105-6.
[2] Quoted by A. Adam in his edition of Tallemant des Réaux, *Historiettes* (Paris, 1961), II, p. 1336.

essay he writes of his favourite authors, of 'jurisprudence', and on moral topics such as ingratitude; but the most important part of the essay is the long concluding section on religion. Here, he briefly discusses, but only to dismiss it as fruitless, metaphysical speculation about the immortality of the soul, and in the passage under consideration turns to the examination of different forms of religion—that is, to religions considered as human institutions.

The religions of the ancient world are judged to be either empty superstitions or political systems manipulated by secular governments; Christianity is superior to these on two counts: its divine revelation, and its wholly admirable ethical teaching. On the subject of revelation, Saint-Évremond has recourse to a conventional fideist distinction between the spheres of faith and reason,[1] though how far his 'submission' denotes a genuine willingness to accept the mysteries of Christian doctrine, at this stage in his intellectual development, it is hard to determine.[2] At all events, his preoccupation is not with the act of faith required by revelation, but with the appeal of the Christian ethical system to the reason; a similar statement of the fideist position is to be found in a passage of 1684, which explains more fully the predominance given to ethics over articles of faith:

Dieu seul nous peut donner une foi sûre, ferme et véritable.[3] Ce que nous pouvons faire de nous, est de captiver l'entendement malgré la répugnance des lumières naturelles, et de nous porter avec soumission à exécuter ce qu'on nous prescrit. L'humanité mêle aisément ses erreurs en ce qui regarde la croyance; elle se mécompte peu dans la pratique des vertus; car il est moins en notre pouvoir de penser juste sur les choses du ciel que de bien faire. Il n'y a jamais à se méprendre aux actions de justice et de charité.[4]

[1] That is to say, he follows those Renaissance thinkers who were prepared to regard articles of faith as immune from the damaging attacks of rationalist criticism. Montaigne's *Essais* are of considerable importance in this respect, as an intermediary between Italian Renaissance thought and the *libertinage* of the seventeenth century.

[2] Saint-Évremond's attitude to the separation of faith and reason has been so variously interpreted that critics have been able to see him as a fideist 'seeker after truth', a deist, and a rationalist precursor of the eighteenth-century *philosophes*. The author of an unpublished thesis on Saint-Évremond, Dr D. C. Potts, suggests that the apparent contradictions in his thought can largely be resolved by a strictly chronological study, and he sees a development from the early agnosticism, through a fideist phase, to his final deism. I am greatly indebted to Dr Potts for the opportunity to consult his thesis.

[3] Cf. the closing paragraphs of Book II, ch. xii of Montaigne's *Essais*.

[4] *Œuvres*, ed. R. de Planhol (Paris, 1927), I, p. 105.

The factor of human 'error' in matters of belief brings about differences of opinion, dissension and strife. As Saint-Évremond says in the concluding paragraph of the letter:

De la diversité des opinions on a vu naître celle des partis; et l'attachement des partis a produit les persécutions et les guerres. Des millions d'hommes ont péri à contester de quelle manière on prenait au sacrement ce qu'on demeurait d'accord d'y prendre. C'est un mal qui dure encore, et qui durera toujours, jusqu'à ce que la religion repasse de la curiosité de nos esprits à la tendresse de nos cœurs; et que, rebutés de la folle présomption de nos lumières, elle aille retrouver les doux mouvements de notre amour.

It is not, he assures us, indifference or scepticism which inspires his own charitable, tolerant attitude towards those who follow other confessions. On the contrary, he has a clear preference for Catholicism, and not only because it was the religion of his fathers: in a later passage he argues the merits of the 'esprit particulier' of Catholicism—namely, the active encouragement of good works—against the more passive character of predestinarian Calvinism. But the stronger one's attachment to a particular branch of the Christian faith, if it is truly based on Christian charity, the stronger should be one's link with those who are just as much Christians, even though they belong to a different confession. In the third paragraph he urges the principle of toleration in forceful terms, first of all on the personal level of charity toward the individual ('un huguenot..., il m'est cher..., qui croit de bonne foi... qu'on le persécute'), and then, as a far-reaching development of this, on the level of public policy. If the last phrase ('notre cœur en est un secret, où il nous est permis d'adorer leur maître') has the flavour of Voltairian deism, rather than of Christian conviction, the whole passage is nevertheless a humane and eloquent plea for liberty of conscience from a standpoint within the Christian tradition. The precise nature of the relationship between Church and State envisaged here is perhaps debatable, but it would seem that the last sentence should be interpreted in the light of the two preceding sentences, and that Saint-Évremond is not advocating an official 'State' religion to which all must pay lip-service, whatever they believe in their hearts, but a more radical freedom, the right to public worship for all, together with equality before the law. Hence the comparision with the ancient world; hence, too, perhaps, the restrictive clause in the penultimate sentence: for minority sects are less likely to become subversive political factions if they enjoy equal citizenship than if they are repressed. The attempts by a sovereign to impose the same religion on all his subjects produces, moreover, precisely that 'feinte' which is here deplored (lines 24-5).

Taken as a whole, the style of the letter to Créqui owes something to that of Montaigne's autobiographical essays; though it lacks the discursive quality of that author's style, and Saint-Évremond is perhaps nearer to Bacon's conception of the essay, with its more orderly treatment of a theme. In the passage under consideration we may distinguish between the personal, 'confessional' flavour of the first two paragraphs (or more precisely, down to 'avec nous', line 14), where the content is matched by an easy, relaxed style, and the more formal, rhetorical style of the remainder, which in any case is more abstract in tone, and where balance and antithesis are very much in evidence.[1]

It is perhaps not easy for a twentieth-century reader to realise to the full the originality of the concept of 'réunion' put forward in this passage. To an orthodox Catholic, the term 'réunion' could have only one meaning: the conversion of heretics to a Catholic way of thinking; and what Saint-Évremond here calls 'la haine de la division' not only inspired such a work as Bossuet's *Histoire des variations des églises protestantes* (1688), but also the polemical writings of Arnauld and Nicole, whose sensitivity to the attacks on Jansenist heterodoxy made them all the more violent in their denunciation of Protestant heresy.[2] On the political implications of religious toleration Arnauld likewise showed himself, in Sainte-Beuve's phrase, to be 'catholique et royaliste plus que chrétien':[3] he approved the Revocation of the Edict of Nantes, and did not condemn the *dragonnades*[4] and other acts of persecution of

---

[1] Though not, I think, to the extent suggested by M. Adam, writing of Saint-Évremond's style in general: 'un style où l'artifice était trop sensible. Il est vrai que les antithèses sont chez lui trop fréquentes et que leur accumulation fatigue quelquefois'—*Histoire de la littérature française au XVIIe siècle*, V, p. 212.

[2] Cf.Sainte-Beuve: 'Dans ses controverses avec les Protestants, Arnauld est bien moins occupé à les persuader et à les convertir qu'à s'en séparer; en écrivant il songe plus aux Catholiques qu'aux Protestants mêmes. Signalé comme le chef d'un «tiers parti», accusé par plusieurs d'incliner au Calvinisme à l'endroit de la Grâce, serré et comme refoulé sur un étroit terrain du côté de Genève, il essaie d'élever une barrière d'autant plus haute, de creuser un fossé d'autant plus profond entre lui et ceux dont on le voudrait faire auxiliaire, et qui eux-mêmes le tirent à eux le plus qu'ils peuvent. On peut dire que là où ils lui tendent de plus près la main, il les repousse, lui, à coups de poing d'autant plus forts'—*Port-Royal*, ed. cit., V, p. 318.

[3] Ibid., p. 320.

[4] The billeting of soldiers on Huguenot families, accompanied by acts of great violence and brutality.

the Huguenots. To Bossuet, too, religious schism was inseparable from political disorder, and he wanted no better illustration of this than the recent history of England:

> Ne croyez pas que ce soit seulement la querelle de l'épiscopat, ou quelques chicanes sur la liturgie anglicane, qui aient ému les Communes. Ces disputes n'étaient encore que de faibles commencements, par où ces esprits turbulents faisaient comme un essai de leur liberté. Mais quelque chose de plus violent se remuait dans le fond des cœurs: c'était un dégoût secret de tout ce qui a de l'autorité, et une démangeaison d'innover sans fin, après qu'on en a vu le premier exemple....
>
> Il ne faut point s'étonner s'ils perdirent le respect de la majesté et des lois, ni s'ils devinrent factieux, rebelles et opiniâtres. On énerve la religion quand on la change, et on lui ôte un certain poids, qui seul est capable de tenir les peuples. Ils ont dans le fond du cœur je ne sais quoi d'inquiet qui s'échappe, si on leur ôte ce frein nécessaire; et on ne leur laisse plus rien à ménager, quand on leur permet de se rendre maîtres de leur religion.[1]

For a nation so beset by the evils of diversity in religion, there could be only one way to salvation: 'par le retour de l'unité, et par la soumission ancienne.'[2]

In such a religious climate, Saint-Évremond's conception of Christian unity was the dream of an idealist: Catholic and Protestant alike continued to think and act in a spirit of mutual hostility,[3] and doctrinal controversy resulted merely in a further hardening of attitudes. Meanwhile, the King was subject to increasing pressure to intensify the political measures against the Huguenots, and the Revocation of the Edict of Nantes in 1685 drove hundreds of thousands into exile; those who remained became, instead of a peaceful minority more or less integrated into the community, a small sect of persecuted martyrs capable of armed revolt (cf. the Camisard risings in the Cévennes).

In England, too, the 1670s and 1680s saw a curtailment of the religious toleration in existence at the Restoration in the Test Act (1673), introduced by Parliament as a check to the designs of Louis XIV and Charles II to restore Catholicism to power in the country. Though French travellers in England in the closing decades of the century remained impressed with the diversity of sects and the freedom of

---

[1] *Oraison funèbre d'Henriette de France.*
[2] Ibid.
[3] Dr Potts points to the single exception of the Calvinist pastor d'Huisseau, whose *Réunion du Christianisme* appeared in 1669.

worship,[1] the events of James II's reign and subsequent Jacobite activities left too much suspicion of political intrigue on the part of Catholics for freedom of worship to be readily extended to this particular minority. Disillusioned by the overwhelming evidence that the existing Christian Churches, far from promoting peace and social order, would continue only to provoke dissension and disorder, Saint-Évremond soon abandoned his ideal of a unified Christian Church as a foundation for a stable society. Henceforward he was to take a more realistic view of the relationship between Church and State, and to concede that a ruler has the right to impose a unified religion in the interests of political security;[2] when in 1681 he advises his friend Justel to abjure his Calvinism if he wishes to return to France, he expresses the prudent conservatism of the sceptic to whom forms of religion are a matter of indifference:

> En effet, ne vaut-il pas mieux recevoir la religion des lois de son pays que de la liberté de sa fantaisie, ou de l'animosité des factions où l'on se trouve ?[3]

Paradoxically, however, he was unwilling to put his own precept into practice. He had refused the permission to return to France which finally came in 1689, preferring the freer intellectual climate that he found in England; but he remained nominally a Catholic until shortly before his death, even though this meant the forfeiting of a salaried sinecure under the Test Act. As regards ethics, on the other hand, his later writings increasingly look to Epicureanism rather than to Christianity for the basis of their ideas: a typical example is the passage in which he quotes with approval Bernier's remark: 'L'abstinence des plaisirs me paraît un grand péché'.[4] His self-portrait, written in 1696, shows his moral goal to be the Epicurean ideal of moderation in all things:

> C'est un philosophe également éloigné du superstitieux et de l'impie; un voluptueux qui n'a pas moins d'aversion pour la débauche que d'inclination pour les plaisirs; un homme qui n'a jamais senti la nécessité, qui n'a jamais connu l'abondance;

---

[1] See G. Ascoli, *La Grande-Bretagne devant l'opinion française au XVIIe siècle* (Paris, 1930), I, pp. 398 ff.

[2] Though he protested in the name of humanity against the harsh methods employed by Louvois against the Protestants; cf. the poem, 'Sur les vaines occupations des savants et des controversistes'—*Œuvres mêlées* (1706), IV, p. 371.

[3] *Œuvres*, ed. Planhol, I, p. 128.

[4] *Œuvres mêlées* (1706), V, p. 392.

and in the picture it gives us of his definitive religious attitude, this same self-portrait contains more than a hint of the optimistic deism that one associates with the following century:

> De justice et de charité,
> Beaucoup plus que de pénitence,
> Il compose sa piété;
> Mettant en Dieu sa confiance,
> Espérant tout de sa bonté,
> Dans le sein de la Providence
> Il trouve son repos et sa félicité.[1]

[1] *Œuvres*, ed. Planhol, I, pp. 5-6.

XI

Boileau

(1636–1711)

Le Lutrin, lines 17–70

Parmi les doux plaisirs d'une paix fraternelle,
Paris voyait fleurir son antique Chapelle.[1]
Ses chanoines vermeils et brillants de santé,
S'engraissaient d'une longue et sainte oisiveté;
Sans sortir de leurs lits plus doux que leurs hermines,
Ces pieux fainéants faisaient chanter matines,
Veillaient à bien dîner, et laissaient en leur lieu
A des chantres gagés le soin de louer Dieu,
Quand la Discorde, encor toute noire de crimes,
10 Sortant des Cordeliers pour aller aux Minimes,
Avec cet air hideux qui fait frémir la Paix,
S'arrêta près d'un arbre au pied de son Palais.
Là, d'un œil attentif, contemplant son empire,
A l'aspect du tumulte, elle-même s'admire:
Elle y voit par le coche et d'Évreux et du Mans,
Accourir à grands flots ses fidèles Normands.[2]
Elle y voit aborder le marquis, la comtesse,
Le bourgeois, le manant, le clergé, la noblesse,
Et partout des plaideurs les escadrons épars,
20 Faire autour de Thémis flotter ses étendards.
Mais une église seule à ses yeux immobile,
Garde au sein du tumulte une assiette tranquille.
Elle seule la brave, elle seule aux procès
De ses paisibles murs veut défendre l'accès.
La Discorde, à l'aspect d'un calme qui l'offense,
Fait siffler ses serpents, s'excite à la vengeance.

---

[1] The Sainte-Chapelle was built in the middle of the thirteenth century in order to house precious relics, including a fragment from the Crown of Thorns. It stands within the precincts of the Palais de Justice; hence the busy traffic of litigants referred to in lines 15 ff.

[2] 'Normands,' because the inhabitants of this province were popularly supposed to be litigious by nature.

Sa bouche se remplit d'un poison odieux,
Et de longs traits de feu lui sortent par les yeux.
«Quoi, dit-elle, d'un ton qui fit trembler les vitres,
30 J'aurai pu jusqu'ici brouiller tous les chapitres,
Diviser Cordeliers, Carmes et Célestins?
J'aurai fait soutenir un siège aux Augustins?
Et cette église seule à mes ordres rebelle
Nourrira dans son sein une paix éternelle?
Suis-je donc la Discorde? et parmi les mortels,
Qui voudra désormais encenser mes autels?»
A ces mots, d'un bonnet couvrant sa tête énorme,
Elle prend d'un vieux chantre et la taille et la forme:
Elle peint de bourgeons son visage guerrier
40 Et s'en va de ce pas trouver le Trésorier.
    Dans le réduit obscur d'une alcôve enfoncée,
S'élève un lit de plume à grands frais amassée.
Quatre rideaux pompeux, par un double contour,
En défendent l'entrée à la clarté du jour.
Là, parmi les douceurs d'un tranquille silence,
Règne sur le duvet une heureuse indolence.
C'est là que le prélat, muni d'un déjeuner,
Dormant d'un léger somme, attendait le dîner.
La jeunesse en sa fleur brille sur son visage:
50 Son menton sur son sein descend à double étage:
Et son corps, ramassé dans sa courte grosseur,
Fait gémir les coussins sous sa molle épaisseur.
    La Déesse en entrant, qui voit la nappe mise,
Admire un si bel ordre, et reconnaît l'***.[1]

Épîtres, Art poétique, Lutrin, ed. C. H. Boudhors
(Paris, 1952), pp. 125-6

'L'envers du Grand Siècle'[2] is nowhere more apparent than in the contrast between the formal, official exterior of the Church and the private lives of some of its dignitaries. There is, it is true, abundant evidence of the spiritual and intellectual vigour of French Catholicism in a period which saw the successful struggle to consolidate a unified Church in the face of movements, such as Jansenism or Quietism, which tended towards disunity. Nor can any student of the seventeenth

[1] Variant: . . . et reconnaît l'Église (1713 and 1716 editions).
[2] See the book bearing this title by F. Gaiffe (Paris, 1924).

century fail to admire the example of austere piety set by the nuns and
the *solitaires* of Port-Royal, as well as by the equally edifying lives of
individual reformers from François de Sales and Vincent de Paul to
Fénelon; while even the less sympathetic figure of Bossuet, the
formidable churchman-politician, commands respect for his sincerity
and devotion to his faith.

On the other hand, however, we have the thoroughly unedifying
spectacle of unprincipled and self-seeking churchmen, whose example
shows only too well that the Church was just as much a lucrative career,
offering great scope for worldly advancement, in seventeenth-century
France, as it had been in Renaissance Italy. Younger sons of the nobility
went into the Church, as they might go into the army; rich benefices
were inherited, from uncle to nephew, down through the generations,
or else were purchased or canvassed for on behalf of young children:
Mère Angélique, the saintly Superior of Port-Royal, and her sister, were
provided for in this way at the respective ages of seven and five, as a
reward for services rendered by their grandfather to Henri IV. Some of
the most responsible offices in the Church were held by young men of
good family hardly out of their teens, even though this was contrary to
canon law: Richelieu, for instance, succeeding to the bishopric of Luçon
at the age of twenty-one, obtained a dispensation enabling him to accept
the nomination, although the canonical age was twenty-six.[1] Bishoprics
and other wealthy benefices were held in plurality, and absenteeism was
common: the Archbishop of Embrun, for instance, celebrated for his
ignorance, was said never to have set foot in his diocese.[2] Anecdotal
histories of the time are full of references to loose living of the most
flagrant kind on the part of princes of the Church: a notorious example
is that of François de Harlay, who succeeded his uncle as Archbishop of
Rouen at the age of twenty-six and was subsequently Archbishop of Paris

---

[1] Originally destined for the military profession, the future Cardinal took up an ecclesiastical career only in order to keep the 'hereditary' bishopric of Luçon in the hands of the
Richelieu family, when a brother, who had intended to go into the Church, chose instead to
enter a monastic Order.

[2] See Sainte-Beuve, *Port-Royal*, ed. cit., IV, pp. 381 ff. And cf. this portrait of the Bishop
of Troyes: 'Il ... passa sa vie dans [la compagnie] la meilleure et la plus distinguée de la cour
et de la ville, recherché de tout le monde, et surtout dans le gros jeu et à travers toutes les
dames: c'était leur favori; elles ne l'appelaient que «le Troyen» et «chien d'évêque» et
«chien de Troyen» quand il leur gagnait leur argent. Il s'allait de temps en temps ennuyer à
Troyes, où, pour la bienséance, et faute de mieux, il ne laissait pas de faire ses fonctions; mais
il n'y demeurait guère, et, une fois de retour, il ne se pouvait arracher'—Saint-Simon,
quoted by Gaiffe, op. cit., pp. 71-2.

from 1671 to 1695. The song-writers of the time celebrated his arrival in Paris in these terms:

> Le pasteur qui nous gouverne
> Fait l'amour toute la nuit
> Et traite de baliverne
> Tout le blâme du déduit.
> Jamais il ne s'en confesse,
> Il n'en dit pas moins la messe:
> Il fait tout ce qu'il défend
> A Paris comme à Rouen

or again:

> Notre archevêque de Paris
> Quoique tout jeune a des faiblesses.
> De crainte d'en être surpris,
> Il a retranché ses maîtresses:
> De quatre qu'il eut autrefois
> Ce prélat n'en a plus que trois.[1]

But Harlay's is an extreme case; a more representative Church dignitary is perhaps to be seen in Le Tellier, brother of Louis XIV's Minister of War, Louvois. Le Tellier had become coadjutor to the Archbishop of Rheims at the canonical age of twenty-six, and succeeded to the archbishopric three years later. A skilful administrator, a noted bibliophile, he was at the same time 'très-décrié du côté de la continence', and is said to have declared that 'on ne pouvait pas être honnête homme si on n'avait dix mille livres de rente'.[2] Saint-Simon's portrait gives an excellent impression of this 'composé fort extraordinaire':

> Extrêmement du grand monde, magnifique, et toutefois avare; grand aumônier,[3] assez résidant chaque année, gouvernant et visitant lui-même son diocèse, qui était le mieux réglé du royaume et le mieux pourvu des plus excellents sujets en tout genre, qu'il savait choisir, s'attacher, employer, et bien récompenser; avec cela, fort de la cour et du plus grand monde, gros joueur, habile en affaires, et fort entendu pour les siennes; lié avec les

---

[1] Reproduced in *Le Nouveau Siècle de Louis XIV, ou Choix de chansons historiques et satiriques* (Paris, 1857), pp. 81-5.

[2] The remark may be apocryphal, but it seems to be in character. The same may be said of the gibe attributed to Boileau, consulted by the Archbishop about the integrity of a mutual acquaintance: 'Monseigneur, il s'en faut de quatre mille livres de rente qu'il soit honnête homme'.

[3] In the sense of 'alms-giving'.

plus doctes et les plus saints de l'épiscopat, aimé et estimé en Sorbonne, qu'il protégeait et gouvernait très bien. C'était un homme fort judicieux, et qui avait le talent du gouvernement.[1]

The excessive worldliness of Church dignitaries, and ecclesiastical laxity generally, aroused abundant criticism during Louis XIV's reign. There was plenty of criticism, first of all, from within the Church itself: Félix Gaiffe has assembled some striking examples from sermons of the time.[2] Outside the Church, criticism was expressed principally in private memoirs, not destined for publication, and in the sort of scurrilous popular song already quoted. One finds very little reflection of it, on the other hand, in the serious literature of the age; as La Bruyère says:

> Un homme né chrétien et Français se trouve contraint dans la satire; les grands sujets lui sont défendus: il les entame quelquefois, et se détourne ensuite sur de petites choses, qu'il relève par la beauté de son génie et son style.[3]

Boileau's approach to his subject in *Le Lutrin* provides an excellent opportunity to examine the inhibitions and taboos to which La Bruyère refers, the restrictions imposed on the seventeenth-century satirist by considerations of taste just as much as by fear of censorship. Satire of a more general kind directed against the clergy was of course nothing new: the lazy, well-fed priest or monk is a familiar figure in medieval and Renaissance literature. *Le Lutrin* certainly owes something to this longstanding tradition: in the extract quoted, the allegorical figure of La Discorde, and the conventional picture of the cleric in the closing lines. Nevertheless, the good-humoured comic tone of the poem conceals some sharp thrusts at particular targets in the manner of the author's own *Satires*, while the subject also gives Boileau the opportunity to declare his position with regard to contemporary theological controversy.

The passage under consideration occurs near the beginning of the first canto of *Le Lutrin*, four cantos of which appeared in 1674 (the fifth and sixth were added in 1683). Boileau had already published nine of his *Satires*, which laid the foundation of his literary reputation; and though

---

[1] *Mémoires*, 'Grands Écrivains' edition (Paris, 1879-1930), XIX, pp. 43-5.

[2] Op. cit., pp. 65 ff. And cf. Fénelon's denunciation of Harlay, Archbishop of Paris: 'Vous avez un archevêque corrompu, scandaleux, incorrigible, faux, malin, artificieux, ennemi de toute vertu, et qui fait gémir tous les gens de bien'—*Correspondance* (Paris, 1827), II, p. 341.

[3] *Caractères*, XIV, para. 65.

he claims in the Preface to *Le Lutrin* that it is a work of pure fantasy, this is not wholly true, for beneath the imaginative embellishment of the theme there lies a basis of topical fact. The particular subject was suggested to him, he tells us in the 'Avis au Lecteur' of the 1683 edition, by Lamoignon, Premier Président du Parlement de Paris, as the result of a dispute which the latter had been asked to settle between the Precentor and the Treasurer of the Sainte-Chapelle in 1667. The Treasurer, as Superior of the chapel (the benefice was of episcopal rank) had suddenly installed, without prior warning, a large lectern in the choir, directly in front of the Precentor's stall; the Precentor objected strongly, since it prevented him from keeping a watchful eye on the choristers, and he had it removed, maintaining that its installation had been a personal insult to himself. This trivial but acrimonious dispute was referred to President Lamoignon, who resolved it by the following compromise: the lectern was to be reinstalled, in deference to the Treasurer's prerogative, but after remaining in place throughout one day's services it was to be removed to satisfy the Precentor.[1]

From this unpromising *fait divers* Boileau has created a minor masterpiece in the genre of the mock-epic (or 'heroicomical poem', as it was called by Pope, who imitated him in *The Rape of the Lock*). Contemporaries who moved in the same legal and ecclesiastical circles as the protagonists of the action recounted in the poem (as Boileau himself did, for his nephew Gilles Dongois was a Canon of the Sainte-Chapelle) must have relished the scarcely-veiled personal allusions. The Treasurer and Precentor were readily identifiable by those 'in the know', as well as some of their prominent supporters, such as the faithful Gilotin (in real life Guironet) who attempts to dissuade the Treasurer from a too-hasty response to the goddess Discord's entreaty:

> Quelle fureur, dit-il, quel aveugle caprice,
> Quand le dîner est prêt, vous appelle à l'office?
> De votre dignité soutenez mieux l'éclat.
> Est-ce pour travailler que vous êtes prélat?[2]

or the 'Perruquier l'Amour'—a transparent disguise for the barber Delamour, whose private life was lampooned in the following lines:

> Ce nouvel Adonis à la blonde crinière
> Est l'unique souci d'Anne sa perruquière.
> Ils s'adorent l'un l'autre, et ce couple charmant

---

[1] See P. Émard and S. Fournier, *La Sainte-Chapelle du Lutrin* (Geneva, 1963).
[2] Canto I, lines 97-100.

S'unit longtemps, dit-on, avant le sacrement;
Mais depuis trois moissons, à leur saint assemblage
L'Officiel a joint le nom de mariage.[1]

Another section of the poem which shows the author in satirical mood is the celebrated 'battle of the books' in canto V. At the climax of their feud, the two factions meet in Barbin's bookshop (situated in the court-yard of the Palais de Justice, next to the Sainte-Chapelle) and bombard each other with volumes of all sorts, and this scene offers scope for a characteristic exercise of the satirist's wit at the expense of contemporary authors. Some tomes, for instance, have a remarkable effect when used as missiles:

Au plus fort du combat le chapelain Garagne
Vers le sommet du front atteint d'un *Charlemagne*,
—Des vers de ce poème effet prodigieux!—
Tout prêt à s'endormir, bâille et ferme les yeux[2]

—but a volume of plays by Quinault, 'doux et tendre ouvrage', proves a useless weapon:

Le sacristain, bouillant de zèle et de courage,
Le prend, se cache, approche, et, droit entre les yeux,
Frappe du noble écrit l'athlète audacieux.
Mais c'est pour l'ébranler une faible tempête,
Le livre sans vigueur mollit contre sa tête.[3]

On the whole, though, in spite of these and other specific references, the form taken by Boileau's satire in this work is clearly very different from that of the *Satires* themselves. In *Le Lutrin* he has achieved a very satisfying blend of comic invention and elevated diction, and he claims in his *Au Lecteur* that this kind of writing is wholly original:

C'est un burlesque nouveau, dont je me suis avisé en notre langue: car, au lieu que dans l'autre burlesque, Didon et Énée parlaient comme des harengères et des crocheteurs,[4] dans celui-ci une horlogère et un horloger parlent comme Didon et Énée.

[1] Ibid., lines 217-22. It is true that Boileau made a perfunctory attempt further to disguise the identity of the unfortunate individual: editions of the poem published during Delamour's lifetime (he died in 1697) refer to him as an 'horloger', not a 'perruquier'.

[2] Lines 165-8. *Charlemagne* was the work of one Le Laboureur, whom Boileau also mocks in his ninth *Épître*.

[3] Lines 194-8.

[4] The reference is to Scarron's *Virgile travesti* (1648-52), perhaps the best-known example of the genre of burlesque poem which flourished in the middle of the century.

The text is full of reminiscences of classical epic style: characteristic turns of phrase, half-quotations such as the opening lines:

> Je chante les combats, et ce prélat terrible
> Qui, par ses longs travaux et sa force invincible,
> Dans une illustre église exerçant son grand cœur,
> Fit placer à la fin un lutrin dans le chœur[1]

and figures of speech such as the apostrophe or the sustained simile. There is a premonitory dream, a Virgilian sibyl called Chicane, and the goddess Thémis who makes an appearance alongside personifications of La Discorde, La Mollesse, La Nuit and La Piété. The noble dignity of seventeenth-century tragedy is parodied by Boileau's use of the same pompous and stately alexandrine for a passage such as the following, where the barber l'Amour is resisting the pleas of his wife not to engage in the hazardous enterprise of installing the lectern:

> Je ne veux point nier les solides bienfaits
> Dont ton amour prodigue a comblé mes souhaits:
> Et le Rhin de ses flots ira grossir la Loire
> Avant que tes faveurs sortent de ma mémoire.
> Mais ne présume pas qu'en te donnant ma foi,
> L'Hymen m'ait pour toujours asservi sous ta loi.
> Si le Ciel en mes mains eût mis ma destinée,[2]
> Nous aurions fui tous deux le joug de l'Hyménée:
> Et sans nous opposer ces devoirs prétendus,
> Nous goûterions encor des plaisirs défendus.
> Cesse donc à mes yeux d'étaler un vain titre.
> Ne m'ôte pas l'honneur d'élever un pupitre:
> Et toi-même donnant un frein à tes désirs,
> Raffermis ma vertu qu'ébranlent tes soupirs.[3]

This comic writing can still be appreciated today, of course; and it is not difficult to see how much more effective it must have been for readers

---

[1] Cf. the opening lines of the *Aeneid*:
> Arma virumque cano, Troiae qui primus ab oris
> Italiam fato profugus Lavinaque venit
> Litora—multum ille et terris iactatus et alto
> Vi superum, saevae memorem Iunonis ob iram.

[2] Cf. Corneille's line:
> Si le Ciel en mon choix eût mis mon hyménée . . .
>   (*Polyeucte*, line 465).

There are other reminiscences of Corneille in this passage.

[3] Canto II, lines 39-52.

of Boileau's own time, who could recognise immediately the parodies of contemporary tragedy, and whose classical culture enabled them readily to identify references to ancient literature. But essentially it was a *jeu d'esprit* for a cultured élite; Boileau himself was not far wrong when he called it 'un ouvrage de pure plaisanterie', and though his contemporary, Pradon, saw fit to accuse him of dangerous anti-clericalism:

> Je ne sais si en faisant voir que son génie pouvait railler jusqu'aux choses les moins susceptibles de raillerie, il n'a point craint de donner une idée un peu trop libre de ses sentiments. . . . Il est vrai que c'est une fiction que ce poème; mais cette fiction est remplie de peintures satiriques qui déchirent les prélats, les moines, les chanoines, et tous les ordres de religieux. . . . Voilà qui a fait dire généralement à tout le monde que M. D***[1] s'était trompé au choix du sujet de son poème, et je crois qu'on lui a fait grâce[2]

it is difficult not to believe that this criticism was inspired by literary jealousy. Generally speaking, in *Le Lutrin* Boileau's satirical purpose is overshadowed by his comic imagination, and rather than being roused to indignation, the reader is invited to share a good-humoured joke.

In spite of these reservations, the passage under consideration presents a concentrated picture of worldliness and corruption in the Church. Reference is made to the quarrels and litigation which continually beset the various religious Orders, and which can be documented from contemporary records: in a footnote to a later edition, for instance, Boileau comments on line 10: 'Il y eut de grandes brouilleries dans ces deux couvents, à l'occasion de quelques supérieurs qu'on y voulait élire'; and in the case of the Augustinian Order (line 32), their house had literally been besieged in 1658 by officers of the Paris Parlement, and the affair had caused bloodshed and even loss of life. One church stands apart from all this strife and dissension, but we soon see that its air of peace and tranquillity is the product of indolence and apathy. This highly critical view of the state of the Church is, however, not expressed in the form of biting satire: instead of the extravagant invective of a d'Aubigné fulminating against Catherine de Médicis, or of a Victor Hugo castigating Louis-Napoléon, Boileau is content with urbane understatement and mild irony. The shortcomings of the Church are, as it were, taken for granted; and the tolerant, if cynical, author asks us to suspend our judgment and appreciate the cultured humour of 'sa

[1] Boileau's full name was Boileau-Despréaux, and he was known to many of his contemporaries as Despréaux.
[2] *Nouvelles Remarques sur tous les ouvrages du Sieur D*** (The Hague, 1685), pp. 100-2.

PLATE IIIa Louis Le Nain (1593–1648): *Repas de paysans*

PLATE IIIb Jacques Callot (1592–1635): *Le Brelan*

PLATE IV   Abraham Bosse (1602–76): *Les Lectures sérieuses des dames*

sainte oisiveté' or of 'nourrira dans son sein *une paix* éternelle'. Where d'Aubigné's *Les Tragiques* or Hugo's *Les Châtiments* make a violent onslaught on the reader's sensibility, Boileau is content to appeal to our intellect; and even the most trenchant criticisms are expressed in such a way that instead of indignation against the object of the satire we feel admiration for the epigrammatic neatness of the expression:

> C'est là que le prélat, muni d'un déjeuner,
> Dormant d'un léger somme, attendait le dîner

or:

> La Déesse, en entrant, qui voit la nappe mise,
> Admire un si bel ordre, et reconnaît l'Église.

The portrait of the worldly cleric (lines 41 ff.) similarly strikes us as a felicitous piece of writing rather than as a stirring denunciation of materialism in the Church: the whole tone is too urbane, the choice of vocabulary too typically classical in its abstraction and tendency to euphemism, for the passage to carry real satirical force; the opportunity for a graphic picture is rejected, and we are given a 'moral' portrait abounding in abstract terms ('un tranquille silence', 'une heureuse indolence', 'la jeunesse en sa fleur', 'sa courte grosseur', 'sa molle épaisseur'). Where commonplace terms are introduced, they are 'elevated' and, by being coupled with unfamiliar verbs ('*muni* d'un déjeuner', '*fait gémir* les coussins'), are accommodated to the prevailing 'style noble'.

It is misleading to suggest, as Brunetière does in his edition of this text, that 'depuis Boileau l'usage s'est introduit d'une raillerie plus âpre et d'un réalisme plus grossier': crude 'realism' was not unknown in the seventeenth-century novel, and the *mazarinades* and other examples of popular satire are certainly not lacking in verve. On this same subject of ecclesiastical laxity, it is interesting to compare Boileau's urbane good humour with La Bruyère's much more telling satire:

> «Moi, dit le chevecier, je suis maître du chœur: qui me forcera d'aller à matines? mon prédécesseur n'y allait point: suis-je de pire condition? dois-je laisser avilir ma dignité entre mes mains, ou la laisser telle que je l'ai reçue?» «Ce n'est point, dit l'écolâtre, mon intérêt qui me mène, mais celui de la prébende: il serait bien dur qu'un grand chanoine fût sujet au chœur, pendant que le trésorier, l'archidiacre, le pénitencier et le grand vicaire s'en croient exempts» . . . Enfin c'est entre eux tous à qui ne louera

10

point Dieu, à qui fera voir, par un long usage, qu'il n'est point obligé de le faire: l'émulation de ne se point rendre aux offices divins ne saurait être plus vive ni plus ardente. Les cloches sonnent dans une nuit tranquille, et leur mélodie, qui réveille les chantres et les enfants du chœur, endort les chanoines, les plonge dans un sommeil doux et facile, et qui ne leur procure que de beaux songes: ils se lèvent tard, et vont à l'église se faire payer d'avoir dormi.[1]

Boileau's own *Satires*, too, have a more earthy flavour, for the most part, since they lack the element of fantasy that characterises *Le Lutrin;* but even the *Satires* and the *Épîtres*, like *Le Lutrin*, on the whole avoid provocative subject-matter. Moreover, they bear the mark of a cultured man of letters for whom there was only one culture, and for whom imitation of the models provided by the literature of the Ancients was an indispensable condition of excellence. If the content of Boileau's *Satires* and *Épîtres* was not dictated by a courtier's opportunism, as in the case of Malherbe's *Odes*,[2] it was frequently determined by the desire to follow Horace or Juvenal on a certain theme; and the indignation which he brought to bear on a particular subject might well be a second-hand indignation, likewise borrowed from his Latin model. He confessed, for instance, in a letter to Brossette:

Quoique j'aie composé, *animi gratia*, une satire contre les méchantes femmes, je suis pourtant du sentiment d'Alcippe, et je tiens comme lui, que pour être heureux sous ce joug salutaire, tout dépend, en un mot, du bon choix qu'on sait faire. Il ne faut point prendre les poètes à la lettre. Aujourd'hui, c'est chez eux la fête du célibat. Demain, c'est la fête du mariage. Aujourd'hui l'homme est le plus sot de tous les animaux. Demain, c'est le seul animal capable de justice, et en cela semblable à Dieu.[3]

[1] *Caractères*, XIV, para. 26. See also para. 16.

[2] With the security offered by his royal pension, and later by his official position as historiographer-royal, Boileau had an independence that a courtier-poet such as Malherbe had never known (see the commentary to passage no. I). Though he did write the formal eulogies of the King that were required of all men of letters under Louis XIV (see the commentary to passage no. XIX), he was entitled to claim:

Je ne sais ni tromper, ni feindre, ni mentir;
Et quand je le pourrais, je n'y puis consentir.
Je ne sais point, en lâche, essuyer les outrages
D'un faquin orgueilleux qui vous tient à ses gages,
De mes sonnets flatteurs lasser tout l'univers,
Et rendre au plus offrant mon encens et mes vers.
Pour un si bas emploi ma Muse est trop altière.
(*Satire* I, lines 43-9).

[3] Letter of 5th July 1706. See E. B. O. Borgerhoff, 'Boileau satirist *animi gratia*' in *Romanic Review* (1952), pp. 241-55.

The phrase 'j'ai composé, *animi gratia*, une satire . . .' helps us to understand Boileau's attitude to the subjects of his *Satires*: in a large measure, these are stylistic exercises on borrowed themes. For Boileau, more than for most of his contemporaries, manner was as important as matter—and matter was in any case subject to the control of the 'bienséances'.

As regards his own religious views, it is clear that Boileau had Jansenist sympathies. If these appear at all in the first four cantos of *Le Lutrin*, it is only in the form of discreet allusions (canto I, 188-90; IV, 201); but in canto VI he comes much more into the open, and attacks the 'morale relâchée' preached by the Jesuits, together with the doctrine that the active love of God was not a necessary feature of repentance, that the receiving of absolution sufficed, without any contrition on the part of the penitent. Here, as well as in his twelfth *Épître* ('Sur l'Amour de Dieu') and his twelfth *Satire* ('Sur l'Équivoque'), Boileau does venture to indulge in the religious controversy of his times; but it must be confessed that the result is not a happy one, and that this is his most tedious writing. The last canto of *Le Lutrin* is frankly dull by comparison with the rest; as H. Busson says: 'La gaieté qui nous amusait du monde clérical, les allusions irrévérencieuses à l'oisiveté, à la gourmandise des chanoines, à leur vanité, aux querelles de préséance . . . ont fait place à un ton sermonneur'.[1] *Satire* XII suffers from the artificiality of its form: it is a long apostrophe to the allegorical figure l'Équivoque; and for every pithy, epigrammatic couplet:

> Et, sans être approuvé par le clergé romain,
> Tout protestant fut pape, une Bible à la main[2]

there are a dozen lines of rambling abstractions:

> Ce chef-d'œuvre devait couronner ton adresse.
> Pour y parvenir donc, ton active souplesse,
> Dans l'École abusant tes grossiers écrivains,
> Fit croire à leurs esprits ridiculement vains
> Qu'un sentiment impie, injuste, abominable,
> Par deux ou trois d'entre eux réputé soutenable,
> Prenait chez eux un sceau de probabilité,
> Qui, même contre Dieu, lui donnait sûreté,

[1] *La Religion des classiques* (Paris, 1948), p. 31.
[2] Lines 223-4.

Et qu'un chrétien pouvait, rempli de confiance,
Même en le condamnant, le suivre en conscience.[1]

At best, this is ingenious versifying; and on the whole, these poems represent Boileau's least distinguished use of the alexandrine, with their cumbersome expository passages, and the artificial literary devices which stand in the way of a warm-blooded, spontaneous polemical style. Yet such was the prestige of the 'style noble' that there could be no question for him of making his contribution to the controversy in a different literary form.

In any case, Boileau was not an original thinker, but a writer whose talent lay in the expression of commonplace ideas in an agreeably harmonious manner. The more 'philosophical' of his poems thus have little to offer beyond the urbane, stylised expression of safe opinions. He is not provocatively pro-Jansenist in the final cantos of *Le Lutrin*, any more than he is provocatively anti-clerical in those published in 1674: in both parts, what he has to say about the world around him seems to be less important than the way in which it is said. There is this difference, however: that whereas the last cantos consist of a rather tedious versified moralising, the earlier ones contain the inspired comic writing of a true *moraliste*.

[1] Lines 261-70

XII

Mme de Lafayette

(1634–93)

From *La Princesse de Clèves*

Il entendit que M. de Clèves disait à sa femme :

— Mais pourquoi ne voulez-vous point revenir à Paris ? Qui vous peut retenir à la campagne ? Vous avez depuis quelque temps un goût pour la solitude qui m'étonne et qui m'afflige parce qu'il nous sépare. Je vous trouve même plus triste que de coutume et je crains que vous n'ayez quelque sujet d'affliction.

— Je n'ai rien de fâcheux dans l'esprit, répondit-elle avec un air embarrassé ; mais le tumulte de la cour est si grand et il y a toujours un si grand monde chez vous qu'il est impossible que le corps et l'esprit ne se lassent
10 et que l'on ne cherche du repos.

— Le repos, répliqua-t-il, n'est guère propre pour une personne de votre âge. Vous êtes, chez vous et dans la cour, d'une sorte à ne vous pas donner de lassitude et je craindrais plutôt que vous ne fussiez bien aise d'être séparée de moi.

— Vous me feriez une grande injustice d'avoir cette pensée, reprit-elle avec un embarras qui augmentait toujours ; mais je vous supplie de me laisser ici. Si vous y pouviez demeurer, j'en aurais beaucoup de joie, pourvu que vous y demeurassiez seul, et que vous voulussiez bien n'y avoir point ce nombre infini de gens qui ne vous quittent quasi jamais.

20 — Ah ! madame ! s'écria M. de Clèves, votre air et vos paroles me font voir que vous avez des raisons pour souhaiter d'être seule, que je ne sais point, et je vous conjure de me les dire.

Il la pressa longtemps de les lui apprendre sans pouvoir l'y obliger ; et, après qu'elle se fut défendue d'une manière qui augmentait toujours la curiosité de son mari, elle demeura dans un profond silence, les yeux baissés ; puis tout d'un coup prenant la parole et le regardant :

— Ne me contraignez point, lui dit-elle, à vous avouer une chose que je n'ai pas la force de vous avouer, quoique j'en ai eu plusieurs fois le dessein. Songez seulement que la prudence ne veut pas qu'une femme de mon âge,
30 et maîtresse de sa conduite, demeure exposée au milieu de la cour.

— Que me faites-vous envisager, madame, s'écria M. de Clèves. Je n'oserais vous le dire de peur de vous offenser.

Mme de Clèves ne répondit point; et son silence achevant de confirmer son mari dans ce qu'il avait pensé:

— Vous ne me dites rien, reprit-il, et c'est me dire que je ne me trompe pas.

— Hé bien, monsieur, lui répondit-elle, en se jetant à ses genoux, je vais vous faire un aveu que l'on n'a jamais fait à son mari; mais l'innocence de ma conduite et de mes intentions m'en donne la force. Il est vrai que
40 j'ai des raisons de m'éloigner de la cour et que je veux éviter les périls où se trouvent quelquefois les personnes de mon âge. Je n'ai jamais donné nulle marque de faiblesse et je ne craindrais pas d'en laisser paraître si vous me laissiez la liberté de me retirer de la cour ou si j'avais encore Mme de Chartres pour aider à me conduire. Quelque dangereux que soit le parti que je prends, je le prends avec joie pour me conserver digne d'être à vous. Je vous demande mille pardons, si j'ai des sentiments qui vous déplaisent, du moins je ne vous déplairai jamais par mes actions. Songez que, pour faire ce que je fais, il faut avoir plus d'amitié et plus d'estime pour un mari que l'on n'en a jamais eu; conduisez-moi, ayez pitié de moi, et aimez-moi
50 encore, si vous pouvez.

ed. E. Magne (Paris, 1946), pp. 123-5

La Princesse de Clèves is by common consent the most distinguished novel written in the seventeenth century. It is the first novel fully to embody the French classical aesthetic, which had already produced masterpieces in other literary genres; and the only one in which can be recognised those characteristics which one associates with the psychological novel as it was developed in the eighteenth and nineteenth centuries. It is also—and these points are not unconnected—a work which illustrates the considerable influence on literature of the *précieux* movement, the social aspect of which has been studied in a commentary to another passage.[1]

Earlier novels in France had mostly been long, shapeless and episodic, with a multiplicity of characters and a lack of artistic focus. The pattern had been set by d'Urfé's *L'Astrée*, the publication of which was spread over two decades (1607-27), and there was a similar lack of urgency and of artistic discipline about the novels of Gomberville, Mlle de Scudéry and La Calprenède in the middle of the century. By the side of

---

[1] See the commentary to passage no. IX.

these leisurely productions, *La Princesse de Clèves* appears a masterpiece of concentration and conciseness: even the interpolated stories are not the episodic digressions of the pastoral or heroic tradition, but are carefully-placed illustrations of the central theme of the novel. What links Mme de Lafayette's novel to those of d'Urfé and his successors—and in this respect all these novels reflect the tastes of the polished *salon* society in which preciosity developed—is the prominent place they give to the study of the psychology of love. But whereas in the earlier novels this had taken the form of long-winded discussion, in abstract terms, of a relationship envisaged in a somewhat superficial light, *La Princesse de Clèves* offers instead the detailed analysis of a single case, presented soberly and without the artificialities of the tradition prevailing in the novel. And Mme de Lafayette breaks with tradition in another important way, again in keeping with the preoccupations of the more serious-minded *précieuses*: *La Princesse de Clèves* is a novel about the real problems of married life. In the pastoral tradition, marriage had always provided a convenient denouement, rounding off the story after the lovers had overcome their innumerable obstacles, while in the different but equally rigid convention of the burlesque or realist novels, married women were introduced only in order to provide episodic love-affairs for the heroes by making cuckolds of their husbands. In 1666 Furetière, bringing Part I of *Le Roman bourgeois* to a close, had written: 'S'ils vécurent bien ou mal ensemble, vous le pourrez voir quelque jour, si la mode vient d'écrire la vie des femmes mariées'.

The feminist aspirations of the *précieuses* derived from their revulsion from the 'mariage de convenance' with its inequality and injustice. Their attitude is well expressed by a character in the abbé de Pure's novel *La Précieuse* (1656), who asks 'quelle règle on pourrait apporter au désordre du mariage pour en adoucir la rigueur de l'esclavage, la dureté des fers; et ce qui peut-être est encore plus fâcheux que tous les deux ensemble, la durée de l'un et de l'autre'; the same character is led to wonder 's'il fallait dire se marier *contre* quelqu'un ou à quelqu'un'.[1] Such a marriage was quite incompatible with their lofty ideal of relations between the sexes as a free and unconstrained exchange between equal partners; and while in practice many women merely sought, as their husbands did, to realise this ideal in an extra-marital relationship, there were many who, with a greater respect for the marriage tie, or because they were dis-illusioned with adultery as well as with marriage, preferred to take

[1] *La Précieuse*, ed. E. Magne (Paris, 1939), II, pp. 15, 17.

refuge in the platonic concept of 'honnête amitié'. A novel like *La Princesse de Clèves*, therefore, in which the author regarded marriage seriously and responsibly, not as the conventional 'happy ending' to a series of far-fetched emotional adventures, but as the starting-point of a moral dilemma leading to a psychological crisis, had a tremendous topicality; and it is no less valuable a reflection of the intellectual climate in which it was produced, because it substitutes realistic analysis for the more typical idealistic escapism.

Mme de Lafayette's own marriage was not an unhappy one by seventeenth-century standards. She had married in 1655, at the age of twenty-one, a man nearly twice her age; there appears to have been a certain affection, based on mutual esteem, between the couple, but for the greater part of the time up to her husband's death in 1683 they preferred to live apart; he on his estates in Auvergne, while her own tastes, as well as indifferent health, kept her in Paris. Her experience of marriage, as a more or less satisfactory *modus vivendi* between two individuals without a great deal in common, may have lent a general colour to the view of marriage put forward in *La Princesse de Clèves;* but there is no autobiographical basis for the principal events of the plot. On the other hand, her attempt to lend remoteness and detachment to these events by situating them in the sixteenth century, at the court of Henri II, is a somewhat transparent literary device: the picture she gives of 'les divers intérêts et les diverses liaisons de la cour' belongs to the seventeenth century as much as to the sixteenth, and contemporaries would have no difficulty in substituting Louis XIV's Versailles for the Louvre of Henri II.[1]

Mlle de Chartres, the heroine, appears as a young beauty at Court after a sheltered upbringing, and is married at the age of sixteen to the young prince de Clèves, an excellent match in every way and a man for whom she feels the greatest esteem. Hardly is she married when she meets the duc de Nemours, who falls violently in love with her, and in spite of herself she finds herself returning his love. Afraid that she might lack the strength of purpose to resist her passion if she is constantly thrown together with Nemours in the atmosphere of a Court so favourable to

---

[1] Mme de Lafayette's *nouvelles*, *La Princesse de Montpensier* (1662) and *La Comtesse de Tende* (not published until 1724) are likewise set in the sixteenth century; they also resemble *La Princesse de Clèves* in that they deal with a moral dilemma caused by the marriage of the heroine. But they are more eventful and melodramatic, and neither shows the psychological penetration of *La Princesse de Clèves*.

intrigue, she confesses her predicament to her husband,[1] and asks him to allow her to live in retirement. But in spite of M. de Clèves' initial confidence in his wife, he is tormented by jealousy and suspicion, which finally prey upon him to such an extent that he goes into a decline and dies. Mme de Clèves feels such remorse at her husband's death, and such distrust of the harmful consequences of passion, that she refuses to marry Nemours despite her love for him, and lives the rest of her life in pious seclusion.

Although the essential theme has the universal relevance which one looks for in a classical work of art, there are features of the plot and setting which firmly establish *La Princesse de Clèves* in the particular context of the Court life of Mme de Lafayette's own time. The young heiress, fresh from a convent education, married before she has had time to acquire any experience of the world in which she has begun to move, and left with inadequate guidance to form her own standards and gain her own experience when she is already committed for life to a man whom she hardly knows: this spectacle must indeed have been a common one at Versailles. Not that the author has 'loaded the dice' against her heroine: Mme de Chartres is a sympathetic and enlightened mother; and in M. de Clèves she has a husband who is civilised and considerate, and who adores her. But her mother's preoccupations in establishing her daughter are of little help to her in forming her own moral standards: Mme de Chartres' morality is the negative one of worldly expediency, in which virtue is to be pursued not for its own sake, but for the tranquillity and the worldly consideration that it brings:

Elle songea aussi à lui donner de la vertu et à la lui rendre aimable. La plupart des mères s'imaginent qu'il suffit de ne parler jamais de galanterie devant les jeunes personnes pour les en éloigner. Mme de Chartres avait une opinion opposée; elle faisait souvent à sa fille des peintures de l'amour; elle lui montrait ce qu'il a d'agréable pour la persuader plus aisément sur ce qu'elle lui en apprenait de dangereux; elle lui contait le peu de sincérité des hommes, leurs tromperies et leur infidélité, les malheurs domestiques où plongent les engagements; et elle lui faisait voir, d'un autre côté, quelle tranquillité suivait la vie d'une honnête femme, et combien la vertu donnait d'éclat et d'élévation à une personne qui avait de la beauté et de la naissance . . . .[2]

---

[1] By an unfortunate concession on the author's part to the popular taste for coincidence, the interview is overheard by Nemours himself (cf. line 1 of the passage). This enables him to infer that his own love is returned, and leads him to commit various imprudences, which increase M. de Clèves' jealous suspicions.   [2] Ed. cit., pp. 17-18.

Mme de Chartres dies soon after her daughter's marriage, but not before she has perceived the growing inclination for M. de Nemours; and her deathbed advice to the Princess is in a similar strain:

> Songez ce que vous devez à votre mari; songez ce que vous vous devez à vous-même, et pensez que vous allez perdre cette réputation que vous vous êtes conquise et que je vous ai tant souhaitée. Ayez de la force et du courage, ma fille, retirez-vous de la cour, obligez votre mari de vous emmener; ne craignez point de prendre des partis trop rudes et trop difficiles, quelque affreux qu'ils vous paraissent d'abord: ils seront plus doux dans les suites que les malheurs d'une galanterie.

The absence of any religious element from this worldly ethic—or more precisely the total separation of 'religion' from the practical problems of life, upon which one so frequently has occasion to remark in the seventeenth century—is well illustrated by the symbolic gesture with which, at the end of this interview, having done with the things of this world and in preparation for the next, Mme de Chartres takes leave of her daughter:

> Elle se tourna de l'autre côté en achevant ces paroles et commanda à sa fille d'appeler ses femmes, sans vouloir l'écouter, ni parler davantage.[1]

Not only is a young woman in Mme de Clèves' position[2] inadequately fortified by any positive morality; Mme de Lafayette also shows how she is subjected to the dangerous, corrupting influence of Court life: the atmosphere of promiscuous *galanteries*, the example of long-established adulterous liaisons, in which the fashion is set by a monarch who is above reproach—in the novel, the liaison between Henri II and Diane de Poitiers, at Versailles those of Louis with Louise de la Vallière and Mme de Montespan. The equivocal attitude of other women to sexual morality, according to which Nemours' reputation as a womaniser is a subject of admiring interest rather than a cause of blame, is illustrated by this fragment of gossip:

> — Nous parlions de M. de Nemours, lui dit cette reine en la voyant, et nous admirions combien il est changé depuis son retour de Bruxelles. Devant que d'y aller il avait un nombre infini de maîtresses, et c'était même

---

[1] Ibid., pp. 56-7.

[2] Cf. 'une femme de mon âge, et maîtresse de sa conduite' (lines 29-30): while convention sheltered the young unmarried woman, it was the young wife, emancipated from the guardianship of her parents and responsible for her own actions, who was morally most vulnerable.

un défaut en lui; car il ménageait également celles qui avaient du mérite et celles qui n'en avaient pas. Depuis qu'il est revenu, il ne connaît ni les unes ni les autres; il n'y a jamais eu un si grand changement; je trouve même qu'il y en a dans son humeur, et qu'il est moins gai que de coutume.[1]

And we are clearly shown the effect of this sort of gossip in providing a stimulus to the heroine's love for Nemours: she feels acute jealousy at the thought that another woman may have caused this change in his behaviour, and a guilty pleasure later at the discovery that she herself is the cause.

There is little doubt that Mme de Lafayette intended to demonstrate the shortcomings of a morality which laid too much stress on external appearances and on worldly reputation: and it seems equally evident that she had little faith in the optimistic psychology in vogue in the middle of the century. Descartes, for instance, had claimed 'qu'il n'y a point d'âme si faible qu'elle ne puisse, étant bien conduite, acquérir un pouvoir absolu sur ses passions';[2] and Corneille's tragedies embody the concept of 'l'amour volontaire' governed by the lover's free-will and lacking the humiliating dependence of an involuntary 'passion'.[3] But for Mme de Lafayette, as for her generation generally, such an heroic assertion of the will was no longer credible: 'J'avoue,' Mme de Clèves tells her lover at the end of the novel, 'que les passions peuvent me conduire; mais elles ne sauraient m'aveugler'.[4] Just as much aware of the strength of her passion for Nemours now as before her husband's death, and unable to resist it except by a prudent retreat, she is nevertheless lucid enough to see that it must be resisted for her own peace of mind: her own experience, and the example of others, have shown her that passion is a destructive force. In the closing pages of the novel, which are a masterpiece of psychological analysis, she acknowledges the mixture of motives which make her still refuse Nemours:

Ce que je crois devoir à la mémoire de M. de Clèves serait faible s'il n'était soutenu par l'intérêt de mon repos; et les raisons de mon repos ont besoin d'être soutenues de celles de mon devoir. Mais, quoique je me défie de moi-même, je crois que je ne vaincrai jamais mes scrupules et je n'espère pas aussi de surmonter l'inclination que j'ai pour vous. Elle me rendra malheureuse et je me priverai de votre vue, quelque violence qu'il m'en coûte;[5]

[1] Ed. cit., p. 53.   [2] *Traité des passions de l'âme* (1649), art. 50.
[3] In addition to Corneille's tragedies, cf. the role of Alidor in his comedy *La Place royale* (1637), and the dedicatory epistle to the same play.
[4] Ed. cit., p. 192.   [5] Ibid., p. 194.

but it is above all her distrust of the destructive force of passion which determines her to avoid the danger by retiring from the world.

More than anything else in the novel, it was the moral problems raised by Mme de Clèves' confession to her husband which appealed to contemporary readers, and this interest was adroitly fostered by an enterprising piece of journalism on the part of the editor of the *Mercure galant*, Donneau de Visé. In the issue which appeared in April 1678 (the novel itself had been published in March) he opened an 'enquête', very much like those conducted by modern literary periodicals, asking for the views of readers on this question: should Mme de Clèves have confided in her husband or not? Though the opinions expressed were overwhelmingly critical of the heroine's action, the volume of correspondence produced by the 'enquête' bears witness to the fascination that the novel had for the cultured *salon* public. For *La Princesse de Clèves*—and particularly the 'scène de l'aveu'—represented the translation into sustained literary form of their principal preoccupation, with the psychology of love and the moral problems arising from it. Since the middle years of the century there had been a considerable vogue for what were called 'questions d'amour': hypothetical problems which provided serious topics for intelligent discussion. The following are examples which have been preserved:

> — je vous demande lequel vous aimeriez mieux, ou à jouir de vos amours sans désirer, ou à désirer sans jouir?
> — lequel est moins avantageux pour la gloire d'un amant, ou qu'il change le premier ou qu'on le change?
> — lequel est le plus difficile, de passer de l'amitié à l'amour ou de retourner de l'amour à l'amitié?[1]

A passage in a letter from Mme de Lafayette in Paris to the absent Mme de Sévigné shows both these ladies to have been followers of this widespread fashion:

> Voici une question entre deux maximes: «On pardonne les infidélités; mais on ne les oublie point». «On oublie les infidélités; mais on ne les pardonne point». Aimez-vous mieux avoir fait une infidélité à votre amant, que vous aimez pourtant toujours; ou qu'il vous en ait fait une, et qu'il vous aime aussi toujours? On n'entend pas par infidélité, avoir quitté pour une autre, mais avoir fait une faute considérable.[2]

[1] Quoted by D. Mornet, *Histoire de la littérature française classique* (Paris, 1947), pp. 33-4.
[2] Letter of 14th July 1673.

One of the interpolated stories in *La Princesse de Clèves* concerns M. de Sancerre, who loves Mme de Tournon, believing his love to be returned; on her death he finds that she did not love him, but another man. Mornet quotes the following passage from this episode:

> Dans un temps où son idée est dans mon cœur comme la plus parfaite chose qui ait été . . ., je trouve que je me suis trompé et qu'elle ne mérite pas que je la pleure. Cependant, j'ai la même affliction de sa mort que si elle m'était fidèle et je sens son infidélité comme si elle n'était point morte. . . . Je suis dans un état où je ne puis ni m'en consoler, ni la haïr

with the comment: 'Ce qui peut se transposer en question d'amour: «si l'on apprend en même temps la mort et l'infidélité d'un objet aimé, qui l'emportera de la douleur ou du ressentiment?»'.[1]

La Bruyère, with his usual down-to-earth criticism of *précieux* extravagance, comments caustically on the fashion:

> Il a régné pendant quelque temps une sorte de conversation fade et puérile, qui roulait toute sur des questions frivoles qui avaient relation au cœur et à ce qu'on appelle passion ou tendresse. La lecture de quelques romans les avait introduites parmi les plus honnêtes gens de la ville et de la cour; ils s'en sont défaits, et la bourgeoisie les a reçues, avec les pointes et les équivoques[2]

—and it is true that at their most banal the 'questions d'amour' were little more than the pretext for a frivolous parlour-game. But they are nevertheless a striking symptom of the intense interest in nuances of psychology and of moral behaviour, the effect of which on the literature of the time cannot be over-emphasised. To quote Mornet: 'Ces questions-conversations . . . ont appris à l'esprit classique à «voir clair dans le cœur de l'homme»'.[3]

The essence of the problem posed by the 'scène de l'aveu' is whether a wife has the right to attempt to purchase her own peace of mind at the expense of that of her husband. As M. de Clèves says on his death-bed: 'Je vous aimais jusqu'à être bien aise d'être trompé, je l'avoue à ma honte; j'ai regretté ce faux repos dont vous m'avez tiré. Que ne me laissiez-vous dans cet aveuglement tranquille dont jouissent tant de maris?';[4] and it is true that it is his wife's confession, as much as his own jealousy or Nemours' imprudence, that is the cause of his mental suffering and early death.

---

[1] Op. cit., p. 314.
[2] *Caractères*, V, para. 68.
[3] Op. cit., p. 34.
[4] Ed. cit., p. 176.

On the other hand, one of Mme de Lafayette's merits is that she succeeds in convincing the reader of the moral anguish, the lack of confidence in her own resources and the lack of any other support except in the person of her husband, which precede the drastic step taken by her heroine; and as the passage under consideration shows, the celebrated 'aveu' is not the outcome of calm deliberation, but of the emotional tension of a particular situation. In spite of the deceptively restrained language of the narrative, one might say that the confession is forced from her as a desperate last expedient, once her husband has rejected her plea for 'solitude' and 'repos'; and that what interested the author herself, at this point in the novel, was not so much the question of moral choice on the heroine's part, as the psychology behind the 'aveu'.

The style is that of the mature classical work of art with its formal dialogue, its abstract, intellectualised vocabulary, its avoidance of emotive effect and its understatement. Even in this passage, the climax of the crucial episode on which the plot of the novel turns, the substance of the vital confession is expressed by means of indirect allusion (lines 39 ff.). But although the author takes refuge in fashionable litotes in order to avoid too uncompromising an expression of feeling (cf. the euphemisms *ne point haïr* for 'aimer', *inclination* for 'amour' throughout the novel), this chastened and conventional language is by no means lacking in precision and subtlety. The heroine may shrink from confessing her unlawful love under its proper name, but the reference to her feelings for her husband is only too explicit, and nothing in the passage is more clear-cut than the distinction to be drawn between 'amitié' and 'estime' on the one hand, and the unacknowledged 'amour' on the other.

A style such as this illustrates the difficulty of determining the relationship between *préciosité* and classicism, largely because of the various implications of the former term. The two concepts are in fact sharply opposed, to the extent to which *préciosité* implied a love of the trivial and the ephemeral, of superficial embellishment, the practice of stylised *galanterie* and the affected jargon which accompanied it— though even this aspect has left its mark on the most 'classical' of authors.[1] But in another sense, it was preciosity and the social life of the *salons* which helped to form that delicacy of psychological analysis

[1] The language of Racine's young lovers has frequently been criticised for its preciosity; and F. Baumal was able to produce a study of Molière under the title *Molière auteur précieux* (Paris, 1924).

that is characteristic of classical literature; once this analysis was brought to bear on real human relationships, instead of operating in the ideal world of Mlle de Scudéry's novels, it is possible to speak of the psychological realism, for want of a better term, of Racine and of Mme de Lafayette.[1] The taste for minute psychological analysis, the most important contribution of the *salons* to seventeenth-century culture, was to survive into the eighteenth century, there to produce, in a different literary field and freed from the fatalistic attitude to sexual love which marked the work of Mme de Lafayette as well as that of Racine, a revival of more recognisably *précieux* literature in the theatre of Marivaux.

[1] Mention must be made, even if only in a footnote, of that masterpiece of psychological penetration, *Les Lettres portugaises* (1669). Long thought to be a translation of genuine letters written by a Portuguese nun, this slender volume has now been proved beyond reasonable doubt (cf. *Les Lettres portugaises*, ed. F. Deloffre and J. Rougeot, Paris, 1962) to be the work of Guilleragues, an *habitué* of Mme de Sablé's *salon* and a friend of La Rochefoucauld and Mme de Lafayette. For a study of the influence of the 'question d'amour' on the composition of *Les Lettres portugaises*, see pp. 15 ff. of the edition referred to above; the editors' description of this work: 'l'œuvre géniale d'une société vouée à l'étude du cœur humain' (p. 32) could equally well be applied to *La Princesse de Clèves*.

XIII

La Fontaine

(1621-95)

Les Deux Rats, le renard et l'œuf

Deux rats cherchaient leur vie; ils trouvèrent un œuf.
Le dîné suffisait à gens de cette espèce:
Il n'était pas besoin qu'ils trouvassent un bœuf.
     Pleins d'appétit et d'allégresse,
Ils allaient de leur œuf manger chacun sa part,
Quand un quidam parut: c'était maître renard,
     Rencontre incommode et fâcheuse:
Car comment sauver l'œuf? Le bien empaqueter,
Puis des pieds de devant ensemble le porter,
10   Ou le rouler, ou le traîner,
C'était chose impossible autant que hasardeuse.
     Nécessité l'ingénieuse
     Leur fournit une invention.
Comme ils pouvaient gagner leur habitation,
L'écornifleur étant à demi-quart de lieue,
L'un se mit sur le dos, prit l'œuf entre ses bras;
Puis malgré quelques heurts et quelques mauvais pas,
     L'autre le traîna par la queue.
Qu'on m'aille soutenir, après un tel récit,
20   Que les bêtes n'ont point d'esprit!
     Pour moi, si j'en étais le maître,
Je leur en donnerais aussi bien qu'aux enfants.
Ceux-ci pensent-ils pas dès leurs plus jeunes ans?
Quelqu'un peut donc penser, ne se pouvant connaître.
     Par un exemple tout égal,
     J'attribuerais à l'animal
Non point une raison selon notre manière,
Mais beaucoup plus aussi qu'un aveugle ressort:
Je subtiliserais un morceau de matière,

30 Que l'on ne pourrait plus concevoir sans effort,
Quintessence d'atome, extrait de la lumière,
Je ne sais quoi plus vif et plus mobile encor
Que le feu; car enfin, si le bois fait la flamme,
La flamme, en s'épurant, peut-elle pas de l'âme
Nous donner quelque idée? et sort-il pas de l'or
Des entrailles du plomb? je rendrais mon ouvrage
Capable de sentir, juger, rien davantage,
    Et juger imparfaitement,
Sans qu'un singe jamais fît le moindre argument.
40   A l'égard de nous autres hommes,
Je ferais notre lot infiniment plus fort;
    Nous aurions un double trésor:
L'un, cette âme pareille en tous tant que nous sommes,
    Sages, fous, enfants, idiots,
Hôtes de l'univers sous le nom d'animaux;
L'autre, encore une autre âme, entre nous et les anges
    Commune en un certain degré;
    Et ce trésor à part créé
Suivrait parmi les airs les célestes phalanges,
50 Entrerait dans un point sans en être pressé,
Ne finirait jamais, quoiqu'ayant commencé:
    Choses réelles, quoique étranges.
    Tant que l'enfance durerait,
Cette fille du ciel en nous ne paraîtrait
    Qu'une tendre et faible lumière;
L'organe étant plus fort, la raison percerait
    Les ténèbres de la matière,
    Qui toujours envelopperait
    L'autre âme imparfaite et grossière.

Fables, ed. R. Radouant (Paris, 1929), pp. 378-80

The above fable is the last in Book IX of the *Fables*, published for the first time in the edition of 1679. To be more precise, the passage quoted forms part (lines 179-237) of a philosophical discussion, the 'Discours à Mme de la Sablière', which consists of a sustained argument illustrated by a series of brief anecdotes; the fable in question, together with the ensuing comment, provides the climax and conclusion to the discussion.

Marguerite de la Sablière was one of the most celebrated *salon* hostesses of her day, and her house in the rue Neuve des Petits Champs, where La Fontaine lived from 1673 until his benefactress's death in 1693, was frequented by intelligent and cultured men of letters. She herself is said to have known Greek, and had been taught mathematics by the eminent professors Roberval and Sauveur. Boileau, indeed, satirises her as the bluestocking *par excellence* :

> . . . cette savante
> Qu'estime Roberval, et que Sauveur fréquente.
> D'où vient qu'elle a l'œil trouble, et le teint si terni ?
> C'est que sur le calcul, dit-on, de Cassini,
> Un astrolabe en main, elle a, dans sa gouttière,
> A suivre Jupiter passé la nuit entière.[1]
> Gardons de la troubler ! Sa science, je croi,
> Aura pour s'occuper ce jour plus d'un emploi :
> D'un nouveau microscope on doit, en sa présence,
> Tantôt chez Dalancé faire l'expérience ;
> Puis, d'une femme morte, avec son embryon,
> Il faut chez du Verney voir la dissection.
> Rien n'échappe aux regards de notre curieuse ;[2]

but it seems that her intellectual qualifications were genuine, and in another fable addressed to her, La Fontaine pays eloquent tribute, in the form of an imaginary temple built as a memorial to her, to her charm as well as to her intellectual gifts :

> Au fond du temple eût été son image,
> Avec ses traits, son souris, ses appas,
> Son art de plaire et de n'y penser pas,
> Ses agréments à qui tout rend hommage. . . .
> J'eusse en ses yeux fait briller de son âme
> Tous les trésors, quoique imparfaitement :
> Car ce cœur vif et tendre infiniment
> Pour ses amis, et non point autrement,
> Car cet esprit, qui, né du firmament,
> A beauté d'homme avec grâce de femme,
> Ne se peut pas, comme on veut, exprimer.[3]

In particular, Mme de la Sablière's *salon* was the meeting-place of a group of people who, while they could not be classed as 'libertins

---

[1] A reply, no doubt, to verses written by Mme de la Sablière herself, in which she had commented on Boileau's ignorance of the function of an astrolabe (in his *Épître*, V, line 28).
[2] *Satire* XII, lines 425-37. See also Plate IV.   [3] *Fables*, XII, 15, lines 20-34.

érudits',[1] were all in some measure followers of the Epicurean philosopher Gassendi. Gassendi himself had died in 1665, but his disciple and former secretary, Bernier, was an *habitué* of the *salon*, and he was responsible for the propagation of the philosopher's ideas to the general public by means of his *Abrégé de la philosophie de Gassendi* (1675-7), for Gassendi himself had written in Latin. A topic of especial interest to this educated *salon* public was the nature of animal intelligence, which was keenly debated by philosophers, physiologists and theologians throughout the second half of the century. The appearance of Descartes' *Discours de la méthode* in 1637 had initiated the debate, and it was Gassendi and his followers who provided the principal opposition to Cartesian thought on the subject.[2]

Before Descartes, attempts to find an answer to this fundamental problem had followed one of three principal lines of thought.[3] First of all, the 'official' view, derived from Aristotle through the intermediary of his scholastic commentators, maintained that there were three kinds of 'soul': vegetative, sensitive and rational. The human intelligence is composed of all three elements, but the rest of animal creation possesses only the vegetative and sensitive elements. A second school of thought, revived by Renaissance Neo-Platonists, held that there is a single pantheistic world-soul (*anima mundi*) to be found in all forms of life; in this case the concept of 'soul' is linked not with the reasoning faculty, as with the first view and as was to be the case with Descartes, but with the essence of life itself. A third view, most notably represented by Montaigne in his 'Apologie de Raymond Sebond',[4] credited animal creation as a whole with rational faculties, and claimed that in many cases animals make more effective use of these than do men.

Descartes seems to have shown an interest in this question from the outset of his scientific career: it has been suggested that as early as 1619, inspired by his view of the regularity and perfection of animal behaviour, he already visualised biology as part of a coherent mechanistic pattern embracing the whole universe.[5] Among the projects which remained

[1] See the commentary to passage no. II.

[2] The interest shown in this and other scientific subjects by the 'honnêtes gens' illustrates the extent to which learning, during the seventeenth century, had left the academic confines of the University, and was more and more becoming the concern of the educated 'layman'. One might mention in this connection the lead given by Descartes, who had chosen to publish his *Discours de la méthode* in French rather than in Latin.

[3] For a full treatment of this whole question, see L. C. Rosenfield, *From Beast-Machine to Man-Machine* (New York, 1941).

[4] *Essais*, II, xii.   [5] See Rosenfield, op. cit., p. 4.

uncompleted at his death was a detailed *exposé* of his systematic physiology, so that the only account of his views on this branch of the sciences
is that given, in a less formal manner than that of the erudite treatise, in
Part V of the *Discours de la méthode*. Here, after a fairly detailed treatment
of the circulation of the blood (Harvey's thesis, setting out his discovery,
had been published in 1628) and a briefer account of the nervous and
muscular systems, Descartes comes on to consider the central question
of 'la différence qui est entre notre âme et celle des bêtes'. Comparing
'divers *automates*, ou machines mouvantes, [que] l'industrie des hommes
peut faire' with the much more complex body of an animal, he sees the
latter as 'une machine qui, ayant été faite dans les mains de Dieu, est
incomparablement mieux ordonnée et a en soi des mouvements plus
admirables qu'aucune de celles qui peuvent être inventées par les
hommes'. If it were possible to construct machines, he continues, which
reproduced exactly the physical appearance and the bodily functions
of a monkey, it would be impossible to distinguish these machines
from real monkeys:

> Au lieu que s'il y en avait qui eussent la ressemblance de nos corps, et
> imitassent autant nos actions que moralement il serait possible, nous
> aurions toujours deux moyens très certains pour reconnaître qu'elles ne
> seraient point pour cela de vrais hommes: dont le premier est que jamais
> elles ne pourraient user de paroles ni d'autres signes en les composant
> comme nous faisons pour déclarer aux autres nos pensées . . .; et le
> second est que, bien qu'elles fissent plusieurs choses aussi bien ou
> peut-être mieux qu'aucun de nous, elles manqueraient infalliblement en
> quelques autres, par lesquelles on découvrirait qu'elles n'agiraient pas par
> connaissance, mais seulement par la disposition de leurs organes.

Descartes proceeds to develop this crucial distinction, 'qu'il n'y a
point d'hommes si hébétés et si stupides, sans en excepter même les
insensés, qu'ils ne soient capables d'arranger ensemble diverses paroles,
et d'en composer un discours par lequel ils fassent entendre leurs
pensées; et qu'au contraire il n'y a point d'autre animal, tant parfait et
tant heureusement né qu'il puisse être, qui fasse le semblable'; and
claims that the sort of example quoted by Montaigne, showing the
apparent use of reason by animals, proves nothing:

> Bien qu'il y ait plusieurs animaux qui témoignent plus d'industrie que
> nous en quelques-unes de leurs actions, on voit toutefois que les mêmes

n'en témoignent point du tout en beaucoup d'autres: de façon que ce qu'ils font mieux que nous ne prouve pas qu'ils ont de l'esprit . . . mais plutôt qu'ils n'en ont point, et que c'est la nature qui agit en eux selon la disposition de leurs organes: ainsi qu'on voit qu'un horloge, qui n'est composé que de roues et de ressorts, peut compter les heures et mesurer le temps plus justement que nous avec toute notre prudence.

Part V of the *Discours* closes with a passage on the immaterial nature of the 'âme raisonnable'—a passage whose importance the author stresses:

Car, après l'erreur de ceux qui nient Dieu, . . . il n'y en a point qui éloigne plutôt les esprits faibles du droit chemin de la vertu, que d'imaginer que l'âme des bêtes soit de même nature que la nôtre, et que par conséquent nous n'avons rien à craindre ni à espérer après cette vie, non plus que les mouches et les fourmis; au lieu que lorsqu'on sait combien elles diffèrent on comprend beaucoup mieux les raisons qui prouvent que la nôtre est d'une nature entièrement indépendante du corps, et par conséquent qu'elle n'est point sujette à mourir avec lui.

In spite of this reservation—and Descartes' dualism was a genuine part of his metaphysical system, not merely a prudent profession of orthodoxy—some theologically-minded contemporaries were not slow to perceive the dangers implicit in his theory: the mechanistic view of animal physiology, reducing all instinct, feeling and intelligence to the automatic functioning of bodily organs, could by extension be applied to the higher faculties of the human organism.[1] It was, however, in the somewhat freer intellectual climate of the following century that this development was to be realised, with the publication of La Mettrie's *L'Homme-machine* in 1747; for the time being the debate centred on the validity of the mechanistic system as applied to animals, not on its possible extension to human beings. However, Descartes' views did give an impetus to the study of human physiology in the seventeenth century, and his influence, together with that of Harvey, helped to establish it as an exact science, subject to laws of cause and effect, and to free it from reactionary theories based on the principle of the 'humours'; though this did not take place without determined opposition from conservative

---

[1] Ibid., p.7. Bossuet was one seventeenth-century churchman who recognised the challenge presented by Cartesian rationalism to the Christian faith, and who denounced it as a pernicious influence.

forces within the Faculty of Medicine (a state of affairs to which Molière
was to make satirical reference in *Le Malade imaginaire*).[1]

Gassendi's objections to Descartes' views on animal intelligence were
based on his own thoroughgoing and sympathetic study of the natural
philosophy of Epicurus. He does not deny that man has an immaterial
soul denied to the rest of animal creation, but he conceives of animal
intelligence as being essentially the same as human. Whereas the soul
gives man certain intellectual faculties beyond the capabilities of other
animals (such as consciousness of his own thinking processes, or the
ability to conceive abstract ideas), the simpler and more straightforward
operations of the intelligence are common to animals and men, and the
difference between an animal's 'reasoning' and that of a man is one of
degree and not of kind. The physiological basis of animal intelligence,
which in man is merely more fully developed than in other animals, is for
Gassendi to be found in Lucretius's minute atoms; these partake of the
nature of fire, and provide the body with heat (though Mrs Rosenfield
suggests that this may in Gassendi's case have been more in the nature
of an illustrative analogy than a literal explanation).[2]

It may seem to a twentieth-century reader that the difference between
the Cartesian view and that of Gassendi is largely one of terminology,
and that the dualism of both these philosophers, who agreed in endowing
man with an immaterial soul, is more important than differences in detail
between their theories of animal physiology. But it was these differences
which not only exercised an intellectual fascination on cultured Frenchmen of the second half of the century, but also had a more practical
bearing on their attitude to animals in their daily lives.

Descartes, it is true, had not himself used the term 'animal-machine',
but it was soon to be in common use among Cartesian thinkers. Mme
Deshoulières, the poetess, referred to her dog as 'la machine aboyante',
and the moralist Nicole wrote of 'ces machines animées'.[3] The latter was
not the only member of the Port-Royal community to think in these
terms, and the following passage shows that in this as in other in-

[1] The doctor, Diafoirus, is singing the praises of his uncouth, pedantic son: 'Mais sur
toute chose ce qui me plaît en lui, et en quoi il suit mon exemple, c'est qu'il s'attache
aveuglément aux opinions de nos anciens et que jamais il n'a voulu comprendre ni écouter
les raisons et les expériences des prétendues découvertes de notre siècle touchant la
circulation du sang, et autres opinions de même farine' (Act II, scene v).
[2] Op. cit., p. 111.
[3] Quoted by H. Busson and F. Gohin in their critical edition of the 'Discours à Mme de la
Sablière' (Paris, 1938), p. 81.

tellectual matters the influence of Cartesian thought on the 'solitaires' was strong:

> Combien aussi s'éleva-t-il de petites agitations dans ce désert touchant les sciences humaines de la philosophie et les nouvelles opinions de M. Descartes? Comme M. Arnauld, dans ses heures de relâche, s'en entrete-nait avec ses amis plus particuliers, insensiblement cela se répandit partout et cette solitude, dans les heures d'entretien, ne retentissait plus que de ces discours. Il n'y avait guère de solitaire qui ne parlât d'*automate*. On ne faisait plus une affaire de battre un chien. On lui donnait fort indifférem-ment des coups de bâton et on se moquait de ceux qui plaignaient ces bêtes comme si elles eussent senti de la douleur. On disait que c'étaient des horloges, que ces cris qu'elles faisaient quand on les frappait n'étaient que le bruit d'un petit ressort qui avait été remué. On clouait de pauvres animaux sur des ais, par les quatre pattes, pour les ouvrir tout en vie et voir la circulation du sang qui était une grande matière d'entretien.[1]

Malebranche likewise, the most renowned Cartesian thinker after Descartes himself, is said to have replied to someone who protested when he kicked his dog: 'Eh quoi! ne savez-vous pas bien que cela ne sent pas?';[2] and Mme de Grignan, daughter of Mme de Sévigné, shows her obedience to Cartesian principles in this passage from a letter:

> Ne vous chargez point ... d'apporter un chien à Pauline: nous ne voulons aimer ici que des créatures raisonnables; et de la secte dont nous sommes, nous ne voulons pas nous embarrasser de cette sorte de *machines;* si elles étaient montées pour n'avoir aucune nécessité malpropre, à la bonne heure; mais ce qu'il en faut souffrir nous les rend insupportables.[3]

This denial of feeling to dogs and other animals seems cruel and heartless; but it was welcomed by some precisely because it absolved the humane conscience of a sense of guilt: 'A favourite argument popular with Cartesians who were not necessarily theologians was based on the Augustinian tenet *sub Deo justo nemo miser nisi mereatur*. Since animals did not commit original sin, and are not rewarded in Heaven, it would be an injustice for them to suffer. Hence they have no feeling, and perforce no soul. The argument touched men's hearts, since it purged them of any consciousness of guilt in causing suffering to dumb brutes'.[4]

---

[1] Fontaine, *Mémoires pour servir à l'histoire de Port-Royal*, quoted by J. S. Spink, *French Free Thought from Gassendi to Voltaire* (London, 1960), p. 227.
[2] Reported by Sainte-Beuve, *Port-Royal*, ed. cit., II, p. 316.
[3] Letter to Coulanges, 17th December 1690, quoted in Mme de Sévigné, *Lettres*, 'Grands Écrivains' edition (Paris, 1862-6), IX, p. 605.   [4] Rosenfield, op. cit., p. 47.

It will be clear to anyone who is acquainted with La Fontaine's *Fables* that the author's opposition to the Cartesian theory of the 'animal-machine' was not merely an intellectual conviction acquired in the pro-Gassendi *milieu* of Mme de la Sablière's *salon*, but also very much a question of temperament. His picture of the animal world as we see it throughout the *Fables* shows such a personal sympathy, such an interest in characteristic details of behaviour, that the notion that animals are unfeeling automata must have been quite abhorrent to him. But it was as a result of discussions with Mme de la Sablière, Bernier and other *Gassendistes* that he was led to express his views explicitly in his fables. He had already, in 'Démocrite et les Abdéritains' (VIII, 26), made a favourable reference to Epicurean atomism, and openly attacked Descartes' mechanistic doctrine in 'Les Souris et le chat-huant' (XI, 9), written in 1675. This fable is based on an anecdote told to Bernier in La Fontaine's presence, and which Bernier also relates in the *Abrégé* : a hollow tree in the forest of Fontainebleau, used as a nest by an owl, had been found to contain scores of mice, still alive but with their legs broken so that they could not escape, together with a small store of ears of wheat to keep them alive and fatten them up for gradual consumption. The poet draws his conclusion as follows:

> Cet oiseau raisonnait: il faut qu'on le confesse . . .
> Sa prévoyance allait aussi loin que la nôtre:
>   Elle allait jusqu'à leur porter
>   Vivres et grains pour subsister.
>   Puis, qu'un Cartésien s'obstine
> A traiter ce hibou de montre et de machine?
>   Quel ressort lui pouvait donner
> Le conseil de tronquer un peuple mis en mue?
>   Si ce n'est pas là raisonner,
>   La raison m'est chose inconnue.[1]

The 'Discours à Mme de la Sablière' treats the whole question much more thoroughly, and puts forward an alternative hypothesis to the

---

[1] MM. Busson and Gohin suggest (op. cit., p. 16) that La Fontaine's attitude at this point is nearer to Montaigne's than to the Epicureanism he adopted later. It is true that when the poem appeared, in the 1679 edition of the *Fables*, it was accompanied by the following note: 'Ceci n'est point une fable; et la chose, quoique merveilleuse et presque incroyable, est véritablement arrivée. J'ai peut-être porté trop loin la prévoyance de ce hibou; car je ne prétends pas établir dans les bêtes un progrès de raisonnement tel que celui-ci; mais ces exagérations sont permises à la poésie, surtout dans la manière d'écrire dont je me sers'.

rejected Cartesian doctrine. The illustrative examples are neither so striking nor so original as the one given in 'Les Souris et le chat-huant', and have a more conventional literary origin (the partridge pretending to be injured in order to draw attention away from its young; the beavers and their complex building operations, etc.) On the other hand, the illustrations have much less importance in this poem (with the exception of the fable contained in the passage under discussion); the normal proportions are reversed, and instead of a fable accompanied by an economical statement of the 'moral', we have a philosophical discussion in poetic form.

Thus the greater part of the poem preceding this passage is devoted to an *exposé* of the mechanistic theory, quite straightforward and perfectly fair to Descartes. The examples already offered of animal 'intelligence' have been explained in Cartesian terms, and it is only in the concluding section of this passage, after the final illustration of the rats and the egg has been given, that the positive alternative to the Cartesian view is elaborated. First of all (lines 21-4 of the passage) a serious attempt is made to meet Descartes on his own ground: if human beings in infancy can 'think' before they are able to 'know' (i.e. to be conscious of their own thought-processes, or to 'reflect'), why should this not be so with animals?[1] From this point on, we have a faithful version of Gassendi's theory: the poet attempts to accommodate the atomistic conception of a material 'soul' common to all animals, composed of infinitesimal flame-like particles, to the orthodox doctrine of an immaterial soul, God-given and immortal. It is a somewhat uneasy compromise, particularly when tentatively expressed in suggestive, poetic terms rather than in the ampler measures of a philosopher's prose; and we may well feel that here, as in 'Les Souris et le chat-huant', the critique of Cartesian automatism is more effective than the philosophical alternative proposed.

[1] Cf. lines 58-68 of this same poem:
Voici, dis-je, comment raisonne cet auteur:
«Sur tous les animaux, enfants du Créateur,
J'ai le don de penser; et je sais que je pense».
Or, vous savez, Iris, de certaine science,
Que quand la bête penserait
La bête ne réfléchirait
Sur l'objet ni sur sa pensée.
Descartes va plus loin, et soutient nettement
Qu'elle ne pense nullement.
Vous n'êtes point embarrassée
De le croire; ni moi . . .

The mechanistic view of animal intelligence continued to make progress throughout the century. Malebranche's *Recherche de la vérité* (1674-5) helped to propagate it in philosophical circles, and such works as Louis Racine's *Épître sur l'âme des bêtes* or Cardinal de Polignac's *Anti-Lucrèce* embodied it in less technical form. It shared in the general disfavour of Descartes' ideas in official academic quarters, in Paris at any rate, where the Church and the University were resolutely opposed to the teaching of 'the new philosophy'. An attempt was in fact made in about 1670 to have the teaching of any philosophy other than that of Aristotle forbidden by a decree of the Paris Parlement, and although this was unsuccessful,[1] an order from the King in 1671 achieved the same effect. Excluded from the University, Cartesianism did, however, make headway in the freer atmosphere of the Académie des Sciences, which had been founded in 1666 on the pattern of the Royal Society in London; and by the end of the century reactionary academicism was powerless to stand in the way of the new ways of thought.[2]

In this field as in others, it was the critical method taught by Descartes that was important; the positive systems with which he sought to replace those which he had helped to overthrow were in their turn proved fallible. Thus Cartesian mechanistic physiology, as the seventeenth century had known it, did not survive for long into the eighteenth century; and the debate about the animal-machine was soon a thing of the past. It still has considerable historical interest, however, as a sample of French intellectual life at a time when important new ideas were stirring, as an episode which helps to illustrate 'how the past became the present, how the old Cartesian mechanism became the new materialistic mechanism, and how the whole development was part of the rationalistic attitude of questioning authority in the search for truth.'[3]

[1] Cf. Boileau, *Arrêt burlesque* (1671). It is worth recalling that in 1625, when certain theses had been defended professing Epicurean atomism, the Parlement had intervened and forbidden anti-Aristotelian theses on pain of death; cf. Spink, op. cit., pp. 189 ff. Although the term 'la nouvelle philosophie' normally referred to Cartesianism (cf. line 28 of this poem: 'On l'appelle nouvelle'), a phrase from the *Arrêt burlesque* indicates that Descartes' Epicurean opponents were equally to be feared by the reactionaries: 'Cartésiens, nouveaux philosophes, circulateurs et Gassendistes'.

[2] On the encouragement given to the Académie des Sciences by the King and Colbert, and the popularisation of science during this period, see F. Brunot, *Histoire de la langue française* (Paris, 1905-), IV (I), pp. 407 ff. Cf. also H. Butterfield, *Origins of Modern Science* (London, 1949), pp. 144 ff.

[3] Rosenfield, op. cit., p. 37.

XIV

Mme de Sévigné

(1626-96)

From letter to Mme de Grignan, 23rd February 1680

Je ne vous parlerai que de Mme Voisin: ce ne fut point mercredi, comme je vous l'avais mandé, qu'elle fut brûlée, ce ne fut qu'hier. Elle savait son arrêt dès lundi, chose fort extraordinaire. Le soir elle dit à ses gardes: «Quoi? nous ne ferons point médianoche!»[1] Elle mangea avec eux à minuit, par fantaisie, car il n'était point jour maigre; elle but beaucoup de vin, elle chanta vingt chansons à boire. Le mardi elle eut la question ordinaire, extraordinaire; elle avait dîné et dormi huit heures; elle fut confrontée à mesdames de Dreux, le Feron, et plusieurs autres, sur le matelas: on ne dit pas encore ce qu'elle a dit; on croit toujours qu'on verra des choses
10 étranges. Elle soupa le soir, et recommença, toute brisée qu'elle était, à faire la débauche avec scandale: on lui en fit honte, et on lui dit qu'elle ferait bien mieux de penser à Dieu, et de chanter un *Ave maris stella*, ou un *Salve*, que toutes ses chansons: elle chanta l'un et l'autre en ridicule, elle mangea le soir et dormit. Le mercredi se passa de même en confrontations, et débauches, et chansons: elle ne voulut point voir de confesseur. Enfin le jeudi, qui était hier, on ne voulut lui donner qu'un bouillon: elle en gronda, craignant de n'avoir pas la force de parler à ces messieurs. Elle vint en carrosse de Vincennes à Paris; elle étouffa un peu, et fut embarrassée: on la voulut faire confesser, point de nouvelles. A cinq heures on la lia; et,
20 avec une torche à la main, elle parut dans le tombereau, habillée de blanc: c'est une sorte d'habit pour être brûlée: elle était fort rouge, et l'on voyait qu'elle repoussait le confesseur et le crucifix avec violence. Nous la vîmes passer à l'hôtel de Sully, madame de Chaulnes et madame de Sully, la comtesse, et bien d'autres. A Notre-Dame, elle ne voulut jamais prononcer l'amende honorable, et à la Grève elle se défendit, autant qu'elle put, de sortir du tombereau: on l'en tira de force, on la mit sur le bûcher, assise et liée avec du fer; on la couvrit de paille; elle jura beaucoup; elle repoussa la paille cinq ou six fois; mais enfin le feu s'augmenta, et on l'a perdue de vue,

---

[1] *médianoche*, from the Spanish: a meal taken at midnight, when a meat-day follows a fast-day.

et ses cendres sont en l'air présentement. Voilà la mort de Mme Voisin,
30 célèbre par ses crimes et par son impiété. Un juge, à qui mon fils disait
l'autre jour que c'était une étrange chose que de la faire brûler à petit feu, lui
dit : «Ah ! monsieur, il y a certains petits adoucissements à cause de la
faiblesse du sexe.»—Eh quoi, monsieur ! on les étrangle ? «Non, mais on
leur jette des bûches sur la tête ; les garçons du bourreau leur arrachent la
tête avec des crocs de fer.» Vous voyez bien, ma fille, que cela n'est pas si
terrible que l'on pense : comment vous portez-vous de ce petit conte ? Il
m'a fait grincer les dents. Une de ces misérables, qui fut pendue l'autre
jour, avait demandé la vie à M. de Louvois, et qu'en ce cas elle dirait des
choses étranges ; elle fut refusée. «Eh bien ! dit-elle, soyez persuadé que
40 nulle douleur ne me fera dire une seule parole.» On lui donna la question
ordinaire, extraordinaire, et si extraordinairement extraordinaire, qu'elle
pensa y mourir, comme une autre qui expira, le médecin lui tenant le
pouls, cela soit dit en passant. Cette femme donc souffrit tout l'excès de ce
martyre sans parler. On la mène à la Grève ; avant que d'être jetée, elle dit
qu'elle voulait parler ; elle se présente héroïquement : «Messieurs, dit-elle,
assurez M. de Louvois que je suis sa servante, et que je lui ai tenu ma
parole ; allons, qu'on achève.» Elle fut expédiée à l'instant. Que dites-
vous de cette sorte de courage ? Je sais encore mille petits contes agréables
comme celui-là : mais le moyen de tout dire ?
50   Voilà ce qui forme nos douces conversations, pendant que vous vous
réjouissez, que vous êtes au bal, que vous donnez de grands soupers. J'ai
bien envie de savoir le détail de toutes vos fêtes ; vous ne ferez autre chose
tous ces jours gras, et vous avez beau vous dépêcher de vous divertir, vous
n'en trouverez pas sitôt la fin : nous avons le carême bien haut.

Lettres, ed. M. Monmerqué
(Paris, 1862-6), VI, pp. 276-80

'Le célèbre préjugé de Stendhal,' wrote the historian Sorel at the end
of the nineteenth century, 'règne obscurément dans nombre d'esprits :
l'extrême politesse, le raffinement social du siècle de Louis XIV en
avaient, dit-on, banni la violence et la volupté, ressorts essentiels du
drame moderne'.[1] Though in a less extreme form, perhaps, this popular
fallacy still persists, and nothing is more capable of exploding it than the
'affaire des poisons', of which the execution here described was one of
the principal events. This sensational scandal, one of the most notorious
in French history, serves to show how thin was the veneer of urbane,
civilised behaviour, and how turbulent and crude were the passions

[1] A. Sorel, Preface to F. Funck-Brentano, *Le Drame des poisons* (Paris, 6th ed., 1903),
p. viii.

which lay beneath the elegant façade; and the demonstration is the more striking in that the setting was the court of Versailles itself, and the dramatis personae of the 'affaire' included some of the most distinguished families of the time.

Catherine Deshayes, wife of a jeweller, Monvoisin, and known professionally as La Voisin, began her career, in order to supplement the family income, by practising as a fortune-teller and as a midwife. Fortune-telling was a fashionable and a lucrative trade, but at this period the interest of ladies of fashion in crystal-gazing and astrology was no mere harmless pursuit: it was exploited by La Voisin and her accomplices in such a way as to make of it a criminal activity. For they made the casting of a horoscope lead on to the prescribing of love potions, and thence, whenever possible, to the much more nefarious traffic in poisons, with the object of removing an unwanted husband, an unfaithful lover or a successful rival. Nor was this all: for the more hardened or unscrupulous of their clients there were the further iniquities of the Black Mass, whose sacrilegious ritual, performed by the renegade priest Guibourg, involved the slaughtering of a newborn child, provided by La Voisin in her other capacity as midwife. Not only do the poisonings and attempted poisonings indicate the criminal lengths to which many men and women were prepared to go in order to satisfy their passions, but the whole atmosphere of sorcery and black magic is evidence of the widespread prevalence of superstition and demonolatry in the Catholic France of Louis XIV.

By a curious coincidence, however, another notorious case of poisoning had come to light a few years earlier which seems to have taken place quite outside the milieu of La Voisin, and in which there is certainly no trace of such phenomena as sorcery and sacrilegious practices; though it is possible that the technical knowledge about poisons derived in each case from a common source. The marquise de Brinvilliers was a woman of extraordinarily strong will and fiery temperament, a living example of a Médée or an Athalie, who was prepared to stop at nothing in order to satisfy her passions or her ambitions. She had poisoned her father as an act of revenge for having her lover Sainte-Croix sent to the Bastille, but before using the poison on her father she had made sure of its efficacy by trying it out on patients during her charitable visits to a hospital;[1] she

---

[1] 'La marquise accomplissait ces besognes horribles avec la sérénité et la méthode d'un chimiste faisant une expérience au laboratoire'—G. Mongrédien, *Mme de Montespan et l'affaire des poisons* (Paris, 1953), p. 23.

had subsequently poisoned her two brothers, so as to secure the whole of her father's succession for herself, and had attempted to kill her sister and her husband. Incriminating evidence left by her lover came to light at his death, and this led to her arrest, trial and execution in 1676.

The marquise de Brinvilliers was a strongminded, ruthless woman of criminal tendencies, for whom poison happened to be the most convenient means of carrying out her crimes (that she was prepared to use other methods is shown by her attempts to dispose of another of her lovers by having him assassinated by Sainte-Croix); the clientele of La Voisin and the other 'sorcières', on the other hand, were in many cases the credulous and weak-willed dupes of charlatans and criminals, rather than criminals themselves; and where they were led to indulge in crime, the choice of poison was an essential feature, because of its associations with alchemy and magic.

The 'affaire des poisons' came to light at the end of 1678 as a result of some unguarded remarks made by one of the fortune-tellers in her cups: the case of Mme de Brinvilliers was so recent that La Reynie, *lieutenant de police*, started an investigation, and this soon led to the discovery of a widespread organisation of 'sorcières', La Voisin herself being arrested in March 1679. In April a special court of carefully-chosen magistrates called the *Chambre ardente* was set up, in order to expedite judicial procedure and to put a stop to these abominable crimes, whose extent the preliminary inquiries had revealed all too clearly. 'La vie de l'homme est publiquement en commerce,' wrote La Reynie; 'c'est presque l'unique remède dont on se sert dans tous les embarras de famille; les impiétés, les sacrilèges, les abominations sont pratiques communes à Paris, à la campagne, dans les provinces'.[1] La Voisin in particular had a great following among the nobility, and made an enormous amount of money, which enabled her to maintain a very lavish way of life; at her trial, her servant gave evidence that 'La Voisin tire aujourd'hui une grande suite après elle, c'est une grande chaîne de personnes de toutes sortes de conditions'.[2] It was not long before La Reynie's investigations were causing alarm, and arousing indignation, in influential circles, and the *Chambre ardente* was presented with some difficult cases of conscience to resolve. In the course of its hearings, thirty-six persons were condemned to death, five sent to the galleys, and twenty-three sentenced to banishment; but it is clear that many who were acquitted or received a comparatively mild sentence, owed this to considerations of rank or

---

[1] Quoted by Funck-Brentano, op. cit., p. 98.   [2] Ibid., p. 117.

influence. Thus Mme le Feron, the wife of a judge, had killed her husband in order to marry a lover, and had also tried to kill the latter on realising that he had married her for her money; she was merely sentenced to banishment from Paris. Mme de Dreux was guilty of several poisonings, and of the attempted poisoning of her husband and her lover's wife; but two of her cousins were members of the *Chambre ardente* and she was acquitted.

But the names of those implicated in the scandal were not confined to the 'noblesse de robe.' The duchesse de Bouillon was accused of seeking the help of La Voisin to dispose of her husband, so as to be free to marry the duc de Vendôme; and the comtesse de Soissons, for whom, as Olympe Mancini, the young Louis XIV had had a tender attachment at the very beginning of his reign, of attempting to poison the royal favourite Mlle de la Vallière. The former was acquitted, though the King forbade her to reappear at Court; while the latter was allowed to leave the country and to take refuge in Belgium, the King confessing apropos of her flight: 'J'ai bien voulu que Mme la comtesse se sauvât; peut-être en rendrai-je un jour compte à Dieu et à mon peuple'.[1] The maréchal de Luxembourg and his sister-in-law the princesse de Tingry, who was said to be his mistress, were both accused of conspiring to poison the maréchal's wife; and it was even rumoured that Henriette d'Angleterre had had a sacrilegious mass said against her husband, the duc d'Orléans, while the Duchess's own sudden death in 1670 had itself been widely attributed to poison.

One can see from Mme de Sévigné's correspondence the effect that accusations and rumours of this nature produced at Court and in the Paris *salons*. 'Ne vous paraît-il pas de loin,' she writes, 'que nous ne respirons tous ici que du poison, que nous sommes dans les sacrilèges et les avortements? En vérité, cela fait horreur à toute l'Europe, et ceux qui nous liront dans cent ans plaindront ceux qui auront été témoins de ces accusations.'[2] But Mme de Sévigné and most of her contemporaries remained unaware of the full gravity of the situation, of the fact that Mme de Montespan, the King's mistress from 1668 to 1680 and mother of seven of his children, was also accused of being a client of La Voisin's. The association was said to date from 1666, when Mme de Montespan had begun her attempt to supplant Mlle de la Vallière in the affections of the King, and to have been renewed whenever she had had reason to doubt the King's fidelity, or to feel jealous of the attractions of a rival.

[1] Ibid., p. 214.   [2] Letter to the comte de Guitaut, 29th January 1680.

To quote the evidence of La Voisin's daughter: 'Toutes les fois qu'il arrivait quelque chose de nouveau à Mme de Montespan, et qu'elle craignait quelque diminution aux bonnes grâces du Roi, elle donnait avis à ma mère, afin qu'elle y apportât quelque remède, et ma mère avait aussitôt recours à des prêtres, par qui elle faisait dire des messes, et donnait des poudres pour les faire prendre au Roi'.[1] In 1676, according to La Voisin and her accomplices, Mme de Montespan's jealousy had driven her to take part, on three occasions, in a Black Mass performed by Guibourg with the full ritual abominations; and finally, in 1679, when the King's liaison with Mlle de Fontanges seemed to mark the irrevocable end of her own reign as Court favourite she had had recourse to La Voisin again, this time to arrange for the poisoning of the new favourite and of Louis himself. One attempt on the King's life by means of a poisoned petition had come to nothing, and the plot was still waiting to be executed at the time of La Voisin's arrest.[2]

Whatever the element of truth contained in the gravest of these accusations,[3] they affected the King's person too nearly for it to be possible to allow them to be investigated in open court. La Reynie's report, containing the depositions of those witnesses who had inculpated Mme de Montespan, was destroyed by the King,[4] and the sittings of the *Chambre ardente* were suspended, and resumed only on condition that none of the testimony involving Mme de Montespan should be proceeded with. Finally, in July 1682, the *Chambre ardente* was closed, and the remaining accused, whose knowledge made them a source of danger, were sentenced by *lettre de cachet* either to exile or to life imprisonment.

---

[1] Quoted by Funck-Brentano, op. cit., p. 154.

[2] When Mlle de Fontanges died suddenly, as a result of childbirth, in 1681, it was commonly suspected that she had been poisoned by her rival.

[3] Funck-Brentano, in *Le Drame des poisons*, presents a convincing case for believing in the complete guilt of Mme de Montespan, and the same view is taken by the authors of a more recent study, P. Émard and S. Fournier—*Les Années criminelles de Mme de Montespan* (Paris, 1938). Some historians, however, while accepting the evidence of her relations with the 'sorcières', regard the more serious charges as malicious inventions of La Voisin; cf. Mongrédien, op. cit.

[4] It is the MS of La Reynie's notes for his report which provides the evidence on which Funck-Brentano's case is based; though La Reynie himself, with a scrupulous regard for justice, seems to have considered the case 'non-proven': 'J'ai fait ce que j'ai pu, lorsque j'ai examiné les preuves et les présomptions, pour m'assurer et pour demeurer convaincu que ces faits sont véritables, et je n'en ai pu venir à bout. J'ai recherché, au contraire, tout ce qui me pouvait persuader qu'ils étaient faux, et il m'a été également impossible'—'Notes manuscrites sur l'affaire des poisons', quoted by Mongrédien, op. cit., p. 7.

LE PORTRAIT DE LA VOISIN.

Source de ... tant de maux maudite creature
Qui par mille poisons destruisois la Nature,
Si la parque en fillant tes detestable jours
A fait regner la Mort, en prolangeant leur cours,
Vn suplice effroyable et plein d'Ignominie
A sceu trancher le fil de ton enorme Vie.

PLATE V Antoine Coypel (1661–1722): *Catherine Deshayes, dite La Voisin*

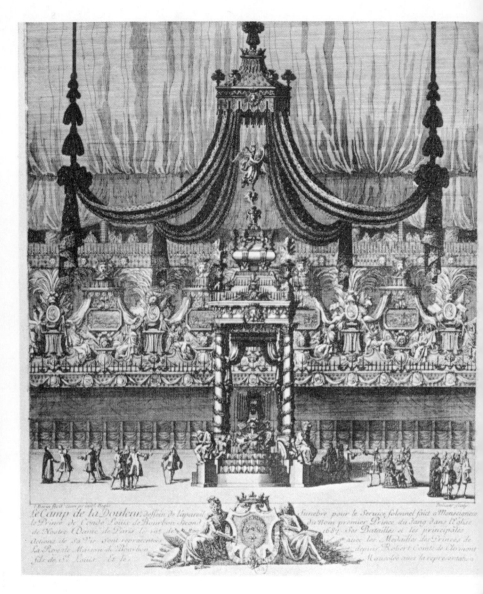

PLATE VI   Jean Berain (1640–1711): The decoration of Notre-Dame for the
funeral service of the Prince de Condé

There seems to be no doubt that the King himself took a most serious view of the 'affaire des poisons'. Indeed, it is possible that his revulsion from the intrigues and scandals surrounding his own person helped to make him more susceptible to the influence of Mme de Maintenon, which was to transform the atmosphere at Versailles into one of *dévotion* and austerity. (It has similarly been argued in the case of Racine that his implication in the affair[1] was a major factor in determining his retiremens from the theatre, though this is contested by most Racine scholars today.)[2] The reaction of the general public, however, which did not have access to the information compiled by La Reynie and Louvois, seems to have been much more detached and even sceptical. Primi Visconti's account is possibly a reflection of public opinion:

> Ce La Reynie, désireux d'être Conseiller d'État, pour mériter la charge, a mis sens dessus dessous toutes les plus honnêtes familles de Paris. Il a fait emprisonner quelques misérables femmes, lesquelles, sous prétexte de divination, vendaient des drogues et attiraient les femmes curieuses par leurs charlatanismes et leurs sortilèges. Elles eurent tôt fait, sur de simples soupçons ou caprices de La Reynie ou de Louvois, de remplir par leurs accusations la Bastille et Vincennes;[3]

though this comment from the memoirs of the marquis de la Fare perhaps betrays personal bias: 'Cela donna un beau champ à Louvois, homme malin et haineux, pour perdre ceux à qui il en voulait'.[4]

Mme de Sévigné's correspondence not only provides an important source of documentation for the historian with regard to the events of her times; it is even more useful as an indication of the intellectual and moral climate in which these events took place. In the present instance, it is clear from her letters that there was a considerable difference between the attitude of persons of quality towards La Voisin and her associates, and their attitude towards women of their own kind who were involved in the scandal. The difference is partly to be accounted for on grounds of scepticism about the charges brought against the latter, and a natural desire to play down the seriousness of the accusations. Thus she writes of 'Mmes de Bouillon et de Tingry': 'Il n'y paraît pas jusqu'ici qu'il y ait rien de noir à leurs sottises; il n'y a pas même du gris brun.

---

[1] He was accused by La Voisin of poisoning his mistress, Mlle du Parc, in 1668; a warrant for his arrest was prepared, but he was never called before the *Chambre ardente*.

[2] See, e.g., R. Picard, *La Carrière de Jean Racine* (Paris, 1956), pp. 329-32.

Quoted by Picard, op. cit., p. 331.

Quoted by P. Bonnefon, *La Société française du XVIIe siècle* (Paris, 1903), p. 297.

Si on ne trouve rien de plus, voilà de grands scandales qu'on aurait pu épargner à des personnes de cette qualité'.[1] But the ambivalent nature of the prevailing moral attitude is shown in this reference to Mme de Soissons: 'La comtesse de Soissons gagne pays, et fait fort bien: il n'est rien tel que de mettre son crime ou son innocence au grand air';[2] in fact, there is apparent a certain admiration, as well as sympathy, for these abandoned women, and in a striking passage about the maréchal de Luxembourg it is clear that Mme de Sévigné is reproaching him for lacking the courage shown by his female counterparts:

> M. de Luxembourg est entièrement déconfit: ce n'est pas un homme, ni un petit homme, ce n'est pas même une femme, c'est une petite femmelette. «Fermez cette fenêtre; allumez du feu; donnez-moi du chocolat; donnez-moi ce livre; j'ai quitté Dieu, il m'a abandonné.» Voilà ce qu'il a montré à Bezemaux [the governor of the Bastille] et à ses commissaires, avec une pâleur mortelle. Quand on n'a que cela à porter à la Bastille, il vaut bien mieux gagner pays, comme le Roi, avec beaucoup de bonté, lui en avait donné les moyens.[3]

But the most surprising example of the equivocal moral attitude shown towards these 'Cornelian' criminals is one which proves that it was not merely a question of class solidarity. Mme de Sévigné's own condemnation of Mme de Brinvilliers, judging by her letters written in 1676, had been quite categorical, but she relates the extraordinary swing of popular feeling in the Marquise's favour at her execution, concluding with the remarkable statement that: 'Le lendemain on cherchait ses os, parce que le peuple croyait qu'elle était sainte.'[4]

The origins and early development of the feminist movement in seventeenth-century France have been studied in the commentary to another passage.[5] It would be an over-simplification to suggest that the heroines of the 'affaire des poisons' were merely a second generation of militant *précieuses;* but it is undeniable that the social inequalities of the 'mariage de convenance', which had caused the *précieuses* of the 1650s to revolt against the very idea of marriage, also helped to form the moral climate in which women from all ranks of society sought the aid of La Voisin and her like to free them from the marriage-tie:

> Ce n'est pas que les quatre cents criminelles découvertes par la police de La Reynie aient été des précieuses authentiques, n :même que les plus

---

[1] Letter of 31st January 1680.
[2] Letter of 2nd February 1680.
[3] Letter of 31st January 1680.
[4] Letter of 22nd July 1676.
[5] See the commentary to passage no. IX.

exaltées des fausses précieuses aient été des émules de la Brinvilliers; mais les unes et les autres ont suscité un mouvement, propagé un état d'esprit favorable à la diffusion des idées de révolte. Leurs paradoxes contre la tyrannie des maris, leur apologie de la liberté des femmes, lorsqu'ils eurent été colportés hors des ruelles et qu'ils se furent répandus dans toutes les classes sociales, devaient, nécessairement, déformés par des cerveaux un peu frustes, dénaturés par des passions trop facilement déchaînées et trop difficilement satisfaites, se transformer en axiomes dissolvants et troubler les consciences.[1]

Mme de Sévigné's own personality was too balanced and mature for her letters to offer any more than a fleeting reflection of this aspect of the contemporary moral climate; but her letters about the 'affaire des poisons' provide an illustration of a peculiar sensibility which seems typical of the cultured society of her time. In the passage under consideration, what stands out from her narrative of the grim events is her detachment: the execution of La Voisin is described, ostensibly at least, as a *spectacle*, just as that of La Brinvilliers had been in her letter of 17th July 1676. Her lack of emotional involvement is shown in the quantity of gossipy detail, which gives such a vivid picture of the event but in so doing reduces it to the proportions of an ordinary *fait divers;* in the short, snappy phrases, and in the avoidance, throughout the entire passage, of all emotive vocabulary. Euphemism and litotes abound: the penitential shroud assumes an easygoing familiarity in the phrase 'C'est une sorte d'habit pour être brûlée', and the solemn climax is evaded by the undramatic 'ses cendres sont en l'air présentement'. In place of emotional reaction, or explicit moral judgment, we have the apparently banal 'c'était une étrange chose que de la faire brûler à petit feu', and the terrible ordeal of the 'question'[2] gives rise to the verbal virtuosity of 'si extraordinairement extraordinare qu'elle pensa y mourir'.

Mme de Sévigné's account of the execution of Mme de Brinvilliers has frequently been criticised for its excessive detachment, for what one critic calls its 'ton plaisant et enjoué';[3] and the same charge could be brought against this passage, no doubt. But the detachment of her narrative style should not be taken to denote callousness: the tone is

---

[1] F. Baumal, *Le Féminisme au temps de Molière* (Paris, 1923), pp. 159-60.

[2] Interrogation under torture, when the victim was made to swallow gallons of water by means of a funnel, and suffered great pain as his stomach was distended; in the 'question extraordinaire' the quantity of water was doubled.

[3] F. Baumal, op. cit., p. 161.

deeply ironical, and this cautious and restrained manner of showing one's humane feelings is very much the manner of the age in which she lived. Not only is the irony obvious in the 'mille petits contes agréables comme celui-là' of the last sentence of the narrative, and in the comment: 'vous voyez . . . que cela n'est pas si terrible que l'on pense' with which she underlines the most shocking passage of the whole account; it also sets the tone of the last paragraph: 'Voilà ce qui forme nos douces conversations . . .'. For this paragraph, with its sudden switch to the gay diversions of her daughter in the provinces, is not merely an example of Mme de Sévigné's charmingly inconsequential manner, her habit of changing abruptly from one subject to another: Mme de Grignan's life of gaiety and pleasure in the week before Lent is introduced with considerable artistry to point the contrast with the grim goings-on in Paris.

It is not, then, that the humane feelings do not exist, but rather that they are indirectly expressed, in accordance with the taste and the conventions of the time. Even in a private letter written by a mother to her daughter, we see the same self-discipline, the same intellectual control of the emotions, as in the imaginative writing of Mme de Sévigné's contemporaries, with the result that the whole passage appears as a sustained exercise in understatement.[1]

[1] For a record of the 'affaire des poisons' which illustrates very different artistic conventions, see Plate V, surely an example of what might be called the 'pop art' of the seventeenth century?

XV

Bossuet

(1627-1704)

From *Oraison funèbre du prince de Condé*

MONSEIGNEUR,

Au moment où j'ouvre la bouche pour célébrer la gloire immortelle de LOUIS DE BOURBON, prince de Condé, je me sens également confondu, et par la grandeur du sujet, et, s'il m'est permis de l'avouer, par l'inutilité du travail. Quelle partie du monde habitable n'a pas ouï les victoires du prince de Condé, et les merveilles de sa vie? On les raconte partout: le Français qui les vante n'apprend rien à l'étranger; et quoi que je puisse aujourd'hui vous en rapporter, toujours prévenu par vos pensées, j'aurai encore à répondre au secret reproche que vous me ferez d'être demeuré beaucoup au-dessous. Nous ne pouvons rien, faibles orateurs, pour la
10 gloire des âmes extraordinaires: le Sage a raison de dire que «leurs seules actions les peuvent louer»: toute autre louange languit auprès des grands noms; et la seule simplicité d'un récit fidèle pourrait soutenir la gloire du prince de Condé. Mais en attendant que l'histoire, qui doit ce récit aux siècles futurs, le fasse paraître, il faut satisfaire comme nous pourrons à la reconnaissance publique, et aux ordres du plus grand de tous les rois. Que ne doit point le royaume à un prince qui a honoré la maison de France, tout le nom français, son siècle, et, pour ainsi dire, l'humanité tout entière? Louis le Grand est entré lui-même dans ces sentiments. Après avoir pleuré ce grand homme, et lui avoir donné par ses larmes, au milieu de toute sa
20 cour, le plus glorieux éloge qu'il pût recevoir, il assemble dans un temple si célèbre ce que son royaume a de plus auguste, pour y rendre des devoirs publics à la mémoire de ce prince; et il veut que ma faible voix anime toutes ces tristes représentations et tout cet appareil funèbre. Faisons donc cet effort sur notre douleur. Ici un plus grand objet, et plus digne de cette chaire, se présente à ma pensée. C'est Dieu qui fait les guerriers et les conquérants. «C'est vous,» lui disait David, «qui avez instruit mes mains à combattre, et mes doigts à tenir l'épée.» S'il inspire le courage, il ne donne pas moins les autres grandes qualités naturelles et surnaturelles, et du cœur et de l'esprit. Tout part de sa puissante main; c'est lui qui

30 envoie du ciel les généreux sentiments, les sages conseils, et toutes les
bonnes pensées; mais il veut que nous sachions distinguer entre les dons
qu'il abandonne à ses ennemis, et ceux qu'il réserve à ses serviteurs. Ce qui
distingue ses amis d'avec tous les autres, c'est la piété; jusqu'à ce qu'on ait
reçu ce don du ciel, tous les autres non seulement ne sont rien, mais encore
tournent en ruine à ceux qui en sont ornés. Sans ce don inestimable de la
piété, que serait-ce que le prince de Condé avec tout ce grand cœur et ce
grand génie? Non, mes frères, si la piété n'avait comme consacré ses autres
vertus, ni ces princes ne trouveraient aucun adoucissement à leur douleur, ni
ce religieux pontife aucune confiance dans ses prières, ni moi-même aucun
40 soutien aux louanges que je dois à un si grand homme. Poussons donc à
bout la gloire humaine par cet exemple; détruisons l'idole des ambitieux;
qu'elle tombe anéantie devant ces autels. Mettons ensemble aujourd'hui,
car nous le pouvons dans un si noble sujet, toutes les plus belles qualités
d'une excellente nature; et, à la gloire de la vérité, montrons, dans un prince
admiré de tout l'univers, que ce qui fait les héros, ce qui porte la gloire du
monde jusqu'au comble, valeur, magnanimité, bonté naturelle, voilà pour
le cœur; vivacité, pénétration, grandeur et sublimité de génie, voilà pour
l'esprit, ne serait qu'une illusion, si la piété ne s'y était jointe; et enfin que
la piété est le tout de l'homme. C'est, messieurs, ce que vous verrez dans
50 la vie éternellement mémorable de très-haut et très-puissant prince LOUIS
DE BOURBON, PRINCE DE CONDÉ, PREMIER PRINCE DU
SANG.

Oraisons funèbres, ed. P. Jacquinet
(Paris, 1948), pp. 459-63

The funeral oration preached in honour of 'le grand Condé', of which
the passage reproduced here forms the exordium, marks the close of
Bossuet's career as a court preacher; it was delivered in Notre-Dame de
Paris on 10th March 1687, Condé having died on 11th December 1686.
A second oration was preached by Bourdaloue some weeks later in the
Jesuit church of Saint-Paul, for the ceremony of the burial of Condé's
heart.

Both occasions were accompanied by great pomp and pageantry, and
produced masterpieces of the baroque art of funeral decoration. This
fashion had been introduced from Italy in the 1660s, its development in
France being largely due to a Jesuit priest, Ménestrier. The 'pompe
funèbre' of both services in memory of Condé was entrusted to Berain,
who had collaborated with Ménestrier in the memorable decoration of
Notre-Dame for Turenne's funeral service in 1675. For the more

intimate ceremony at the Jesuit chapel the decoration was less spectacular in style, though the engraving makes it appear imposing enough;[1] but in Notre-Dame, 'ces tristes représentations et tout cet appareil funèbre', to which Bossuet refers here, exploited all the devices of the decorator's art, and combined to form a spectacle as impressive as any that has been recorded of its kind.[2] The whole nave of the cathedral was draped with dark hangings, and richness and colour were supplied by ermine and cloth of gold; bas-reliefs alternated with medallions, commemorating the hero's victories. The centrepiece was a masterpiece of solemn magnificence:

> D'immenses colonnes droites à chapiteaux corinthiens s'élevèrent, guirlandées de lauriers. Sur l'entablement qu'elles portaient, un autre édifice se dressa, compliqué sans doute, puisque formé de plusieurs gradins, avec, aux angles, de grands vases à l'antique, d'où jaillissaient des flammes, puis dans la partie centrale, une urne de lignes élégantes, au-dessus d'elle une autre urne, plus étroite, et pour terminer, la statue traditionnelle de l'Immortalité, ses voiles gonflés par le vent et présentant, selon l'usage, le portrait du Prince. . . . Aux angles du catafalque, des statues symboliques; à l'intérieur du baldaquin, le cercueil drapé, recouvert d'un immense coussin avec la couronne princière; aux pieds du cercueil, un immense trophée.
>
> Entre l'entablement et le cercueil, un poêle, de proportions parfaites, tenait sa juste place, avec ses tentures discrètement relevées. Un autre poêle, suspendu à la voûte, surmontait le *castrum doloris* et le reliait à la décoration générale.[3]

This ostentatious mixture of pagan pomp and Christian ceremony aimed at realising the ideal of the 'pompe funèbre' as expressed by Ménestrier: 'ajouter aux tentures noires, aux lumières et au chant lugubre de l'Église des inscriptions, des peintures et des représentations qui font revivre les vertus et les actions illustres des morts, à l'exemple de ces anciennes apothéoses, si célèbres parmi les Grecs et si connues

[1] Reproduced in V. L. Tapié, *Baroque et classicisme* (Paris, 1957), facing p. 192. For a discussion of the 'pompe funèbre' as an art-form, see pp. 239-50. Cf. also R. A. Weigert, *Jean I Berain, 1640-1711* (Paris, 1937), I, pp. 41 ff. and 87 ff.

[2] See Plate VI; and cf. Mme de Sévigné's account of 'la plus belle, la plus magnifique et la plus triomphante pompe funèbre qui ait jamais été faite depuis qu'il y a des mortels', in a letter to the comte de Bussy, 10th March 1687.

[3] Tapié, op. cit., pp. 247-8. The cost amounted to over 135,000 francs, and the King, never noted for his liberality, refused to bear the expense out of the royal purse, though this had been done in the case of Turenne, who had died in action. See G. Mongrédien, *Le Grand Condé* (Paris, 1959), p. 248.

parmi les Romains'.[1] If we are tempted to assume too readily, suggests Tapié, that the purpose of edification must have been defeated by 'la beauté gratuite d'un spectacle',[2] we should remember how much the sensibility of one age differs from that of another; and it is certainly not difficult to imagine the powerful theatrical effect derived from hearing a funeral oration in such a *décor*, or the dynamic force with which Bossuet was able to deliver his tremendous peroration:

> Venez, peuples, venez maintenant; mais venez plutôt, princes et seigneurs, et vous qui jugez la terre, et vous qui ouvrez aux hommes les portes du ciel, et vous, plus que tous les autres, princes et princesses, nobles rejetons de tant de rois, lumières de la France, mais aujourd'hui obscurcies et couvertes de votre douleur comme d'un nuage; venez voir le peu qui nous reste d'une si auguste naissance, de tant de grandeur, de tant de gloire; jetez les yeux de toutes parts: voilà tout ce qu'a pu faire la magnificence et la piété pour honorer un héros; des titres, des inscriptions, vaines marques de ce qui n'est plus; des figures qui semblent pleurer autour d'un tombeau, et de fragiles images d'une douleur que le temps emporte avec tout le reste; des colonnes qui semblent vouloir porter jusqu'au ciel le magnifique témoignage de notre néant, et rien enfin ne manque dans tous ces honneurs que celui à qui on les rend.

For Bossuet's theme, outlined in the passage under consideration, is far from being merely the glorification of a great military commander. Condé's accomplishments in the field are subordinated to his moral qualities, and he is eulogised less for his military exploits than for his edifying life, above all for 'ce don inestimable de la piété . . . [qui] avait comme consacré ses autres vertus', and by the side of which 'la gloire humaine' is a thing to be despised. Bourdaloue was to take a similar theme for his address, and portrayed Condé as the truly Christian hero, 'ce cœur que toute la gloire du monde n'a pu remplir, parce qu'il était né pour cette gloire éternelle que Dieu prépare à ses élus'.[3]

One does not need to be excessively cynical to suspect that these eulogies contain a good measure of deliberate idealisation; just as do,

---

[1] Quoted by Tapié, op. cit., p. 242.

[2] Ibid., p. 240. Some support is lent to this view, I think, by the letter of Mme de Sévigné referred to above. Whereas in earlier letters she had confessed her emotion at the news of Condé's death, she describes the decoration of Notre-Dame, with considerable detachment, as pure spectacle.

[3] Bourdaloue, *Ora son funèbre de Louis de Bourbon, prince de Condé* in *Œuvres* (Paris, 1838), IV, p. 436.

in other genres, Mlle de Scudéry's portrait of Condé as the hero of *Le Grand Cyrus*:

> En effet, ce prince était si dissemblable à lui-même, dès qu'il s'agissait de combattre ou seulement de donner des ordres militaires, qu'il n'arrivait pas un plus grand changement au visage de la Pythie, lorsqu'elle rendait des oracles, que celui qu'on voyait en Cyrus, dès qu'il avait les armes à la main. On eût dit qu'un nouvel esprit l'animait, et qu'il devenait lui-même le dieu de la guerre. . . . Sa présence avait quelque chose de si divin et de si terrible tout ensemble, que l'on peut dire que, quand il était à la tête de son armée, il ne faisait pas moins trembler ses amis que ses ennemis [1]

or La Bruyère's picture of his employer and benefactor in his portrait of Æmile:

> Æmile était né ce que les plus grands hommes ne deviennent qu'à force de règles, de méditation et d'exercice. Il n'a eu dans ses premières années qu'à remplir des talents qui étaient naturels et qu'à se livrer à son génie. Il a fait, il a agi, avant que de savoir, ou plutôt il a su ce qu'il n'avait jamais appris. Dirai-je que les jeux de son enfance ont été plusieurs victoires? Une vie accompagnée d'un extrême bonheur joint à une longue expérience serait illustre par les seules actions qu'il avait achevées dès sa jeunesse.[2]

But Mme de Sévigné's opinion, expressed in a private letter, is much less suspect of extravagant praise: 'Enfin on sent la douleur de voir sortir du monde un si grand homme, un si grand héros, dont les siècles entiers ne sauront point remplir la place';[3] and there is no doubt at all that Condé made a remarkable impression on all his contemporaries.[4] He was clearly one of the outstanding men of his century, and it is all the more interesting to ask what was the historical reality behind the idealised portraits, and to what extent Bossuet's exemplar of noble piety corresponds to the facts.

[1] *Le Grand Cyrus* (1649-53), III, Book ii.
[2] *Caractères*, II, para. 32. The portrait first appeared in the seventh edition of the *Caractères*, in 1692.
[3] Letter to Président de Moulceau, 13th December 1686.
[4] In the following portrait by Bussy-Rabutin, however, the conventional eulogy is tempered by a cynical realism characteristic of the author: 'Tyridate avait les yeux vifs, le nez aquilin et serré, les joues creuses et décharnées, la forme du visage longue, la physionomie d'un aigle, les cheveux frisés, les dents mal rangées et malpropres, l'air négligé, et peu de soin de sa personne, la taille belle; il avait du feu dans l'esprit, mais il ne l'avait pas juste; il riait beaucoup et fort désagréablement; il avait le génie admirable pour la guerre; et particulièrement pour les batailles. Le jour du combat il était doux aux amis, fier aux ennemis; il avait une netteté d'esprit, une force de jugement et une facilité sans égales. Il était né fourbe; mais il avait de la foi et de la probité aux grandes occasions; il était né insolent et sans égard, mais l'adversité lui avait appris à vivre'—*Histoire amoureuse des Gaules* (Paris, 1868), p. 105.

Born in 1621,[1] Condé did in fact perform prodigious feats of general-ship in his early twenties (the victories of Rocroi (1643), Freiburg (1644) and Nordlingen (1645)). In the first Fronde, he was a loyal supporter of Mazarin and Anne of Austria, and the suppression of the revolt was largely due to his energetic action. But Mazarin's suspicion of him, and his own haughty bearing, drove him into opposition: a year's imprison-ment was followed by the unsuccessful 'Fronde des Princes', and finally in 1652 by his flight to join the forces of Spain. This unhappy episode in his career lasted until the Peace of the Pyrenees in 1659, when he was pardoned by the young King and reinstated in his possessions. During the years of peace which followed he made of Chantilly one of the most magnificent houses in the country, and began seriously to patronise the arts; but the renewal of war with Spain called for his services, and he again won some notable victories in the war with Holland (1672-5). The last years of his life were spent in retirement at Chantilly.

It was not only the fact of his having borne arms with the Spaniards against his own country which constituted a blemish in the eyes of Condé's panegyrists. Though he did incur the criticism of some of his contemporaries,[2] feeling among the nobility in the years of Louis XIV's minority had been so universally hostile to Mazarin that Condé's attitude, if not his actions, was generally applauded; and his activities during this period had in any case been abundantly compensated for by his final victories. What required possibly more indulgence on the part of his supporters were certain defects of character: his hotheadedness and fiery temper, his arrogant pride in his rank, and consciousness of what was due to him as 'premier prince du sang'—though for all his pride and prestige, this great prince was himself the victim of the dynastic ambitions of his father. The elder Condé, just as suspect in his way to Richelieu as his son was to be to Mazarin, had schemed to win favour for his family by an alliance with the Cardinal, and his son was forced into marriage, very much against his will, with Richelieu's half-mad niece. The worst possible kind of 'dynastic' marriage, it brought misery and bitterness to both parties; and Condé had virtually no further dealings with his wife, once she had borne him an heir: the 'Monseigneur' to whom Bossuet's oration is formally addressed, and

---

[1] The son of Charlotte, princesse de Condé, to whom Malherbe's ode 'Pour Alcandre...' is addressed. See passage no. I and commentary.

[2] For Corneille's attitude towards Condé's activities at this period, see the commentary to passage no. VIII.

who inherited the temperamental instability of his mother's family. This early affront could only intensify the proud susceptibility of the already arrogant Condé, and almost certainly helped to make of him the hardened and unprincipled libertine of the years leading up to the Fronde.

For during his campaigns with the army, and in his winter quarters in Paris, Condé became notorious as the leader of a band of rich young noblemen given over to all kinds of debauchery, the 'petits-maîtres' whose name was to become a byword for licentious and unruly behaviour:

> Ses favoris, qui étaient la plupart des jeunes seigneurs qui l'avaient suivi dans l'armée et participant à sa grandeur comme ils avaient eu part à la gloire qu'il y avait acquise, avaient été les *petits-maîtres*, parce qu'ils étaient à celui qui le paraissait être de tous les autres.[1]

A letter from Saint-Évremond to the duc de Candale describes the behaviour of Monsieur le Prince at Brussels:

> Il y était logé chez l'archiduc, faisant un bruit de diable pendant que l'autre priait Dieu, et disant qu'il fallait ou qu'il pervertît l'archiduc ou que l'archiduc le convertît, et qu'enfin il le mènerait au bordel ou l'autre le mènerait à confesse. Ces paroles si licentieuses ont fort choqué les jésuites qui environnent ce bon prince allemand, et les bourgeois de Bruxelles le prennent du moins pour un hérétique[2]

and the lengths to which his impiety went are illustrated by an anecdote related by Sainte-Beuve of his attempt, with the Princess Palatine, to burn a fragment of the True Cross.[3]

As regards sexual licence, contemporary satirists accused Condé of flagrant homosexuality and even of incest; and a phrase from a letter written by his father bears witness to the scandal caused by his unrestrained debauch: 'Il vaut mieux vous poignarder que de continuer la vie que vous menez'.[4] At this period of his life there seems to be nothing

[1] Mme de Motteville, *Mémoires*, quoted by Mongrédien, op. cit., p. 70.
[2] Letter of 12th May 1653, quoted by R. Ternois, 'Quelques Lettres inédites de Saint-Évremond' in *Revue d'histoire littéraire de la France* (1933), p. 245.
[3] *Port-Royal*, ed. cit., III, p. 303. Sainte-Beuve adds: 'On ajoute que, malgré tous leurs efforts, ils n'en purent venir à bout, et que cela même contribua à la conversion de la princesse Palatine. Le fait est qu'il y a loin encore de cette jeune incrédulité qui tente le sacrilège, à l'indifférence finale qui n'essaye même pas. Après tout, ces esprits-forts qui mettaient tant de prix à un brûlement de Vraie Croix étaient bien du même temps que ces autres jeunes esprits qui croyaient à la guérison par la Sainte-Épine'.
[4] Quoted by Mongrédien, op. cit., p. 60.

wanting to complete the picture of the free-thinker and loose-liver ruthlessly bent on satisfying his passions, whether in his personal relationships or in his political ambitions.

The enormous discrepancy between such a picture and the image of patriarchal piety which emerges from Bossuet's funeral oration does not of course mean that this image is apocryphal. The failure of the Fronde and of the Spanish adventure brought disillusionment and time for reflection; the Condé who retired to Chantilly in 1660 was older and more mature than the turbulent libertine of the 1640s; and above all the prince of the blood royal who had been so arrogantly insistent on his prerogatives in his dealings with Mazarin and other inferiors, had a profound sense of loyalty to his King. For all that, the first phase of the 'retirement' at Chantilly was marked by indifference in religious matters, not by piety; and if Condé's new way of life was such as to satisfy the Epicurean Saint-Évremond:

> Après avoir réduit mille peuples divers
> Par l'effort glorieux d'une valeur extrême,
>   Pour vaincre tout dans ce vaste univers
> Il ne te restait plus qu'à te vaincre toi-même,
>   Le dernier de tes ennemis:
> A tes vertus, Condé, tu t'es enfin soumis. . . .
>
>   Jamais condition mortelle
>   Ne fut si douce ni si belle;
>   Condé, le premier des héros,
>   Unit la gloire et le repos,
> Et jouit pleinement de l'heureux avantage
>   Dont les Dieux ont fait leur partage;
>   Tranquille et glorieux
> Il vit à Chantilly comme on vit dans les cieux[1]

it could hardly at this stage have satisfied a Bossuet or a Bourdaloue. The intellectual atmosphere at Chantilly was tolerant and progressive: Jesuits and Jansenists, Protestants and free-thinkers were made welcome there; Condé was the protector of enlightened scientists such as his doctor, Bourdelot, and he championed Molière against the 'cabale des dévots' on the occasion of the banning of *Tartuffe*.

But in 1685 a variety of factors: his own illness; the example of so many of his contemporaries who had forsworn their early *libertinage*,

---

[1] 'Sur la retraite de M. le prince de Condé à Chantilly' in *Œuvres mêlées* (Amsterdam, 1706), IV, pp. 305-6.

including his own sister, Mme de Longueville, and his brother the prince de Conti;[1] the deaths of Retz, Mme de Longueville, the Princess Palatine and other close friends; and possibly the example of official *dévotion* set by the Court under the influence of Mme de Maintenon— all combined to bring about his conversion, and he made his Easter communion for the first time for seventeen years. The conversions which form such a common feature of the anecdotal history of the seventeenth century may be divided into various categories. First there is the purely formal profession of faith on the part of the agnostic: the acceptance of the outward form of Catholicism by men quite indifferent in the matter of religious belief; secondly, the 'fausse dévotion' castigated by Molière, La Bruyère and others: the hypocritical mask of the self-seeking *libertin;* and finally, the genuine acceptance of Christian values in place of the values of the world, the true conversion of the repentant sinner. In the new climate of austerity and *dévotion* which prevailed at Versailles it is only natural that the first two kinds of conversion should have predominated; in La Bruyère's memorable phrase, 'un dévot est celui qui, sous un roi athée, serait athée',[2] and the advantages of appearing to be a practising Catholic were too obvious to be neglected by the assiduous courtier. But there does not seem to be any reason to doubt the genuineness of Condé's conversion, any more than that of Louis XIV himself; accounts of the closing months of his life, and in particular the terms of his death-bed letter to the King, testify to a true piety.

When one considers that Condé's conversion took place only some eighteen months or so before his death, and that his early impiety had been so notorious, one can appreciate the extent of Bossuet's reticence. Just as Condé's defection to join the forces of Spain is treated with the utmost discretion ('puisqu'il faut une fois parler de ces choses dont je voudrais me taire éternellement. . . .'), and indeed largely blamed on the indignity of his imprisonment, so the scandals of his early life are glossed over in a perfunctory reference to his conversion:

> L'heure de Dieu est venue, heure attendue, heure désirée, heure de miséricorde et de grâce. Sans être averti par la maladie, sans être pressé par le temps, il exécute ce qu'il méditait,

[1] Conti's conversion, which had taken place in 1655, under the direction of Pavillon, Bishop of Aleth, was one of the most sensational of the century. It led him to withdraw his patronage from Molière's troupe, then touring the provinces, and subsequently (1666) to write a *Traité de la comédie et des spectacles*, a violent attack on the theatre. See the commentary to passage no. XX.   [2] *Caractères*, XIII, para. 21.

—and in what is no more than the conventional picture of the repentant sinner receiving the last sacraments. A good deal of reading between the lines is necessary in order to restore the true historical perspective, and it is clear that Bossuet had deliberately projected over the whole of Condé's career the edifying piety which marked its close. This tendency is also evident in Bourdaloue, though it is not carried to the same extreme: he speaks of 'une espèce d'oubli de Dieu, ce refroidissement où nous l'avons vu dans la pratique des devoirs de la religion', but he too plays down Condé's *libertinage*, and claims that he was at heart always a believer:

> Malgré son relâchement dans la pratique des devoirs de la religion, il n'a jamais, dans le secret de son cœur, abandonné la religion, il n'a jamais perdu la foi, il n'a jamais douté de nos mystères.

It would be wrong, however, to think that this embellishment of Condé's moral character merely reflects the flattery of the Court preacher, or an idealising convention inseparable from the style of the 'oraison funèbre'. Bossuet's funeral oration in memory of the Princess Palatine (1685) shows him to have been perfectly capable of dwelling on the early failings of the deceased, in order, it is true, to draw the lesson of the miracle of divine Grace, but also in order to deliver an awful warning against the dangers of *libertinage* in high places:

> En cet état, chrétiens, où la foi même est perdue, c'est-à-dire où le fondement est renversé, que restait-il à notre princesse, que restait-il à une âme qui, par le juste jugement de Dieu, était déchue de toutes les grâces, et ne tenait à Jésus-Christ par aucun lien?[1]

If he preferred to draw a veil over the impiety of Condé (who, as we have seen, had been not only a kindred spirit, but also an active partner in the Princess's impiety), it was not in deference to any inhibiting convention, but because he saw in the career of Monsieur le Prince the theme for a very different kind of sermon. For the piety he extols in Condé is not merely the crowning Christian virtue of an individual, however illustrious; it is the exemplary devotion to Church and State of the 'premier prince du sang'. After succumbing temporarily, at the time of the rebellion against Mazarin, to the temptation to use his power and prestige for his own ends, Condé had never wavered in his zeal to serve his King, and this is Bossuet's theme: the devotion of the greatest

---

[1] *Oraisons funèbres*, ed. cit., p. 303.

of his subjects to one who was himself '[le] plus grand de tous les rois'. In this panegyric to 'un prince qui a honoré la maison de France, tout le nom français, son siècle, et, pour ainsi dire, l'humanité tout entière' it is at times difficult to separate praise of Condé from eulogy of the King himself:

> Qui croiriez-vous voir, messieurs, sous cette figure, Alexandre, ou le prince de Condé? Dieu donc lui avait donné cette indomptable valeur pour le salut de la France durant la minorité d'un roi de quatre ans. Laissez-le croître, ce roi chéri du Ciel, tout cédera à ses exploits: supérieur aux siens comme aux ennemis, il saura tantôt se servir, tantôt se passer de ses plus fameux capitaines; et seul, sous la main de Dieu, qui sera continuellement à son secours, on le verra l'assuré rempart de ses États.

The whole address is inspired by Bossuet's fervent conviction of the divinely-ordained role of the French monarchy, and in Condé he chose to praise the example of one who had served God (at least at the close of his life) as nobly as he had served the King:

> Voilà que dans son silence son nom même nous anime, et ensemble il nous avertit que pour trouver à la mort quelque reste de nos travaux et n'arriver pas sans ressource à notre éternelle demeure, avec le roi de la terre il faut encore servir le roi du ciel.

'Le roi de la terre' is no fortuitously-chosen phrase; in the funeral oration to Le Tellier (1686) Bossuet had used the same terms to congratulate the King on the Revocation of the Edict of Nantes:

> Par vous, l'Hérésie n'est plus: Dieu seul a pu faire cette merveille. Roi du ciel, conservez le roi de la terre: c'est le vœu des Églises; c'est le vœu des évêques.[1]

Towards God's elect, seen in this light, no adulation could be too extravagant, and the blatant flattery of the passage under consideration ('Louis le Grand est entré *lui-même* dans ces sentiments . . . le plus glorieux éloge qu'il pût recevoir') finds a striking parallel in the exordium to Bourdaloue's oration where the preacher, taking as his text II Samuel iii, 38: 'Le roi lui-même, touché de douleur et versant des larmes, dit à ses serviteurs: «Ignorez-vous que le prince est mort, et que dans sa personne nous venons de perdre le plus grand homme d'Israël?»', comments:

[1] Ibid., p. 410.

Après un témoignage aussi illustre et aussi authentique que celui-là, comment pourrions-nous ignorer la grandeur de la perte que nous avons faite dans la personne de ce prince? Comment pourrions-nous ne la pas comprendre après que le plus grand des rois l'a ressentie, et qu'il a bien voulu s'en expliquer par des marques si singulières de sa tendresse et de son estime?

There is at least a hint here of the courtier's religion satirised by La Bruyère:

Ces peuples d'ailleurs ont leur dieu et leur roi. Les grands de la nation s'assemblent tous les jours, à une certaine heure, dans un temple qu'ils nomment église. Il y a au fond de ce temple un autel consacré à leur dieu, où un prêtre célèbre des mystères qu'ils appellent saints, sacrés et redoutables. Les grands forment un vaste cercle au pied de cet autel, et paraissent debout, le dos tourné directement au prêtre et aux saints mystères, et les faces élevées vers leur roi, que l'on voit à genoux sur une tribune, et à qui ils semblent avoir tout l'esprit et tout le cœur appliqués. On ne laisse pas de voir dans cet usage une espèce de subordination, car le peuple paraît adorer le prince, et le prince adorer Dieu.[1]

But in fact the profane, almost sacrilegious cult paid to the King at Versailles had its serious Christian counterpart in Bossuet's political theory based on the Divine Right of Kingship: 'Vous devez donc considérer, sire,' he wrote in a letter, 'que le trône que vous remplissez est à Dieu, que vous y tenez sa place, et que vous devez y régner selon ses lois.' In the hierarchical system of absolute monarchy, with the King at the apex of the pyramid, set apart from other men by his divine mission, no other subject had such an exalted and conspicuous place as Condé. Illustrious by birth, he gained lustre from the service of his King; and since the cause of the French monarchy was God's cause, in serving his King he was also serving God. So that in spite of the plan carefully established in the exordium, which provides the formal dialectical framework of Bossuet's oration (the vanity of worldly glory redeemed by Christian piety), the picture of Condé which emerges most clearly is the almost feudal one of a great princely vassal who has died in the glorious service of his overlord and his God. In spite of—or perhaps because of—the magnificent pomp of the setting in Notre-Dame, and the sublime eloquence of France's greatest preacher, both so much bound up with the temporal glories of Church and State, there is something rather

[1] *Caractères*, VIII, para. 74.

PLATE VIIa Philippe de Champaigne (1602–74):
Louis XIII couronné par la Victoire

PLATE VIIb Jacques Callot (1592–1635):
Scene from *Les Grandes Misères de la Guerre*

PLATE VIII   Pierre Mignard (1612–95): *Louis XIV*

ambiguous about Bossuet's treatment of the theme of worldly fame. How much more direct and unequivocal are the following lines by Saint-Évremond:

> Que vous servent, Condé, ces tableaux de batailles?
> Que vous sert ce pompeux orgueil
> De pavillons et de murailles?
> Ce chef-d'œuvre nouveau de tristesse et de deuil;
> Tout ce grand art de funérailles,
> Condé, que vous sert-il dans le fond du cercueil?
>
> Des célèbres Condoms[1] les oraisons funèbres
> Ne perceront point vos ténèbres;
> Les éloges des Bourdaloûs
> Hélas! n'iront point jusqu'à vous.
> Vous n'êtes qu'une belle idée
> En nos cœurs encore gardée;
> Tout l'être qui vous reste est notre propre bien,
> Hors de nous vous n'êtes plus rien.
>
> Ô Mort, ô funeste puissance,
> Qui pourra résister à ton cruel effort?
> La valeur n'a point de défense;
> Le sang qu'on respecte si fort,
> Ce sang t'oppose en vain l'honneur de la naissance:
> Tout se confond à ton abord;
> Le savoir et l'intelligence
> De la stupidité trouvent le même sort.
> Ô Mort, ô funeste puissance,
> Qui pourra résister à ton cruel effort?[2]

If this poem lacks the extra, spiritual dimension which gives Bossuet's oration its majestic splendour, Saint-Évremond's approach is equally free from the consequences of Bossuet's political absolutism, and the secular 'oraison funèbre' of the exiled Epicurean has a critical detachment which that of the Gallican prelate could not possess.

[1] Bossuet was Bishop of Condom from 1669 to 1681, before becoming Bishop of Meaux.
[2] 'Sur la mort de M. le prince, et sur son catafalque' in *Œuvres mêlées*, ed. cit., IV, pp. 373 ff.

XVI

Dancourt

(1661-1726)

From *Le Chevalier à la mode*, Act I, scene iii

LISETTE

Au moins, madame, il faut prendre cette affaire-ci du bon côté. Ce n'est pas à votre personne qu'ils ont fait insulte, c'est à votre nom. Que ne vous dépêchez-vous d'en changer ?

MME PATIN

J'y suis bien résolue, et j'enrage contre ma destinée, de ne m'avoir pas fait tout d'abord une femme de qualité.

LISETTE

Eh ! vous n'avez pas tout à fait sujet de vous plaindre ; et si vous n'êtes pas encore femme de qualité, vous êtes riche au moins ; et comme vous savez, on achète facilement de la qualité avec de l'argent ; mais la naissance ne donne pas toujours du bien.

MME PATIN

10 Il n'importe ; c'est toujours quelque chose de bien charmant qu'un grand nom.

LISETTE

Bon ! bon ! madame, vous seriez, ma foi, bien embarrassée si vous vous trouviez comme certaines grandes dames de par le monde, à qui tout manque, et qui malgré leur grand nom ne sont connues que par un grand nombre de créanciers, qui crient à leurs portes depuis le matin jusqu'au soir.

MME PATIN

C'est là le bon air. C'est ce qui distingue les gens de qualité.

LISETTE

Ma foi, madame, avanie pour avanie, il vaut mieux, à ce qu'il me semble, en recevoir d'une marquise que d'un marchand ; et, croyez-moi, c'est un

20 grand plaisir de pouvoir sortir de chez soi par la grande porte sans craindre qu'une troupe de sergents vienne saisir le carrosse et les chevaux. Que diriez-vous si vous vous trouviez réduite à gagner à pied votre logis, comme quelques-unes à qui cela est arrivé depuis peu ?

MME PATIN

Plût au ciel que cela me fût arrivé, et que je fusse marquise!

LISETTE

Mais, madame, vous n'y songez pas.

MME PATIN

Oui, oui, j'aimerais mieux être la marquise la plus endettée de la cour, que de demeurer veuve du plus riche financier de France. La résolution en est prise, il faut que je devienne marquise, quoi qu'il en coûte; et, pour cet effet, je vais absolument rompre avec ces petites gens dont je me suis
30 encanaillée. Commençons par Monsieur Serrefort.

LISETTE

Monsieur Serrefort, madame! votre beau-frère!

MME PATIN

Mon beau-frère! mon beau-frère! Parlez mieux, s'il vous plaît.

LISETTE

Pardonnez-moi, madame, j'ai cru qu'il était votre beau-frère, parce qu'il était frère de feu monsieur votre mari.

MME PATIN

Frère de feu mon mari, soit; mais, mon mari étant mort, Dieu merci, monsieur Serrefort ne m'est plus rien. Cependant il semble à ce crasseux-là qu'il me soit de quelque chose; il se mêle de censurer ma conduite, de contrôler toutes mes actions. Son audace va jusqu'à vouloir me faire prendre de petites manières comme celles de sa femme, et faire des com-
40 paraisons d'elle à moi. Mais est-il possible qu'il y ait des gens qui se puissent méconnaître jusqu'à ce point-là?

LISETTE

Oui, oui, je commence à comprendre qu'il a tort, et que vous avez raison, vous. C'est bien à lui et à sa femme à faire des comparaisons avec vous! Il n'est que votre beau-frère, et elle n'est que votre belle-sœur, une fois.

MME PATIN

Il n'y a pas jusqu'à sa fille qui ne se donne aussi des airs. Allons-nous en carrosse ensemble, elle se place dans le fond à mes côtés. Sommes-nous à pied, elle marche toujours sur la même ligne, sans observer aucune distance entre elle et moi.

LISETTE

La petite ridicule! Une nièce vouloir aller de pair avec sa tante!

MME PATIN

50 Ce qui m'en déplaît encore, c'est qu'avec ses minauderies, elle attire les yeux de tout le monde, et ne laisse pas aller sur moi le moindre petit regard.

LISETTE

Que le monde est fou! Parce qu'elle est jeune et jolie, on la regarde plus volontiers que vous.

MME PATIN

Cela changera, ou je ne la verrai plus.

LISETTE

Vous la corrigerez aisément; et en devenant sa belle-mère, madame, vous aurez des droits sur elle, que la qualité de tante ne vous donne pas.

MME PATIN

Comment donc sa belle-mère? Tu crois qu'après ce qui vient d'arriver je me piquerai de tenir parole à Monsieur Migaud, que je l'épouserai?

LISETTE

60 Oui, madame. Et qu'a de commun ce qui vient de vous arriver avec les deux mariages que l'on a conclus de vous avec Monsieur Migaud, et du fils de Monsieur Migaud avec Lucile, votre nièce?

MME PATIN

Vraiment, je serais bien avancée. C'est un beau nom que celui de Madame Migaud! J'aimerais autant demeurer Madame Patin.

LISETTE

Oh, il y a bien de la différence. Le nom de Migaud est un nom de robe, et celui de Patin n'est qu'un nom de financier.

MME PATIN

Robe ou finance, tout m'est égal; et depuis huit jours je me suis résolue d'avoir un nom de cour, et de ceux qui emplissent le plus la bouche.

LISETTE

Ah! ah! ceci ne vaut pas le diantre pour Monsieur Migaud.

MME PATIN

70 Que dis-tu?

LISETTE

Je dis, madame, qu'un nom de cour vous siéra à merveille; mais que ce n'est pas assez d'un nom, à ce qu'il me semble, que je crois qu'il vous faut un mari, et que vous devez bien prendre garde au choix que vous ferez.

MME PATIN

Je me connais en gens, et j'ai en main le plus joli homme du monde.

LISETTE

Comment! ce choix est déjà fait, et je n'en savais rien!

MME PATIN

Le chevalier n'a pas voulu que je te le dise.

LISETTE
Quel chevalier ? Le chevalier de Villefontaine ?

MME PATIN
Lui-même.

LISETTE
Quoi ! c'est le chevalier de Villefontaine que vous voulez épouser ?

MME PATIN
80 Justement.

Théâtre choisi (Paris, Garnier ; n.d.),
pp. 79-81

Molière's greatest comedies derive their universality from the abstract, intellectual way in which the subject is conceived. The comic foible of the central character is seen as an inherent flaw in his mental make-up, which although it expresses itself in terms appropriate to a given social context, is not determined by it; thus *Le Misanthrope* is not primarily a study of the conventions and pretences of polite society in the 1660s, but of an 'atrabilaire amoureux', and Orgon (in *Tartuffe*), Harpagon (in *L'Avare*) and Argan (in *Le Malade imaginaire*) all have their counterpart in other societies than Molière's own. With his successors in the field of comedy this largely ceases to be the case, for while Molière, in keeping with the purest classical aesthetic, had subordinated the element of direct moralising ('instruire') to that of artistic pleasure ('plaire'), writers like Baron and Boursault, Dancourt and Lesage preferred to regard comedy as a vehicle for comment on the society of their time, and to write as satirists. The distinction is not an absolute one, of course, and there has been a tendency in recent years to underestimate the satirical element in Molière's own theatre; but in the case of Dancourt, for instance, it was certainly his excessive preoccupation with contemporary social phenomena, rather than lack of literary ability, which prevented even his better plays from achieving more than ephemeral success. In spite of its merits, *Le Chevalier à la mode* did not succeed in remaining on the repertory of the Comédie-Française as long as the plays of Regnard, who alone of Molière's successors was able to achieve some of the 'timeless' quality of the latter's comedy.[1]

---

[1] While *Le Chevalier à la mode* was performed only eighty-four times in the nineteenth century, and came off the repertory in 1854, at least three plays of Regnard's were performed several hundred times, and remained on the repertory into the twentieth century.

It is instructive in this respect to compare Molière's *Le Bourgeois gentilhomme* with a play by Dancourt on a similar theme, *Les Bourgeoises à la mode* (1692) or *Les Bourgeoises de qualité* (1700). Molière demonstrates the absurdity of M. Jourdain's social aspirations by referring them to a norm of robust common-sense; his actions are the product of an intellectual aberration, of a clouded judgment. There is a strong element of fantasy in the characterisation: Jourdain is an 'imaginaire' like the other great comic roles in Molière's theatre; he actually believes that by wearing fine clothes, learning to fence, and having an affair with a lady of quality, he is proving himself to be a gentleman; and when Covielle flatters him by pretending that his tradesman father was of noble birth:

> Lui marchand! C'est pure médisance, il ne l'a jamais été. Tout ce qu'il faisait, c'est qu'il était fort obligeant, fort officieux; et comme il se connaissait fort bien en étoffes, il en allait choisir de tous les côtés, les faisait apporter chez lui, et en donnait à ses amis pour de l'argent [1]

he is ready to believe him. All this is richly comic, and it is this element of fantasy in Molière's comedy that has enabled it to keep its freshness for the modern reader, when mere topical satire has become dated. Dancourt by comparison is much more of a satirist: he is concerned with the *behaviour* of his characters rather than with their faulty thought-processes; moreover, his 'bourgeoises' belong to a society where such behaviour no longer represents an eccentric departure from the normal standard, but is itself fast becoming normal. There is certainly more direct rendering of observed social phenomena in Dancourt's theatre, and we are easily persuaded that his characters are representative types; in the case of Molière, the observed social phenomenon is material for his comic fantasy, and M. Jourdain is above all an extravagant individual.

Not that Dancourt's comedy is lacking in inspired comic invention: the *greffière* of *Les Bourgeoises de qualité*, for instance, is a particularly vivid embodiment of extravagant social ambition; cf. this scene with her brother-in-law:

> —Vous devez bien aussi vous attendre, quand je serai comtesse, et vous procureur, que nous n'aurons pas grand commerce ensemble.
> — Comment, comtesse? Allez, vous êtes folle.
> — Je débute par là, c'est assez pour un commencement: mais cela augmen-

[1] Act IV, scene iii.

tera dans la suite, et de mari en mari, de douaire en douaire, je ferai mon
chemin, je vous en réponds, et le plus brusquement qu'il me sera possible.
— Il faudra la faire enfermer.
— Holà, ho! [this to a quite imaginary retinue of servants]: laquais, petit
laquais, grand laquais, moyen laquais, qu'on prenne ma queue. Avancez,
cocher; montez, madame [this again to an imaginary acquaintance], après
vous, madame; eh! non, madame, c'est mon carrosse. Donnez-moi la
main, chevalier; mettez-vous là, comtin. Touche, cocher. La jolie chose
qu'un équipage! la jolie chose qu'un équipage![1]

On the whole, however, the characterisation and dialogue remain on
this side of fantasy, and Dancourt provides an accurate enough indication of the preoccupations of the social-climbing bourgeois and reproduces convincingly the flavour of their speech. For instance,
Angélique, one of the two heroines of *Les Bourgeoises à la mode*, conceives
the idea of starting gaming-parties to attract the nobility to her house,
and elaborates a programme for her new life as a lady of quality:

> — Hors Araminte, qui a des manières de condition, je ne veux voir que des
> femmes de qualité, s'il vous plaît.
> — Eh bien oui, des femmes de robe?
> — Non, monsieur, des femmes d'épée. C'est mon faible que les femmes
> d'épee, je vous l'avoue. . . . Nous donnerons des concerts quelquefois.
> — Des concerts, ici, dans ma maison?
> — Oui . . . comme vous voulez que j'y demeure toujours, il faut bien que
> je m'y divertisse . . . . Il me faut de la musique trois jours de la semaine
> seulement; trois autres après-dînées, on jouera quelques reprises d'hombre
> et de lansquenet, qui seront suivies d'un grand souper, de manière que
> nous n'aurons qu'un jour de reste, qui sera le jour de conversation; nous
> lirons des ouvrages d'esprit; nous débiterons des nouvelles; nous nous
> entretiendrons des modes; nous médirons de nos amis; enfin, nous
> emploierons tous les moments de cette journée à des choses purement
> spirituelles.[2]

The emphasis throughout his theatre is on the harmful consequences of this passion for social advancement in the womenfolk of the
bourgeois, which is frequently contrasted with a more sensible attitude
on their husbands' part. In *Le Moulin de Javelle* (1696) two bourgeois
friends dining out at a country inn are surprised to meet their wives

---

[1] Act I, scene iii.   [2] Act IV, scene vi.

dining with two noblemen, while in *La Maison de campagne* (1688) M. Bernard is forced to the expedient of putting up an inn-sign outside his house, in order to frighten away all the penniless nobility who take advantage of his wife's extravagant hospitality and threaten to ruin him. Similarly, in *Les Bourgeoises à la mode*, the two husbands, Simon and Griffard, are tired of paying for their wives' extravagances, and Simon's humiliating situation is summed up by the servants of the two families:

> — Pour faire la dame de qualité, on dit que ta maîtresse le fait quelquefois passer pour son homme d'affaires?
> — Le grand malheur! Est-ce ici la seule maison de ta connaissance où les maris ne sont que les premiers domestiques de leurs femmes?[1]

The whole adds up to a picture of a society in which considerations of wealth and pleasure seem to have taken the place of family life, a fluid society in which the rich bourgeois were able to buy offices which conferred nobility on the holder, and in which impoverished noblemen could restore their fortunes by marrying the daughters of the bourgeoisie.

As early as 1665, in his fifth *Satire*, Boileau had castigated those members of the nobility who demeaned themselves by a misalliance:

> Alors, le noble altier, pressé de l'indigence,
> Humblement du faquin rechercha l'alliance;
> Avec lui trafiquant d'un nom si précieux,
> Par un lâche contrat vendit tous ses aïeux;
> Et, corrigeant ainsi la fortune ennemie,
> Rétablit son honneur à force d'infamie;[2]

and La Bruyère, in the opening paragraphs of 'De quelques usages', comments sarcastically on the mania for 'titres de noblesse' among the magistracy and financiers. In the 1660s, the Conseil du Roi had instituted extensive inquiries into the improper use of such titles,[3] but La Bruyère makes it clear that in the twenty years that had elapsed since then, the border-line between 'noblesse' and 'roture' had become considerably blurred, and that it was not always necessary for the would-be nobleman to obtain letters patent by the purchase of an office:

---

[1] Act I, scene iii.   [2] Lines 117-22.

[3] In 1661, 1664 and 1666; in addition, an order of 1664 had annulled all letters patent of nobility granted since 1634. Cf. J. Marion, 'Molière a-t-il songé à Colbert en composant le personnage de M. Jourdain?' in *Revue d'histoire littéraire de la France* (1938), p. 145.

Réhabilitations, mot en usage dans les tribunaux, qui a fait vieillir et rendu gothique celui de *lettres de noblesse*, autrefois si français et si usité. Se faire réhabiliter suppose qu'un homme, devenu riche, originairement est noble, qu'il est d'une nécessité plus que morale qu'il le soit; qu'à la vérité, son père a pu déroger ou par la charrue, ou par la houe, ou par la malle, ou par les livrées; mais qu'il ne s'agit pour lui que de rentrer dans les premiers droits de ses ancêtres, et de continuer les armes de sa maison, les mêmes pourtant qu'il a fabriquées, et tout autres que celles de sa vaisselle d'étain; qu'en un mot, les lettres de noblesse ne lui conviennent plus; qu'elles n'honorent que le roturier, c'est-à-dire celui qui cherche encore le secret de devenir riche.[1]

Le Chevalier à la mode, first performed in 1687, was the joint work of Dancourt and of Saint-Yon, a *moraliste* who had written a comedy, *Les Façons du temps*, under his own name a year or two earlier, and who now, since the latter play had been criticised as showing technical inexperience, sought the collaboration of a promising young actor-author of the Théâtre-Français.[2] It treats a theme similar to that of a successful play of the previous year, Baron's *L'Homme à bonnes fortunes* : Baron's hero, Moncade, is the handsome, conceited ladies' man, carrying on several affairs at the same time; though, unlike Dancourt's chevalier, he does this partly from vanity, partly from a love of excitement and risk: he does not make it into a full-time commercial proposition. Moncade and the chevalier de Villefontaine are two of the earliest literary incarnations of a well-defined social type, that of the *petit-maître*—the label is applied to Moncade in the course of Baron's play—which was to continue as a prominent feature of the life of the capital for the next fifty years or more, and which was to be so frequently represented in dramatic literature of the time as to become something of a stereotype:

Le petit-maître joue un rôle très curieux sur la scène française, entre 1685 et 1765 environ. Ce n'est pas un caractère, comme l'avare ou le misanthrope: tandis que les auteurs s'efforcent de trouver sans cesse de nouveaux caractères, ils n'éprouvent aucun besoin de remplacer celui-ci. Il ne représente pas une catégorie sociale, comme le noble ou le financier, puisqu'il existe des petits-maîtres de diverses classes, indifféremment riches ou pauvres. C'est un type, presque un emploi, au même titre que le père ou la soubrette. On dirait que, de même que le rôle d'amoureuse s'est

---

[1] *Caractères*, XIV, para. 3.
[2] It is impossible to assess the respective contributions of Saint-Yon and Dancourt to the finished work. See E. Lintilhac, *La Comédie au XVIIe siècle* (Paris, n.d.), pp. 396-402.

divisé en ingénue et en coquette, celui d'amoureux s'est subdivisé en amoureux sérieux et en petit-maître.[1]

The *petit-maître*, in the person of the chevalier himself, motivates the action of *Le Chevalier à la mode* : a series of comic situations arises out of his attempts to play off the elderly baronne and Mme Patin against each other, and to prevent his designs on the fortunes of these two older women from standing in the way of his intrigue with the young Lucile, Mme Patin's niece. But the comic character of the play is undoubtedly Mme Patin, the rich widow of a *partisan*,[2] whose social ambitions make her an easy victim for the chevalier; and the passage under consideration contains one of the most sustained demonstrations of her overriding obsession with rank and status.

In the two brief expository scenes with which the play opens, we learn of the affront (the 'avanie' of line 18) that Mme Patin has received at the hands of a lady of quality. Out for the first time in her new carriage, attended by 'six grands laquais plus chamarrés de galons que les estafiers d'un carrousel', as her maid describes them, she has been forced to give way to 'une marquise de je ne sais comment' in a shabby carriage, accompanied by 'des laquais déguenillés'; and the crowning mortification was the marquise's 'Taisez-vous, bourgeoise!' in reply to her protests. 'Bourgeoise!' comments Lisette ironically, 'bourgeoise! Dans un carrosse de velours cramoisi à six poils entouré d'une crépine d'or!'

[1] Marivaux, *Le Petit-maître corrigé*, ed. F. Deloffre (Geneva, 1955), p. 88. The term *petit-maître* had come into the language a generation earlier, when it denoted a more dangerous social type: the unprincipled *libertin* of Condé's entourage. See the commentary to passage no. XV.

[2] 'Un homme qui fait des traités, des partis avec le Roi, qui prend ses revenus à ferme'—Furetière, *Dictionnaire universel* (1690). Furetière informs us that *traitant* was by this time used in preference to *partisan* 'qui est devenu odieux'. The following passage helps to show how it was that these men were able to amass great fortunes so quickly: 'On appelle *traitants* des gens d'affaires qui se chargent du recouvrement des impôts, qui traitent avec le souverain en toutes sortes de taxes, revenus, projets de finances, etc., moyennant des avances en deniers qu'ils fournissent sur-le-champ. Ils reçoivent dix à quinze pour cent de leurs avances, et ensuite gagnent un quart, un tiers sur leurs traités. . . . C'est chez eux que la France vit pour la première fois en argent ces sortes d'ustensiles domestiques, que les princes du sang royal n'avaient qu'en fer, en cuivre et en étain: spectacle insultant à la nation'—*Encyclopédie* (1751-65), s.v. *traitant*. To a Treasury in desperate need of ready money, the existence of this class of wealthy bourgeois (their wealth made in the first place in commerce, or in the lower ranks of the financial hierarchy) was a godsend. They needed enough free capital to be able to make the considerable advance involved in such a *traité*, but the return on the advance, as the above passage shows, was enormous, so that the *traitant* was soon able to extend the scale of his operations by negotiating further *traités*.

Now, in scene iii, led on by Lisette's discreet mockery, Mme Patin indignantly resolves not to be exposed any longer than she can help to indignities of this sort. She is well aware of the truth of Lisette's opening remark, and is resolved to do all she can to buy the social status of which her bourgeois birth deprived her. Her chagrin, and her jealousy of the penniless marquise, are much more convincing as an expression of the social aspirations of the bourgeoisie in real life than M. Jourdain's wishful thinking; she is too conscious of the gulf that separates her from the nobility to be able to pretend, even to herself, that she is already one of them. She envies the ease with which they can avoid paying their creditors: a trait which Molière had illustrated in his unprincipled Dom Juan, and which Bourdaloue and other preachers had condemned from the pulpit, but which Mme Patin admires as characteristic of 'le bon air'. Not only that: when Lisette consoles her with the reminder that some persons of quality actually fall victims to the importunities of the bailiffs, her recent mortification forces from her the sublime *cri du cœur* : 'Plût au ciel que cela me fût arrivé, et que je fusse marquise!' This line is a stroke of genius on the playwright's part, the sort of larger-than-life touch that transforms otherwise 'life-like' dialogue into brilliant comic writing.

As for Mme Patin's own relations, 'ces petites gens dont je me suis encanaillée',[1] they are a stumbling-block in her path towards her goal; particularly her brother-in-law, whom she scornfully dismisses as 'ce crasseux-là'. Yet she is in the power of the aptly-named M. Serrefort, and if the chevalier is eager to lay his hands on Mme Patin's fortune, her bourgeois brother-in-law is equally determined to prevent its being squandered. Lintilhac has perceptively analysed the niceties of the situation: why is it, he asks, that Mme Patin, secure in the possession of her late husband's fortune, is unable to snap her fingers at M. Serrefort and marry her chevalier?

> Il faut se reporter à l'état social des personnages et au moment historique de la pièce, pour avoir le sens exact de la situation.
>
> Mme Patin est la veuve d'un partisan qui n'a pas gagné trop honnête-ment son argent, au service du roi, comme elle en convient elle-même. Un scandale peut tout gâter. Le pouvoir avait la main lourde envers les financiers, et Colbert venait de leur faire rendre gorge, avec une brutalité

---

[1] *S'encanailler*, a most expressive term, was a *précieux* neologism: 'hanter et fréquenter la canaille. Dégénérer. Se ravaler à des choses basses et indignes'—Richelet, *Dictionnaire français* (1680).

qui s'appelle dans l'histoire «la Terreur de Colbert»: on en sortait à peine.[1]
... M. Serrefort lui fait entrevoir quelque grosse taxe qui la ruinerait du
coup; et il est même homme à demander une lettre de cachet pour sa belle-
sœur, si elle fait mine d'épouser le chevalier. . . . Il n'aurait pas eu besoin
d'en venir là, et le fisc, toujours aux expédients, dès cette date, toujours prêt
à se donner barres sur les partisans—à les faire chanter, pour employer le
mot propre—se fût vite fait son complice. Nous en avons des preuves,
multiples et piquantes.

Si évaporée que soit Mme Patin, elle sent tout cela à demi-mot, comme
faisait le parterre du temps, et voilà justement le nœud de la pièce. On
aperçoit ici comment il prend ses plis et replis dans le fond même des
mœurs du temps, combien l'action en est datée avec précision.[2]

At least, as Lisette points out, in marrying M. Migaud[3] Mme Patin
would be moving up in the world, from 'la finance' to 'la robe'. For if the
magistracy, straddling as it did the border-line between bourgeoisie and
nobility, lacked the unequivocal social status of the 'noblesse d'épée', at
any rate it was free from the stigma which attached to the various orders
of financier. But for Mme Patin it is all or nothing: 'Robe ou finance,
tout m'est égal'; and if she has a chance of acquiring a 'nom de cour',
then she will be able to look down on the Migauds of her acquaintance
as well as the Serreforts. The chevalier possesses the charm of a fine
figure as well as the prestige of a noble name, and however dubious his
title to the latter may be (this point is not emphasised in the play, but at
all events he has not scrupled to introduce himself to Lucile under the

---

[1] As well as bringing order into the future financial administration of the country when he
assumed control in 1661, Colbert set up a *Chambre de justice* to inquire into past irregularities,
going as far back as 1635. As a result of these investigations, several *partisans* were hanged or
sent to the galleys, and many more were heavily taxed. In 1669, the *Chambre de justice* had
been suppressed, but an *arrêt du conseil* was prepared, invoking the death penalty against
anyone advancing funds against a concession in respect of new taxes. But the *arrêt* was never
enforced: new wars demanded new fiscal measures, and Colbert was driven to make use of
the system whose grave defects he had already exposed. Boileau's portrait of the *partisan*
in his eighth *Satire* (1667):

Prends au lieu d'un Platon, le guidon des finances,
Sache quelle province enrichit les traitants. . . .
Et trompant de Colbert la prudence importune,
Va par tes cruautés mériter la fortune (lines 188-95)

dates from the height of Colbert's punitive campaign.

[2] Op. cit., pp. 411-12.

[3] Surely a name just as expressive, with its suggestion of 'nigaud', as is that of Mme Patin
herself: cf. '*patin*: soulier à semelle fort épaisse, que les femmes portaient autrefois pour se
grandir'—Littré.

false name of the marquis des Guérêts), these advantages make him quite irresistible to the gullible Mme Patin.

The chevalier de Villefontaine's counterparts in real life were common enough, as were those of Mme Patin and her niece: the *Mercure galant*, reviewing the play in November 1687, commented that 'l'on y voit des peintures vives et naturelles de beaucoup de choses qui se passent tous les jours dans le monde et qui pourraient faire devenir beaucoup de gens sages, si l'homme pouvait prendre assez d'empire sur lui pour se corriger'.[1] But though the moralist in Dancourt is in evidence throughout his theatre, the tone is not over-didactic. What he in fact achieved in *Le Chevalier à la mode* was the prototype of a new genre, the 'comédie de mœurs', which was to have a long and honourable tradition in the French theatre. Fluid, unsettled societies such as that in which Dancourt himself lived are a fertile source of subject-matter for the writer of social comedy, and one of the masterpieces of the genre was Lesage's *Turcaret* (1709), which deals with the same unscrupulous financiers and confidence-tricksters. In the eighteenth century, social comedy for the most part ceases to be amusing and becomes heavily didactic, taking the form of *comédie larmoyante* with Nivelle de la Chaussée, and of the over-solemn *drame bourgeois* later in the century; but the nineteenth century saw a great revival of amusing 'comédies de mœurs', and the genre was to have its heyday amid the restless pursuit of money and pleasure in the Second Empire.

---

[1] Quoted by C. Barthélemy, *La Comédie de Dancourt* (Paris, 1882), p. 61.

XVII

Fontenelle

(1657-1757)

From *Digression sur les anciens et les modernes*

Toute la question de la prééminence entre les anciens et les modernes étant une fois bien entendue, se réduit à savoir si les arbres qui étaient autrefois dans nos campagnes étaient plus grands que ceux d'aujourd'hui. En cas qu'ils l'aient été, Homère, Platon, Démosthène, ne peuvent être égalés dans ces derniers siècles, mais si nos arbres sont aussi grands que ceux d'autrefois, nous pouvons égaler Homère, Platon et Démosthène.

Éclaircissons ce paradoxe. Si les anciens avaient plus d'esprit que nous, c'est donc que les cerveaux de ce temps-là étaient mieux disposés, formés de fibres plus fermes ou plus délicates, remplis de plus d'esprits animaux;
10 mais en vertu de quoi les cerveaux de ce temps-là auraient-ils été mieux disposés? Les arbres auraient donc été plus grands et plus beaux; car si la nature était alors plus jeune et plus vigoureuse, les arbres aussi bien que les cerveaux des hommes auraient dû se sentir de cette vigueur et de cette jeunesse.

Que les admirateurs des anciens y prennent un peu garde; quands ils nous disent que ces gens-là sont les sources du bon goût et de la raison, et les lumières destinées à éclairer tous les autres hommes, que l'on n'a d'esprit qu'autant qu'on les admire, que la nature s'est épuisée à produire ces grands originaux, en vérité ils nous les font d'une autre espèce que nous,
20 et la physique n'est pas d'accord avec toutes ces belles phrases. La nature a entre les mains une certaine pâte qui est toujours la même, qu'elle tourne et retourne sans cesse en mille façons et dont elle forme les hommes, les animaux, les plantes; et certainement elle n'a point formé Platon, Démosthène ni Homère d'une argile plus fine ni mieux préparée que nos philosophes, nos orateurs et nos poètes d'aujourd'hui. Je ne regarde ici dans nos esprits qui ne sont pas d'une nature matérielle, que la liaison qu'ils ont avec le cerveau qui est matériel, et qui par ses différentes dispositions produit toutes les différences qui sont entre nous.

Mais si les arbres de tous les siècles sont également grands, les arbres de
30 tous les pays ne le sont pas. Voilà des différences aussi pour les esprits. Les

différentes idées sont comme des plantes ou des fleurs qui ne viennent pas également bien en toutes sortes de climats. Peut-être notre terroir de France n'est-il pas propre pour les raisonnements que font les Égyptiens, non plus que leurs palmiers; et sans aller si loin, peut-être les orangers qui ne viennent pas aussi facilement ici qu'en Italie, marquent-ils qu'on a en Italie un certain tour d'esprit que l'on n'a pas tout à fait semblable en France. Il est toujours sûr que par l'enchaînement et la dépendance réciproque qui est entre toutes les parties du monde matériel, les différences de climats qui se font sentir dans les plantes, doivent s'étendre jusqu'aux
40 cerveaux, et y faire quelque effet.

ed. R. Shackleton (Oxford, 1955),
pp. 161-2

This passage forms the opening paragraphs of the *Digression sur les anciens et les modernes*, which was published together with the *Discours sur l'églogue* in 1688. Its author, Bernard Le Bovier de Fontenelle, was then aged thirty-one; he had already gained a considerable literary reputation with his *Dialogues des morts* (1683), the *Entretiens sur la pluralité des mondes* (1686) and the *Histoire des oracles* (1687).

The 'Querelle des anciens et des modernes', to which the *Digression* is one of the principal contributions, is usually considered to have been inaugurated by the reading of Perrault's poem *Le Siècle de Louis le Grand* at a meeting of the Academy in January 1687. In this poem, Perrault not only glorifies the literary achievements of his contemporaries, but incidentally makes disparaging comparisons with ancient writers; he was to take the actual attack on the literature of antiquity much further in his *Parallèle des anciens et des modernes* (1688). In the meantime Fontenelle, who had treated the issues involved in the controversy in the third of his *Dialogues des morts* (between Socrates and Montaigne), had also written the *Digression* in support of the Moderns. Perrault's poem had already provoked brief replies from La Fontaine and Boileau; with the intervention of La Bruyère (in his *Discours de réception* on election to the Academy in 1693, and his portrait of Fontenelle as Cydias in the 1694 edition of his *Caractères*), the replies became sharper and more personal, so that the controversy had taken on the character of a trivial personal squabble by the time that the mediation of the venerable Arnauld brought about a reconciliation between Boileau and Perrault in 1694.

It would be wrong, however, to dismiss the 'Querelle' as nothing but a personal dispute, and to overlook the important aesthetic issues that were involved; for the controversy of the 1680s and 1690s is really one important phase of a debate of long standing. Du Bellay's *Défense et illustration de la langue française* (1549) considers the authority and tradition of ancient literature to be the surest guides for French writers wishing to enhance the prestige and glory of their own language, and the problem of combining originality with the imitation of recognised models was one which had preoccupied creative writers and theorists since the time of the Pléiade. Until about 1660 the debate had been an open one, although a writer like Corneille found himself forced to pay lip-service in his theoretical writings to a greater degree of orthodoxy and respect for the authority of the ancients than he was prepared to observe in practice. The outstanding literary achievements of the 1660s and 1670s, however, reflect a more homogeneous aesthetic,[1] in which imitation of recognised classical models plays a much greater part; indeed, the principle of imitation, inherited from the literary theories of the Pléiade, was probably the most important single influence in the formation of the doctrines of French classicism.[2] Not that Boileau and his contemporaries recognised any debt to the Pléiade: Boileau himself is particularly patronising in his reference to Ronsard in the *Art poétique*.[3] However, Racine's tragedy, Boileau's satire, and even La Fontaine's *Fables*, were so very much in keeping with Du Bellay's programme of 'creative imitation' that the Moderns were to some extent on the defensive at this time. But ironically, it was the very success of the aesthetic principles to which the Ancients subscribed, that was to provide the Moderns with their strongest argument; for when the latter urged the pre-excellence of the literature of seventeenth-century France, this claim was largely based on the recent achievements of their opponents in the controversy.[4]

This debate about aesthetic theory should not, of course, be seen in isolation from the wider question of the seventeenth century's intellectual debt to antiquity in a more general sense; for it was not only on matters of aesthetic principle affecting imaginative writing that there

---

[1] Even if the idea of the 'quatre amis'—Boileau, La Fontaine, Molière and Racine—meeting regularly to discuss each other's works and to make helpful criticism, is no longer accepted nowadays.

[2] See R. Bray, *La Formation de la doctrine classique en France* (Paris, 1927).

[3] Canto I, lines 123-30.

[4] Cf. Fénelon: 'Si jamais il vous arrive de vaincre les anciens, c'est à eux-mêmes que vous devrez la gloire de les avoir vaincus'—*Mémoire sur les occupations de l'Académie française* (1716), Letter 1.

was a cleavage between the supporters of old and new. The Ancients remained much more conscious of this debt than their opponents: they looked back to Greek and Latin literatures not only as examples of literary and linguistic excellence, but also as providing a storehouse of wise teaching and moral example. While the Ancients were prepared to continue this obligation by perpetuating a classically-inspired literature based on the twin principles of 'instruire et plaire', the Moderns were ready to turn their backs on the past, to find their example and instruction in themselves and in the world around them, and, like true Cartesians, to emancipate themselves from the authority of the past in philosophical as well as aesthetic matters, now that French civilisation had, as it were, come of age, and could stand on an equal footing with that of the Graeco-Roman world.

It was natural that Fontenelle should lend his support to the party of the Moderns. Antagonism between the partisans of Racine and those of Corneille was one of the factors superimposed on the purely theoretical issues in the debate, and as Corneille's nephew, Fontenelle had a stronger personal interest than most of the participants. But in any case, his temperament and intellectual training predisposed him inevitably to take sides against the supporters of traditional authority in literary matters. He had already, in *L'Histoire des oracles*, used the methods of Cartesian rationalism to attack superstitious belief in supernatural occurrences, and as a thoroughgoing rationalist he sees the *a priori* belief in the superiority of ancient literature as equally contrary to the proper exercise of one's reason. The closing paragraphs of the *Digression*, however, show a healthy reservation on the subject of Descartes as a guide to thought: 'Si on s'allait entêter un jour de Descartes, et le mettre en la place d'Aristote, ce serait à peu près le même inconvénient'. Uncritical admiration of Descartes by posterity will be no less pernicious than uncritical admiration of the ancients on the part of some of his own contemporaries. In other words, Cartesian *method*, as an intellectual tool, is already seen to be of more permanent value than Cartesian science, and here Fontenelle anticipates the judgment of the eighteenth-century *philosophes*: D'Alembert, for instance, was to write: 'Respectons toujours Descartes, mais abandonnons sans peine des opinions qu'il eût combattues lui-même un siècle plus tard'.[1]

The opening comparison sets the tone for the style of the passage as a whole. It is the agreeable, urbane manner of the polished man of letters,

[1] *Discours préliminaire de l'Encyclopédie.*

not the technical style of the professional philosopher. In this respect
Fontenelle in particular among the Moderns had a considerable
advantage over some of his adversaries: the tone of the *Digression*
compares favourably with that of La Bruyère's *Discours de réception*, for
instance, which is much more openly polemical, altogether less subtle,
and betrays a certain touchiness on the author's part; or with the more
technical subject-matter and pedantic tone of Boileau's *Réflexions sur
Longin* (1694), which constitute the eminent critic's most substantial
contribution to the controversy. Fontenelle's prose is metaphorical and
figurative—albeit in a conventional way—rather than analytical and
formally logical in structure (cf. for instance the personification of
Nature; the use of terms like 'pâte', 'argile'; the illustration developed in
paragraph 4). It is suggestively rather than logically persuasive: the
same style of writing that Fontenelle had already used to excellent effect
in his *Entretiens sur la pluralité des mondes*, where Copernican astronomy
is expounded in an agreeable, attractive manner by means of a series of
conversations with a lady of noble birth. Above all, though the *Digression*
is obviously controversial in purpose, the tone is strikingly detached; for
instance, further on, when developing the conventional comparison
between the progress of mankind throughout history and the growth of a
single human being (from which the conclusion might be drawn that
the ancients represented the childhood of mankind, while modern
writers represented its mature state), he is capable of interrupting
himself in this way:

> Il est fâcheux de ne pouvoir pousser jusqu'au bout une comparaison qui
> est en si beau train, mais je suis obligé d'avouer que cet homme-là n'aura
> point de vieillesse. . . .

From the point of view of literary technique, again, it can be said that
Fontenelle's *Digression* looks forward to the manner of Voltaire and the
philosophes.

In the first three paragraphs of the passage under discussion, the
writer clearly hopes to appeal to the reader's imagination by his striking
analogy between men and trees, and by the appearance of a coherent
sequence of thought, so as to disguise the logical deficiencies of his
argument. In particular, the attempt to reduce all literary and artistic
accomplishment to the intellectual endowment of the artist or writer,
and to assess this in measurable material terms ('fibres plus fermes ou
plus délicates', 'esprits animaux') reveals a limitation of the exclusively

rational approach to aesthetic matters; for the reservation contained in the last sentence of paragraph 3 is evidently not intended to invalidate the comparison developed up to that point: it is perhaps more in the nature of a prudent safeguard against the charge of taking a materialistic approach to physiology too far.[1]

A more serious and far-reaching limitation is shown in the assumption (not made explicitly in the passage itself, but to which the argument under discussion serves as a basis, and which is common to all supporters of the Moderns) that a quantitative progress in human knowledge over the centuries must imply a qualitative progress in the arts: an assumption which is particularly insidious whenever the approach to artistic creation lays great stress on the technique and *métier* of the artist. Thus Perrault, enumerating the causes for believing in the superiority of modern literature, writes:

> La première est le temps, dont l'effet ordinaire est de perfectionner les arts et les sciences. La seconde, la connaissance, plus profonde et plus exacte, qu'on s'est acquise du cœur de l'homme et de ses sentiments les plus délicats et les plus fins, à force de le pénétrer. La troisième, l'usage de la méthode, presque inconnue aux anciens, et si familière aujourd'hui à tous ceux qui parlent ou qui écrivent. . . .[2]

Fontenelle, it is true, shows considerable moderation on this point: he does discriminate later between the arts and the sciences, though in a manner which is very disparaging towards the former:

> Afin que les modernes puissent toujours enchérir sur les anciens, il faut que les choses soient d'une espèce à le permettre. L'éloquence et la poésie ne demandent qu'un certain nombre de vues assez borné, et elles dépendent principalement de la vivacité de l'imagination; or les hommes peuvent avoir amassé en peu de siècles un petit nombre de vues, et la vivacité de l'imagination n'a pas besoin d'une longue suite d'expériences, ni d'une grande quantité de règles pour avoir toute la perfection dont elle est capable.

He goes on to compare Cicero favourably with Demosthenes, and Virgil with Homer; it is interesting to observe, incidentally, that he cites three *Greek* authors in this opening passage: the preference accorded to their Latin counterparts, particularly Virgil, was a critical commonplace, acknowledged even by the Ancients, so that he is thereby setting himself a less formidable task; while in any case this very acknowledgment of the superiority of the Latin writers over the Greek

---

[1] Cf. the commentary to passage no. XIII.   [2] *Parallèles . . .*, II, iiie Dialogue.

within the field of 'ancient' literature provided an argument in support of the Moderns' cause, as Fontenelle himself points out further on: 'Les Latins étaient des modernes à l'égard des Grecs'.

In the conclusion to the *Digression*, Fontenelle seems to disregard the distinction between arts and sciences, and claims that the general superiority of modern 'philosophical' literature applies equally well to the craft of poetry:

> Nous voyons par *L'Art poétique* et par d'autres ouvrages de la même main que la versification peut avoir aujourd'hui autant de noblesse, mais en même temps plus de justesse et d'exactitude qu'elle n'en eut jamais.

On the whole, one can say that as regards the basic aesthetic problem of whether progress is possible in the arts, the participants in this phase of the controversy begged the question.

If the Moderns erred in trying to apply a too rigidly rationalistic critical approach to aesthetic matters, in the long run it was the Ancients who were shown to have been at fault, in their inflexible adherence to a single universal aesthetic, valid for all time and place. This was never clearly demonstrated at the time by their opponents, but not the least interesting aspect of this passage from the *Digression* is that its fourth paragraph does contain in germ that relativist approach to literature which was to grow in importance in the eighteenth century. The notion that intellectual formation and habits of thought are conditioned by climatic influence was not a new one: it is found in Montaigne and in other sixteenth-century writers; but the classical ideal of the second half of the seventeenth century ignored such possibilities (and here, curiously, Descartes seems to be in line with the Ancients, his fundamental principle being that the minds of all men will function in the same way, if only they are guided by the right 'method'.[1] In this passage, Fontenelle hints (lines 29 ff.) that there may be a reason for difference of taste in literary matters, in the different national characteristics produced by climate. He develops this argument in subsequent paragraphs by suggesting that while *European* writers, whether ancient or modern, all have similar aptitudes and therefore the same creative potential, the climates of Greece, Italy and France being sufficiently similar, this is not so with negroes and Laplanders, and there will therefore probably never be 'de grands auteurs lapons ou nègres'. This is evidently a rather special and limited application of the principle of relativism, and one cannot

---

[1] Cf. the opening lines of the *Discours de la méthode*.

help feeling that Fontenelle could have made more effective use of it in support of the Moderns' cause; but there is at any rate more than a suggestion here of that fruitful aesthetic principle which forms a basic assumption of the modern critical approach to literature and the arts: that each country and age will naturally develop its own independent aesthetic standards. If Fontenelle seems a little timid in freeing himself from the narrower habits of thought of his contemporaries, it should be borne in mind that the principle of relativism made slow progress in the field of the arts: it was quickly adopted by forward-looking thinkers in other fields, forming the basis, for instance, of Montesquieu's *De l'esprit des lois*, but it is Mme de Staël, at the very end of the eighteenth century, who first embodies it in a major work of literary criticism.[1]

[1] *De la littérature considérée dans ses rapports avec les institutions sociales* (1800).

XVIII

Racine

(1639-99)

Esther, lines 31-88

Peut-être on t'a conté la fameuse disgrâce
De l'altière Vasthi, dont j'occupe la place,
Lorsque le Roi, contre elle enflammé de dépit,
La chassa de son trône, ainsi que de son lit.
Mais il ne put sitôt en bannir la pensée.
Vasthi régna longtemps dans son âme offensée.
Dans ses nombreux États il fallut donc chercher
Quelque nouvel objet qui l'en pût détacher.
De l'Inde à l'Hellespont ses esclaves coururent.
10 Les filles de l'Égypte à Suse comparurent.
Celles même du Parthe et du Scythe indompté
Y briguèrent le sceptre offert à la beauté.
On m'élevait alors, solitaire et cachée,
Sous les yeux vigilants du sage Mardochée.
Tu sais combien je dois à ses heureux secours.
La mort m'avait ravi les auteurs de mes jours.
Mais lui, voyant en moi la fille de son frère,
Me tint lieu, chère Élise, et de père et de mère.
Du triste état des Juifs jour et nuit agité,
20 Il me tira du sein de mon obscurité,
Et sur mes faibles mains fondant leur délivrance,
Il me fit d'un empire accepter l'espérance.
A ses desseins secrets tremblante j'obéis.
Je vins. Mais je cachais ma race et mon pays.
Qui pourrait cependant t'exprimer les cabales
Que formait en ces lieux ce peuple de rivales,
Qui toutes disputant un si grand intérêt,
Des yeux d'Assuérus attendaient leur arrêt ?
Chacune avait sa brigue et de puissants suffrages :
30 L'une d'un sang fameux vantait les avantages ;

L'autre, pour se parer de superbes atours,
Des plus adroites mains empruntait le secours.
Et moi, pour toute brigue et pour tout artifice,
De mes larmes au ciel j'offrais le sacrifice.
    Enfin on m'annonça l'ordre d'Assuérus.
Devant ce fier monarque, Élise, je parus.
Dieu tient le cœur des rois entre ses mains puissantes;
Il fait que tout prospère aux âmes innocentes,
Tandis qu'en ses projets l'orgueilleux est trompé.
40 De mes faibles attraits le Roi parut frappé.
    Il m'observa longtemps dans un sombre silence;
Et le ciel, qui pour moi fit pencher la balance,
Dans ce temps-là sans doute agissait sur son cœur.
Enfin avec des yeux où régnait la douceur:
'Soyez reine', dit-il; et dès ce moment même
De sa main sur mon front posa son diadème.
Pour mieux faire éclater sa joie et son amour,
Il combla de présents tous les grands de sa cour;
Et même ses bienfaits, dans toutes ses provinces,
50 Invitèrent le peuple aux noces de leurs princes.
    Hélas! durant ces jours de joie et de festins,
Quelle était en secret ma honte et mes chagrins!
«Esther, disais-je, Esther dans la pourprè est assise;
La moitié de la terre à son sceptre est soumise;
Et de Jérusalem l'herbe cache les murs!
Sion, repaire affreux de reptiles impurs,
Voit de son temple saint les pierres dispersées,
Et du Dieu d'Israël les fêtes sont cessées!»

Œuvres complètes, ed. R. Picard
(Paris, 1950), I, pp. 818-19

Racine's retirement from the theatre after *Phèdre* in 1677 has never ceased to be a subject for conjecture on the part of historians. The abandonment of his career as a dramatist, in the prime of his life and at the height of his powers, has been variously attributed to disillusionment with the theatre after the cabal which had been organised against *Phèdre*, to remorse as a result of the death of Mlle du Parc,[1] and to a desire for reconciliation with the community of Port-Royal who had

---

[1] See the commentary to passage no. XIV.

condemned the theatre on moral grounds.[1] But as M. Picard has recently stressed, it is a complete anachronism to speak of the poet as consciously 'sacrificing' his creative genius and 'retiring' into an unproductive obscurity as historiographer to the King. For a born courtier like Racine, 'l'entrée dans la charge d'historiographe, bien loin d'être, comme on l'a tant répété, une retraite, étrange en effet à cet âge, marque bien plutôt un départ':[2] the office of historiographer was a coveted one which brought with it status at Court and released him from the sometimes humiliating social disadvantages of the mere 'métier' of dramatist.[3]

Seen in this light, the retirement after *Phèdre* poses much less of a problem; and by the same token, what has been considered as a re-emergence from retirement—the writing of *Esther* in 1688 and of *Athalie* in 1690—can be explained naturally as part and parcel of the life of the courtier-historian. For Racine to have returned to writing tragedies for the Hôtel de Bourgogne would have meant associating again on equal terms with actors and actresses, and would have been impossible without derogating from his acquired nobility and his function at Court; whereas in writing plays on religious subjects for private performance at Saint-Cyr he was showing his zeal in the service of Mme de Maintenon, and at the same time adding to his lustre as a man of letters without incurring any of the stigma attached to the professional theatre. In the case of *Esther* the undertaking succeeded beyond the expectations of even the most ambitious courtier, and as Racine himself says in his Preface: 'Un divertissement d'enfants est devenu le sujet de l'cmpressement de toute la cour.'

The Institut des Filles de Saint-Louis had been founded by Mme de Maintenon in 1686 at Saint-Cyr, a small town conveniently near to Versailles, for the education of 'jeunes filles nobles et sans fortune'. The performance of suitably edifying plays had a recognised place in the educational programme of this and other similar establishments, particularly during the Carnival season before Lent. But since even such masterpieces on religious subjects as Corneille's *Polyeucte* contained profane elements not entirely appropriate to the purposes of Saint-Cyr, Mme de Maintenon approached Racine with the request that he should write a play to meet her requirements. The Preface to *Esther* gives an

[1] The 'quantité de personnes célébrées par leur piété et par leur doctrine' mentioned in the Preface to *Phèdre*.

[2] R. Picard, *La Carrière de Jean Racine* (Paris, 1956), p. 290.

[3] Cf. Boileau's revealing comment on his own nomination as historiographer: 'ce glorieux emploi qui m'a tiré du métier de la poésie', quoted by Picard, op. cit., p. 289.

account of this request and—with a suitable assumption of modesty—of Racine's response. It is probable that the performances were never intended to be private in the strictest sense of the word: the thoroughness of the rehearsals, the richness of the costumes, the sums of money spent on the stage and the sets, suggest an entertainment on the lines of the polished and elaborate Court 'divertissement'; in fact it was a composite spectacle created by the acknowledged masters of this art, in which Racine's verse was accompanied by the music of J.-B. Moreau, Master of the King's Music, and the sets entrusted to Berain, 'décorateur des spectacles de la Cour'.[1] And indeed, the preparations aroused such interest at Court that there was tremendous competition for the privilege of an invitation: 'L'engouement du Roi pour ce divertissement et la faveur reconnue de Mme de Maintenon firent [de ces représentations] des manifestations mondaines d'une suprême élégance, où ce fut un immense honneur d'être convié'.[2] The first performance of *Esther* took place on 26th January 1689, and this pressure was maintained right up to the last performance on 19th February at which Mme de Sévigné was present, and of which she has left such a graphic account. It is a courtier's account of a social occasion; and if Mme de Sévigné finds time to praise the play in passing:

> Je ne puis vous dire l'excès de l'agrément de cette pièce: c'est une chose qui n'est pas aisée à représenter, et qui ne sera jamais imitée: c'est un rapport de la musique, des vers, des chants, des personnes, si parfait et si complet, qu'on n'y souhaite rien

she makes it abundantly clear that she was a most self-conscious spectator, herself playing to the gallery:

> Nous écoutâmes, le maréchal et moi, cette tragédie avec une attention qui fut remarquée, et de certaines louanges sourdes et bien placées, qui n'étaient peut-être pas sous les fontanges[3] de toutes les dames

and that the most memorable part of the evening was the conversation that she was privileged to have with the King himself, and which she reports verbatim.[4]

Esther, then, is far from being a detached and disinterested exercise in piety written purely with the edification of Mme de Maintenon's young

[1] For mention of Berain in another capacity, see the commentary to passage no. XV.
[2] Picard, op. cit., p. 397.
[3] The current fashion in *coiffures* was named after the King's mistress, Mlle de Fontanges.
[4] Letter of 21st February 1689.

ladies in mind, by a dramatist who had prematurely renounced the active pursuit of his career; on the contrary, it has a good claim to be considered of all his plays the one most calculated to further his ambitions. In writing *Esther*, he was paying court not only to Mme de Maintenon by satisfying her requirements for Saint-Cyr, but also, in a more subtle fashion, to the King, by enabling him to indulge his liking for the theatre without offending against the devout austerity now prevailing at Versailles. Although the 'Querelle du théâtre' did not break out until 1694,[1] the issues underlying it were already clearly defined, and it is a tribute to Racine's courtiership that he was able to enhance his prestige as a dramatist with a play that Bossuet himself was prepared to watch, and whose edifying nature was further guaranteed by a *privilège* which forbade its performance on the professional stage.

In his treatment of the subject of Esther, Racine was content to follow his Biblical source fairly closely, and he did not attempt to develop a tragic conflict of character, as he was to do in *Athalie*. His contemporaries appreciated the play rather as a sacred poem, with particular admiration for the musical effect of the choruses, and in so far as the characters themselves were the subject of interest, this was largely because of the possibilities they offered of allegorical interpretation. The question of allegorical reference to topical events in the tragedies of the period has already been discussed elsewhere;[2] in the case of Racine's theatre, it can be said that there is little trace of such intention in his 'profane' tragedies, though an exception should possibly be made for *Bérénice*, which has been interpreted as an allegorical treatment of the young Louis XIV's renunciation of his love for Marie de Mancini.[3] But there is more evidence of this sort of allegorical intention in *Esther* and *Athalie*: not only have modern critics found more scope here for their ingenuity in searching out parallels, but there is some indication that Racine's contemporaries too were more ready to interpret these plays in a topical light than the plays written up to 1677. In any case, it is not uncommon in Christian communities to take Old Testament situations and characters as symbolic, and to relate them to topical events; we may compare the Biblical tragedies of the late sixteenth century, produced at the height of the Wars of Religion.[4]

[1] See the commentary to passage no. XX.
[2] See the commentary to passage no. VIII.
[3] For a discussion of this question, see Picard, op. cit., pp. 154 ff.
[4] See the commentary to passage no. IV.

Once again, however, as in the case of the passage from *Sertorius*, it is prudent to remember that we are not dealing with anything so clearly defined as a *pièce à clef*, in which there is a complete correspondence between the events and characters of the play, and those of real life. Racine's use of allegory, like Corneille's, is perhaps less deliberate than that, and certainly less thoroughgoing, but it is more subtle. What he offers us is the fragmentary and suggestive allusion to real life, which never permits of complete identification.

How far, then, is one justified in attributing any such allegorical purpose to Racine in the case of *Esther*? And what are the topical events to which the story of an oppressed minority, rescued from annihilation by the timely intervention of the King's consort, herself a member of the oppressed race, might be taken to refer? To begin with, the religious context of the play led some contemporaries to look for an analogy with religious affairs in seventeenth-century France, and in particular to see a parallel between the plight of Esther's co-religionaries and that of the persecuted Huguenots: a parallel all the closer because in addition to the identification of Louis with Assuérus and Louvois with Aman, that of Mme de Maintenon with Esther was supported by her own Protestant ancestry.[1] But while this particular allegorical interpretation was even canvassed by some non-Protestant commentators,[2] and while it appealed to the Protestants themselves so much that an edition of the play appeared under Huguenot auspices at Neuchâtel in 1689, the publisher of this edition acknowledged that such an interpretation was quite contrary to the author's intentions:

> L'on espère que l'illustre auteur de cette tragédie ne trouvera pas mauvais qu'on en ait fait une application si éloignée de sa pensée.[3]

Moreover, if proof were needed of the unlikelihood of Racine's composing a pro-Huguenot apologia so soon after the Revocation of the Edict of Nantes, it is to be found in the Prologue to the play itself, where Protestantism is clearly stigmatised as 'l'affreuse hérésie'.

A second interpretation which has tempted commentators since Racine's day is one which seeks to identify the persecuted Jews of *Esther* with the community of Port-Royal. It appears that in Jansenist circles it had been common practice, before the date at which Racine wrote his play, to refer to the members of Port-Royal and their great leader Arnauld in the allegorical guise of Mordecai and the Israelites,

---

[1] She was the grand-daughter of the poet Agrippa d'Aubigné.
[2] See Picard, op. cit., pp. 407-8.					[3] Ibid., p. 409.

while the name of Haman was similarly used to designate their enemies and persecutors. But although Sainte-Beuve's speculation may seem to be psychologically convincing:

> *Esther* et les chants de ces jeunes filles proscrites, exilées du doux pays de leurs aïeux, ces aimables chants qui, chantés devant Mme de Maintenon, lui rappelaient peut-être, a-t-on dit, les jeunes filles protestantes qu'elle n'osait ouvertement défendre ni plaindre, nous paraîtront à coup sûr, dans l'âme de Racine, la voix, à peine dissimulée, des vierges de Port-Royal qu'on disperse et qu'on opprime [1]

there is no evidence at all that contemporaries did interpret the play itself in this light, and any such application must remain a mere hypothesis.

A third interpretation, still within the field of contemporary religious affairs, has been advanced by J. Orcibal in *La Genèse d'Esther et d'Athalie*.[2] According to M. Orcibal, the young companions of Esther represent a religious community called Les Filles de l'Enfance, founded at Toulouse in 1662, which had been virtually dissolved by royal order in 1686, at the instance of the Jesuits, and on whose behalf Arnauld himself had written *L'Innocence opprimée par la calomnie, ou l'Histoire de la Congrégation des Filles de l'Enfance de N.S. J.-C. Et de quelle manière on a surpris la religion du Roi Très-Chrétien* in 1687. In this volume, an explicit comparison had been made between the persecution of the Jews by Ahasuerus, misled by Haman, and Louis' mistaken policy with regard to the Filles de l'Enfance; and Orcibal's thesis is that Racine, in sympathy with the argument of Arnauld's book, which had made quite a stir in Paris in 1688, intended *Esther* to be a further plea on behalf of the persecuted nuns, with Mardochée to represent their champion Arnauld, and Esther to suggest Mme de Maintenon, to whom the Filles de l'Enfance had appealed for protection in 1686. Attractive though this thesis is, the interpretation it proposes does not appear to have suggested itself to contemporaries, and once more it would seem prudent to suspend judgment, in the absence of more convincing evidence.

This does not mean, however, that one is not justified in attributing to Racine some sort of allegorical purpose in writing *Esther*. Mme de Lafayette tells us that 'tout le monde crut toujours que cette comédie était allégorique', and indeed her account of the performances at Saint-Cyr lays quite a lot of stress on this aspect of the play:

[1] *Port-Royal*, ed. cit., I, p. 25.   [2] Paris, 1950. See especially pp. 32 ff.

La comédie représentait en quelque sorte la chute de Mme de Montespan et l'élévation de Mme de Maintenon. Toute la différence fut qu'Esther était un peu plus jeune, et moins précieuse en fait de piété. L'application qu'on lui faisait du caractère d'Esther, et de celui de Vasthi à Mme de Montespan, fit qu'elle ne fut pas fâchée de rendre public un divertissement qui n'avait été fait que pour la communauté et pour quelques-unes de ses amies particulières. . . . Tout le monde crut toujours que cette comédie était allégorique, qu'Assuérus était le Roi, que Vasthi, qui était la femme concubine détrônée, paraissait pour Mme de Montespan. Esther tombait sur Mme de Maintenon, Aman représentait M. de Louvois, mais il n'y était pas bien peint, et apparemment Racine n'avait pas voulu le marquer.[1]

These lines offer a most interesting commentary on the passage from *Esther* under consideration. Provided that one bears in mind the reservations indicated by Mme de Lafayette ('la comédie représentait *en quelque sorte* la chute de Mme de Montespan', 'M. de Louvois . . . *n'y était pas bien peint*'), and that one does not look for too precise or too detailed a correspondence between the historical figures concerned and the characters of the play, it would seem reasonable enough to see in the passage a reflection of the changes which had taken place at court in the last decade. For if we remember that the play was commissioned by Mme de Maintenon, to be performed in her own establishment at Saint-Cyr, it is impossible not to recognise in Racine's Esther a portrait of his protector, who had so quickly gained such an ascendancy over the King and his court, and whom Boileau, in 1692, was also to compare flatteringly to the Jewish queen:

> A Paris, à la cour, on trouve, je l'avoue,
> Des femmes dont le zèle est digne qu'on le loue,
> Qui s'occupent du bien en tout temps, en tout lieu.
> J'en sais une, chérie et du monde et de Dieu,
> Humble dans ses grandeurs, sage dans la fortune,
> Qui gémit, comme Esther, de sa gloire importune,
> Que le vice lui-même est contraint d'estimer. . . .[2]

A passage at the end of Act I, scene i seems to refer specifically to Saint-Cyr:

---

[1] 'Mémoires de la cour de France, 1688-9' in *La Princesse de Clèves, Lettres, Mémoires*, ed. Calvet (Paris, 1937), pp. 366-7. The 'Mémoires' provide an invaluable background to the study of *Esther*.

[2] *Satire* X, lines 513-19.

> Cependant mon amour pour notre nation
> A rempli ce palais de filles de Sion,
> Jeunes et tendres fleurs, par le sort agitées,
> Sous un ciel étranger comme moi transplantées.
> Dans un lieu séparé de profanes témoins,
> Je mets à les former mon étude et mes soins;
> Et c'est là que fuyant l'orgueil du diadème,
> Lasse de vains honneurs, et me cherchant moi-même,
> Aux pieds de l'Éternel je viens m'humilier,
> Et goûter le plaisir de me faire oublier

—and even M. Picard, who is extremely cautious with regard to the allegorical content of the play, has to admit that this allusion admits of no doubt at all.[1]

If we accept that Esther represents Mme de Maintenon—even with Picard's reservation that the resemblance is 'vague et comme flottante', for, as he points out with a touch of pedantry, 'après tout, le peuple n'avait pas été invité à ses noces avec le Roi, comme c'est le cas pour Esther'[2]—then there seems to be every reason to take 'l'altière Vasthi' to refer to Mme de Montespan. Picard will not have it that this is so: 'Mme de Maintenon aurait trouvé de très mauvais goût qu'on mît dans sa bouche le vers d'Esther sur «l'altière Vasthi dont j'occupe la place»: l'épouse du Roi ne considérait nullement qu'elle remplaçait Mme de Montespan.'[3] But however tactless this line may be considered to be, and however indiscreet the reference in lines 5-6 to Louis' difficulties in breaking with Mme de Montespan, it is surely quite inconceivable that a poet so experienced in the scandal and gossip of Court life as Racine undoubtedly was could have written the opening lines of this passage and remained unconscious of the interpretation that would be put on them. Once again, the allusion is vague and suggestive, not detailed or precise: the 'enflammé de dépit' of line 3 may correspond to certain historians' views of the King's reaction to Mme de Montespan's part in the 'affaire des poisons',[4] but it would be an exaggeration in the eyes of contemporaries, who were in any case not generally aware of the extent of the scandal. Similarly, the details Esther gives of her early life (lines 13-18) have no biographical validity when applied to Mme de Maintenon, and there is no individual who had filled in her life the role attributed to Mardochée. Nevertheless, the subtler allusions and half-hints are there:

---

[1] Racine, *Œuvres complètes*, ed. cit., I, p. 1157.　　　　[2] Ibid., p. 1158.
[3] Picard, op. cit., p. 407.　　　　[4] See the commentary to passage no. XIV.

the 'race' and 'pays' of line 24 hint at her Protestant ancestry, and the references to Esther's state of dependence (lines 15-16) and 'obscurité' (line 20) at any rate do not conflict violently with the facts about Mme de Maintenon's early poverty, marriage to the poet Scarron and widowhood.

As regards the complimentary allusions to Louis XIV in the person of Assuérus, the references are imprecise enough (lines 35-50) to lend themselves perfectly well tol the desired interpretation; while the passage devoted to Esther's rivals (lines 25-32), even if there is no recognisable counterpart for the particular portraits of lines 30 and 31-2, must have reminded courtiers who watched the play of the succession of ephemeral affairs which marked the closing period of the King's liaison with Mme de Montespan.

Analysis of the passage, then, in conjunction with Mme de Lafayette's commentary on the play, seems to bear out at least a limited allegorical interpretation of *Esther*. Whether or not Racine intended the play to be a more sustained allegory it is impossible to say without further evidence, though it should be noted that the interpretation placed on this passage does not rule out the more extensive interpretations discussed above. However, it would be prudent to assume that Racine did not set out to write a coherent, self-consistent *pièce à clef*, even if he was prepared to stimulate the interest of his audience of courtiers by transparent references, in certain episodes and situations, to the world to which they belonged. In addition to being an edifying Biblical tragedy, *Esther* is Racine's most notable contribution to the aulic literature of his time.

XIX

La Bruyère

(1645–96)

Les Caractères ou les Mœurs de ce siècle, chapter X ('Du souverain ou
de la république'), para. 24

La science des détails, ou une diligente attention aux moindres besoins
de la république, est une partie essentielle au bon gouvernement, trop
négligée, à la vérité, dans les derniers temps, par les rois ou par les
ministres, mais qu'on ne peut trop souhaiter dans le souverain qui l'ignore,
ni assez estimer dans celui qui la possède. Que sert en effet au bien des
peuples et à la douceur de leurs jours que le prince place les bornes de
son empire au-delà des terres de ses ennemis; qu'il fasse de leurs
souverainetés des provinces de son royaume; qu'il leur soit également
supérieur par les sièges et par les batailles, et qu'ils ne soient devant
10 lui en sûreté ni dans les plaines ni dans les plus forts bastions; que
les nations s'appellent les unes les autres, se liguent ensemble pour se
défendre et pour l'arrêter; qu'elles se liguent en vain; qu'il marche
toujours et qu'il triomphe toujours; que leurs dernières espérances soient
tombées par le raffermissement d'une santé qui donnera au monarque
le plaisir de voir les princes ses petits-fils soutenir ou accroître ses
destinées, se mettre en campagne, s'emparer de redoutables forteres-
ses, et conquérir de nouveaux États; commander de vieux et expérimentés
capitaines, moins par leur rang et leur naissance que par leur génie et leur
sagesse; suivre les traces augustes de leur victorieux père, imiter sa bonté,
20 sa docilité, son équité, sa vigilance, son intrépidité? Que me servirait, en
un mot, comme à tout le peuple, que le prince fût heureux et comblé de
gloire par lui-même et par les siens, que ma patrie fût puissante et
formidable, si, triste et inquiet, j'y vivais dans l'oppression ou dans
l'indigence; si, à couvert des courses de l'ennemi, je me trouvais exposé,
dans les places ou dans les rues d'une ville, au fer d'un assassin, et que je
craignisse moins, dans l'horreur de la nuit, d'être pillé ou massacré dans
d'épaisses forêts que dans ses carrefours; si la sûreté, l'ordre et la propreté
ne rendaient pas le séjour des villes si délicieux, et n'y avaient pas amené,

avec l'abondance, la douceur de la société; si, faible et seul de mon parti,
30 j'avais à souffrir dans ma métairie du voisinage d'un grand, et si l'on avait
moins pourvu à me faire justice de ses entreprises; si je n'avais pas sous
ma main autant de maîtres, et d'excellents maîtres, pour élever mes enfants
dans les sciences ou dans les arts qui feront un jour leur établissement; si,
par la facilité du commerce, il m'était moins ordinaire de m'habiller de
bonnes étoffes, et de me nourrir de viandes saines et de les acheter peu; si
enfin, par les soins du prince, je n'étais pas aussi content de ma fortune
qu'il doit lui-même, par ses vertus, l'être de la sienne?

Caractères, ed. G. Servois and M. Rébelliau
(Paris, Hachette; n.d.), pp. 278-9

Some critics, looking for an overall pattern in the *Caractères*, have
suggested that the chapter 'Du souverain ou de la république' was
intended to form the conclusion of the first half of the work, which may
be said to deal in general with outward or social features of contemporary
life; whereas the second half, according to this view, deals rather with
men's private or individual lives, and leads up to the chapter 'Des
esprits forts'. Whether or not one accepts such a view of La Bruyère's
intentions as regards the plan of his work as a whole, the chapter on the
King (the original title was merely 'Du souverain') certainly concludes
a central section of three chapters dealing with the court at Versailles,
and is itself brought to an end by a long, extravagant panegyric of Louis
XIV. As Sainte-Beuve says:

Un livre composé sous Louis XIV ne serait pas complet, et j'ajouterai,
ne serait pas assuré contre le tonnerre, s'il n'y avait au milieu une image
du Roi. La Bruyère n'a manqué ni à la précaution ni à la règle. . . .L'autel
est au centre, au cœur de l'œuvre, un peu plus près de la fin que du
commencement et à un endroit élevé, d'où il est en vue de toutes parts.[1]

Unashamed adulation of Louis XIV, in the form of idealised portraits
of imaginary rulers, when it was not in the form of more directly
personal flattery, was indeed a commonplace of the literature of the
time. It is to be found not only in such formal academic exercises as La
Bruyère's own 'discours de réception' on his admission to the Academy

[1] *Causeries du lundi* (Paris, n.d.), V, p. 333.

in 1694,[1] but also in such diverse literary works as Boileau's *Satires* (cf. the end of *Satire* V), Corneille's tragedy *Attila*, with its artificially interpolated portrait of Mérovée, Racine's Prologue to *Esther*, and Molière's *Tartuffe* with its well-known eulogy of the King: 'Nous vivons sous un prince ennemi de la fraude . . . .' This latter group of writers, and others one might quote, were of course in receipt of royal pensions, and it was openly recognised that one important reason for these was to 'hire' a body of writers who would sing the royal praises; Chapelain had acknowledged as much in his letter to Colbert in 1663 submitting a list of recommendations: 'Je ne fais, Monsieur, que vous indiquer ceux que je crois dignes de ces faveurs, suivant l'ordre que vous m'avez donné, afin d'avoir plusieurs trompettes des vertus du Roi. . . .'[2] La Bruyère, however, was not so placed—by virtue of his employment as tutor in Condé's household he enjoyed rather more independence—and in the fact that the *Caractères* contain the same sort of formal eulogy, we may see an indication that in the intellectual climate then prevailing any serious writer had not only to refrain from subversive or tendentious writing, but also to give positive proof of support for the absolutist régime.

Chapter X was much augmented from one edition to another, however, and the passage under discussion, where the eulogy of the King is neither so extravagant nor so straightforward, comes in first in the fourth edition, in 1689. M. P. Richard has commented on the effect of the successive revisions of this chapter:

Ce chapitre, qui n'avait dans la première édition que neuf petites pages, dont l'éloge de Louis XIV prenait à lui seul les deux tiers, en occupa, dans la huitième, 35 d'un texte beaucoup plus serré. L'auteur semblait vouloir y corriger les hyperboles justifiées par le besoin de s'assurer un tout-puissant patron, en traçant un idéal de souveraineté patriarcale.[3]

Indeed, only at a casual, superficial reading could the passage under consideration appear to present the same unqualified panegyric as the paragraph which closes the chapter.

[1] Cf. this particularly fulsome piece of flattery from an academic address by Racine, who claimed that to work on the Academy dictionary was a pleasure because 'tous les mots de la langue, toutes les syllabes nous paraissent précieuses, parce que nous les regardons comme autant d'instruments qui doivent servir à la gloire de notre auguste protecteur'. Quoted by R. Picard in *La Carrière de Jean Racine* (Paris, 1956), p. 443.

[2] Quoted by G. Mongrédien, *La Vie littéraire au XVIIe siècle* (Paris, 1947), p. 264.

[3] *La Bruyère et ses Caractères* (Amiens, 1946), p. 77.

Louis XIV's 'personal' reign had begun in 1661 with great promises of stability and prosperity. With bourgeois ministers in charge of the various sections of a departmentalised administration, and effective power firmly in the hands of the King, there was no longer a danger of ambitious nobles conspiring or rebelling against the tyranny of an all-powerful minister. Louis' administrators were capable, too: Colbert in particular, up to his death in 1683, developed overseas trade and internal communications as a basis for economic prosperity. But by 1689 this economic progress was already being largely undermined by an expansionist and aggressive foreign policy; the War of Devolution against Spain (1667-8) had been followed by the Dutch War of 1672-8, and the War of the League of Augsburg was to last from 1688 to 1697. At home the ruinous extravagance at Versailles was combined with an ineffective fiscal policy, while the Revocation of the Edict of Nantes (1685) and the large-scale emigration of Protestants which ensued, was a further blow to the nation's economy. It is not easy to pinpoint a precise date at which the tide of events began to turn, but the peak of the prosperity and glory of Louis' reign may be said to have been about 1680. His early wars had on the whole been successful, and the nation seems largely to have identified itself with the ambitions and achievements of the King; but by the time this passage was written a certain disillusionment was beginning to be apparent, and serious writers were increasingly to turn their attention to the realities behind the showy façade of Versailles.

It is tempting for the modern reader, looking at the passage through twentieth-century eyes, to see it as the ironical expression of scathing criticism under the mask of conventional flattery; particularly, perhaps, in view of the curious stylistic feature of the interrogative 'Que sert . . . ?' (line 5) followed by a parallel question in the conditional tense, 'Que me servirait . . . ?' (line 20), which may at first sight give the impression that the redeeming aspects of Louis' reign are referred to only as a prudent afterthought. However, although it is not treated fully until the final sentence, the subject of the internal administration of the country has already been introduced in the short sentence with which the paragraph begins. 'La science des détails' is in fact the dominant theme of the whole paragraph, which is constructed so as to emphasise the domestic realities of everyday life by a forceful contrast with the glory and prestige conventionally associated with military exploits and foreign affairs. It is by no means easy, nevertheless, to assess the proportions of sincere appreciation and of ironical criticism in the passage, but it does seem to contain some measure at least of genuine appreciation of the real benefits enjoyed by Louis' subjects. The emphasis is not on the disastrous foreign wars—and the worst in any case were still to come —nor on the wasteful cult of splendour at Versailles, but rather on the stability and administrative efficiency of the State. We must not forget, moreover, how stable and settled the government of the country must have seemed under Louis XIV after the disturbances of the Fronde, the turbulence of Louis XIII's reign, and the remoter memories of the Wars of Religion.

It would be possible, no doubt, to invalidate nearly all the claims made in the second half of the passage, by confronting them with personal memoirs, reports of *intendants* and provincial governors, and other similar documentary evidence. The modern historian has access to this material, so that our picture of Louis XIV's reign is more complete and less one-sided than that painted by earlier historians (for instance, that given in *Le Siècle de Louis XIV* by Voltaire, who in any case perhaps tends to overpraise Louis XIV as a means of expressing indirect criticism of Louis XV); but we must remember that La Bruyère's comments are the individual comments of a private person, whose view of contemporary events, however well-informed, was necessarily limited. Still, there are cases where the favourable picture which he is at least ostensibly painting here, does not tally with what he himself says elsewhere in the *Caractères*.

The tribute expressed in the opening sentence would appear to be sincere enough; elsewhere (X, 35) La Bruyère praises the King for his ability to 'se renfermer au dedans, et comme dans les détails de tout un royaume', and this characteristic is also recognised by other writers, though not all regard it as a virtue: both Fénelon and Saint-Simon criticise the King for an excessive attention to detail. The second sentence contains the familiar subject-matter of the conventional eulogy of the King, however unorthodox the form in which it is presented here ('Que sert . . . ?'); it is noticeable that it is this part of the passage which approximates most closely to the extravagant panegyric of the concluding paragraph (no. 35) of 'Du souverain . . .', not only in content but also in the carefully-contrived rhetorical style. The long final sentence—still rhetorical in its style, but with a more spontaneous flavour (though this may merely be the effect of the repetition of the personal pronoun) and a more urgent, vehement tone—offers most scope for careful analysis.

In it, La Bruyère proceeds in effect from the general to the particular, the two terms *oppression* and *indigence* covering, more or less, the specific hardships and abuses which he subsequently details. We may think at once of the celebrated passage from 'De l'homme' in which the utter destitution of the French peasantry is so eloquently revealed:

> L'on voit certains animaux farouches, des mâles et des femelles, répandus par la campagne, noirs, livides et tout brûlés du soleil, attachés à la terre qu'ils fouillent et qu'ils remuent avec une opiniâtreté invincible: ils ont comme une voix articulée, et, quand ils se lèvent sur leurs pieds, ils montrent une face humaine; et en effet ils sont des hommes.[1]

This passage was also published for the first time in the fourth edition, but we need not necessarily conclude, for all that, that the reference to *indigence* in the passage under discussion must be ironical. Here, La Bruyère is speaking on behalf of the whole nation (*peuple* should clearly be taken in an inclusive sense, and not as for instance in IX, 25, in opposition to the nobility: 'Faut-il opter? Je ne balance pas, je veux être peuple'), and he seems to be acknowledging that the vast majority of Frenchmen are quite comfortably off; in the other passage, though there is no doubting its sincere humanitarian tone, there is no evidence that the plight of the peasants is primarily connected in his mind with the evils of a particular administration: indeed, its position in the chapter 'De l'homme' might suggest the contrary, and it is certain that some of the most graphic accounts of poverty and destitution during the century refer to the period of the Fronde.

The reference to brigandage and highway robbery inevitably recalls, particularly by the juxtaposition of 'd'épaisses forêts' and 'carrefours', a couplet from Boileau's sixth *Satire* (1666):

> Le bois le plus funeste et le moins fréquenté
> Est, au prix de Paris, un lieu de sûreté.[2]

If this might appear at first sight to provide evidence that La Bruyère's claim is ironical, we should remember that the twenty-odd years since Boileau's lines were written had brought about a considerable increase in orderliness, in Paris at any rate. As regards the claim of *propreté*, and the 'séjour [des] villes si délicieux', these are material characteristics, and relate to aspects of life where progress is measurable; and we can see in 'la douceur de la société' an appreciative reference to the stability and

[1] XI, 128.   [2] Lines 89-90.

relative security of Louis' reign. *L'abondance* is the one term in this sentence that it is difficult to accept. For if the worst years of famine, as a result of bad harvests, were still to come, even in a normal year the whole of the grain-producing economy was precarious with factors such as internal tariffs between provinces and hoarding by profiteers preventing the equitable distribution of what supplies there were; and reports of *intendants*, or memoirs of foreign ambassadors show how hard a life was that of the whole community in some provinces.[1] But once again, it is doubtful whether La Bruyère is using the term ironically: he seems to be writing in much the same spirit as in the following passage from 'Des biens de fortune':

> Il y a des misères sur la terre qui saisissent le cœur. Il manque à quelques-uns jusqu'aux aliments; ils redoutent l'hiver, ils appréhendent de vivre. L'on mange ailleurs des fruits précoces; l'on force la terre et les saisons pour fournir à sa délicatesse: de simples bourgeois, seulement à cause qu'ils étaient riches, ont eu l'audace d'avaler en un seul morceau la nourriture de cent familles. Tienne qui voudra contre de si grandes extrémités; je ne veux être, si je le puis, ni malheureux, ni heureux; je me jette et me réfugie dans la médiocrité.[2]

We may call this an escapist attitude, but it is surely the sort of escapism which brings comfort to the consciences of most of us.

In the case of the remarks about oppression and injustice, we must again allow that from a relative point of view there had been progress during the century. Oppression there certainly was, but not on the whole from the nobles; and if Colbert could write to an *intendant* at Limoges, in 1681:

> Je suis bien aise de vous faire observer que l'on a toujours accusé les gentilshommes et personnes puissantes de votre généralité de faire un grand nombre de vexations sur les peuples,[3]

many cases could be quoted of noblemen championing the poor against the oppression of the tax-farmers. It was this that impartial observers recognised as the principal source of the sufferings of the poor; for instance, the Venetian ambassadors reported in 1664:

[1] See F. Gaiffe, *L'Envers du Grand Siècle* (Paris, 1924); P. Sagnac, *La Formation de la société française moderne* (Paris, 1945), vol. 1.

[2] VI, 47.   [3] Quoted by Sagnac, op. cit., p. 103.

Les provinces sont ruinées par la pauvreté du menu peuple, qui souffre moins du poids excessif des tailles que de l'avidité des partisans,[1]

and again in 1680:

A Paris, on ne peut voir l'état nécessiteux du peuple de France; c'est dans les provinces qu'apparaissent la misère et la détresse des peuples accablés par les charges sans nombre et par les logements des gens de guerre auxquels ils sont obligés de faire face, quoique réduits à la mendicité.[2]

Cases of iniquitous oppression on the part of noble landlords do not appear to have been numerous, and contemporary records show that noble offenders did not enjoy any immunity before the law.[3] Finally, the last of the specific references contained in the passage, the acknowledgment of increased commerical prosperity, is an obvious half-truth. There had undoubtedly been considerable progress in this field, but there were still great obstacles to economic development, not least the feeling of social inferiority on the part of the merchant classes themselves: 'Il suffit d'être négociant' says a contemporary text, 'pour être regardé avec mépris. . . . Alors le négociant quitte son commerce pour se retirer à la campagne ou achète une charge pour lui-même pour sortir de cet esclavage'.[4] The result was, of course, that there was a tremendous wastage of the money and the ability which should have been devoted to developing business interests.[5]

The more carefully one reads the passage in the light of contemporary references to the topics it alludes to, and in the light of the author's own pronouncements elsewhere, the more difficult it is to interpret it either as conventional eulogy or as deliberately disguised criticism; and perhaps one might be justified in concluding that its tone is purposely ambiguous. We must not overlook the prudent conservatism with which this chapter opens: after admitting that all forms of government have their good and bad points, La Bruyère observes: 'Ce qu'il y a de plus raisonnable et de plus sûr, c'est d'estimer celle où l'on est né la meilleure de toutes, et de s'y soumettre'.[6] A paternal sort of absolutism seems to be his ideal

[1] Quoted by Gaiffe, op. cit., p. 343.
[2] Ibid., p. 346.
[3] See, e.g., Fléchier, *Mémoires sur les Grands-Jours d'Auvergne*, ed. P. A. Chéruel (Paris, 1856), pp. 67, 230, 259 ff., etc.
[4] Quoted by Sagnac, op. cit., p. 162. See the commentary to passage no. XVI.
[5] Cf. Voltaire's favourable comment on the absence of this prejudice in England (*Lettres philosophiques*, ed. cit., I, pp. 120-2).
[6] X, 1.

of government; but whereas the conventional eulogy with which he had rounded off the chapter in the first edition of the *Caractères* had automatically identified the realities of Louis' reign with this ideal, in the passage we are considering he is very careful not to do that: both the appreciation and the implied criticism are more sincere. In X, 35, warfare is shown merely as contributing to the glory of the monarch and of his people; but here there is more than a hint that war is not always desirable, and that other considerations must come first. We may compare the following denunciation of war on humanitarian grounds, also first included in the fourth edition:

> La guerre a pour elle l'antiquité. . . . De tout temps les hommes, pour quelque morceau de terre de plus ou de moins, sont convenus entre eux de se dépouiller, se brûler, se tuer, s'égorger les uns les autres. . . . De l'injustice des premiers hommes, comme de son unique source, est venue la guerre, ainsi que la nécessité où ils se sont trouvés de se donner des maîtres qui fixassent leurs droits et leurs prétentions. Si, content du sien, on eût pu s'abstenir du bien des voisins, on avait pour toujours la paix et la liberté.[1]

In some of the additions of the seventh edition, published in 1692, La Bruyère goes about as far as a subject of Louis XIV could go in reminding the King where his first endeavours should lie;[2] in criticising, for instance, the extravagant follies of Versailles:

> Le faste et le luxe dans un souverain, c'est le berger habillé d'or et de pierreries, la houlette d'or en ses mains; son chien a un collier d'or, il est attaché avec une laisse d'or et de soie. Que sert tant d'or à son troupeau ou contre les loups?[3]

and in denouncing the evils of irresponsible warmongering:

> Les huit ou les dix mille hommes sont au souverain comme une monnaie dont il achète une place ou une victoire: s'il faut qu'il lui en coûte moins,

---

[1] X, 9. For a contrast between the 'official' attitude to war in the seventeenth century and a much more realistic private attitude, see Plates VII a and VII b.

[2] Cf. Bossuet, in a letter to the King: 'La guerre qui oblige Votre Majesté à de si grandes dépenses l'oblige en même temps à ne laisser pas accabler le peuple par qui seul elle les peut soutenir. Ainsi leur soulagement est autant nécessaire pour votre service que pour leur repos. Votre Majesté ne l'ignore pas; et pour lui dire sur ce fondement ce que je crois être de son obligation précise et indispensable, elle doit avant toutes choses s'appliquer à connaître à fond les misères des provinces, et surtout ce qu'elles ont à souffrir sans que Votre Majesté en profite, tant par les désordres des gens de guerre que par les frais qui se font à lever la taille, qui vont à des excès incroyables' (10th July 1675). If Bossuet is more outspoken than La Bruyère, we must remember not only that this text comes from a private letter, but that Bossuet also enjoyed the privilege of his cloth.

[3] X, 25.

s'il épargne les hommes, il ressemble à celui qui marchande et qui connaît mieux qu'un autre le prix de l'argent.[1]

In 1689, he was obviously much less open in his criticism; and it is probable that he was much less critically disposed. Disillusionment was only beginning to set in, and the interest of a passage like paragraph 24 is that it seems to represent a half-way stage between the rather hollow praise of paragraph 35 and the sharp criticism expressed in the additions of 1692: tending neither to one extreme nor the other, it is a balanced, prudent and thoughtful piece of writing.

[1] X 29.

XX

Bourdaloue

(1632-1704)

From *Sermon pour le troisième dimanche après Pâques, sur les Divertissements du monde*

Ainsi, par exemple, ces représentations profanes, ces spectacles où assistent tant de mondains oisifs et voluptueux, ces assemblées publiques et de pur plaisir, où sont reçus tous ceux qu'y amène, soit l'envie de paraître, soit l'envie de voir; en deux mots, pour me faire toujours mieux entendre, comédies et bals, sont-ce des divertissements permis ou défendus? Les uns, éclairés de la véritable sagesse, qui est la sagesse de l'Évangile, les réprouvent; les autres, trompés par les fausses lumières d'une prudence[1] charnelle, les justifient, ou s'efforcent de les justifier. Chacun prononce selon ses vues, et donne ses décisions. Pour moi, mes chers auditeurs, si je
10 n'étais déjà d'une profession qui, par elle-même, m'interdit de pareils amusements, et que j'eusse comme vous à prendre parti là-dessus et à me résoudre, il me semble d'abord que pour m'y faire renoncer, il ne faudrait rien davantage que cette diversité de sentiments. Car pourquoi, dirais-je, mettre ma conscience au hasard dans une chose aussi vaine que celle-là, et dont je puis si aisément me passer? D'une part, on m'assure que ces sortes de divertissements sont criminels; d'autre part, on soutient qu'ils sont exempts de péché. Ce qui doit résulter de là, c'est qu'ils sont au moins suspects; et puisque ceux qui soutiennent que l'innocence y est blessée sont, du reste, les plus réglés dans leur conduite, les plus attachés à leurs
20 devoirs, les plus versés dans la science des voies de Dieu, n'est-il pas plus sûr et plus sage que je m'en rapporte à eux, et que je ne risque pas si légèrement mon salut? Voilà comme je conclurais, et ce serait sans doute la conclusion la plus raisonnable et la plus sensée.

Mais ce n'est pas là que je me voudrais arrêter, et il y a encore de plus fortes considérations qui me détermineraient. Que ferais-je? Suivant le conseil du Saint-Esprit, j'interrogerais ceux que Dieu m'a donnés pour maîtres; ce sont les Pères de l'Église: *interroga patrem tuum, et annuntiabit*

---

[1] *prudence*, 'sagesse'.

tibi majores tuos, et dicent tibi ; et après les avoir consultés, il serait difficile,
s'il me restait quelque délicatesse de conscience, que je ne fusse pas
30 absolument convaincu sur cette matière. Car ils m'apprendraient des
vérités capables, non seulement de me déterminer, mais de m'inspirer pour
ces sortes de divertissements une espèce d'horreur. Suivez-moi, je vous
prie.

Ils m'apprendraient que les païens mêmes les ont proscrits, comme
préjudiciables et contagieux. Il n'y a qu'à lire ce que Saint-Augustin en a
remarqué dans les livres de la Cité de Dieu, et les belles ordonnances qu'il
rapporte à la confusion de ceux qui prétendaient maintenir dans le
christianisme ce que le paganisme a rejeté. Ils m'apprendraient que
d'abandonner ces spectacles et ces assembleés, dans les premiers siècles
40 de l'Église, c'était une marque de religion, mais une marque authentique;
et en particulier ils ne blâmaient pas seulement le théâtre, parce que de leur
temps il servait à l'idolâtrie et à la superstition, mais parce que c'était une
école d'impureté. Or vous savez s'il ne l'est pas encore plus aujourd'hui,
et si la contagion de l'impureté n'y est pas d'autant plus à craindre qu'elle y
est plus déguisée et plus raffinée. Il est vrai, le langage en est plus pur, plus
étudié, plus châtié; mais vous savez si ce langage en ternit moins l'esprit,
en corrompt moins le cœur, et si peut-être il ne vaudrait pas mieux entendre
les adultères d'un Jupiter et des autres divinités, dont les excès, exprimés
ouvertement et sans réserve, blessant les oreilles, feraient moins d'im-
50 pression sur l'âme. Ils m'apprendraient que, dans l'estime commune des
fidèles, on ne croyait pas pouvoir garder le serment et la promesse de son
baptême, tandis qu'on demeurait attaché à ces frivoles passetemps du
siècle. Car c'est vous jouer de Dieu même, mon frère, écrivait Saint-
Cyprien, d'avoir dit anathème au démon, comme vous avez fait en recevant
sur les sacrés fonts la grâce de Jésus-Christ, et de rechercher maintenant les
fausses joies qu'il vous présente dans une assemblée ou dans un spectacle de
vanité. Ils m'apprendraient que sur cela l'Église usait d'une sévérité
extrême dans sa discipline, et que cette sévérité alla même à un tel point que
ce fut quelquefois un obstacle à la conversion des infidèles. Jusque-là, dit
60 Tertullien, que l'on en voyait presque plus s'éloigner de notre sainte foi par
la crainte d'être privés de ces divertissements qu'elle condamnait, que par
la crainte du martyre et de la mort dont les tyrans les menaçaient.

Œuvres (Paris, 1838), II, pp. 391-2

There is plenty of evidence from contemporary records of the great
following enjoyed by the leading preachers of Louis XIV's time. Copies
were taken of their sermons, to serve as a basis for pirated editions which

were eagerly read and discussed, even in apparently worldly circles; one
text refers to a score of shorthand-writers grouped round the pulpit of a
fashionable preacher. Of all the preachers of his time, Bourdaloue had
by far the biggest reputation. A Jesuit from Bourges, he first preached in
Paris in 1669, and at Versailles in the following year; he was soon given
the official title of 'prédicateur du Roi', and for the rest of his life preached
at court and in various churches in the capital, with only occasional
excursions into the provinces. Mme de Sévigné is particularly eloquent
in praise of Bourdaloue's gifts as a preacher, and her letters testify to his
extraordinary popularity. She writes to her daughter in 1671:

> J'ai entendu la Passion du Mascaron, qui en vérité a été très belle et très
> touchante. J'avais grande envie de me jeter dans le Bourdaloue; mais
> l'impossibilité m'en a ôté le goût: les laquais y étaient dès mercredi [in order
> to reserve seats for a Good Friday sermon!], et la presse était à mourir. Je
> savais qu'il devait redire celle que M. de Grignan et moi nous entendîmes
> l'année passée aux Jésuites, et c'est pour cela que j'en avais envie: elle
> était parfaitement belle, et je ne m'en souviens que comme d'un songe.[1]

Compared with those of Bossuet, who had ceased to preach (except
for funeral orations) by 1669, Bourdaloue's sermons make a more direct
appeal to the intellect. If they lack the emotional appeal of Bossuet's
rhetoric, they have a remarkable dialectical force, and the passage under
consideration is a good example of Bourdaloue's closely-knit argumentative style. The sermon from which it is taken has as its text St John xvi,
20: 'Verily, verily, I say unto you, that ye shall weep and lament, but the
world shall rejoice', and it is constructed according to the following
argumentative scheme:

Introduction: consolation of the just, whose grief will become ever-
lasting joy, while worldly pleasures will lead to eternal misery.

Division: most worldly pleasures are to be condemned, as being
(i) impure by nature, (ii) excessive in their extent, or (iii) scandalous in
their effects.

First part: pleasures naturally impure: (i) theatres and balls; (ii)
novels.

Second part: pleasures dangerous because excessive: especially
gambling. Excessive (i) in time consumed, (ii) in money wasted,
(iii) in passions aroused.

[1] Letter of 27th March 1671.

Third part : pleasures which may be the occasion of sin in others, e.g. fashionable display or 'la promenade.'

Conclusion : distinction between these pleasures and 'divertissements honnêtes, sans excès et sans danger.'

The Church's attitude towards the theatre, with which this passage is particularly concerned, hardened considerably in the closing decades of the century. It is a curious paradox that in a period which had seen as splendid a flowering of dramatic literature as any in the world's history, the French theatre should come under the anathema of the Church, and that this condemnation should manifest itself at the Court of a monarch whose enlightened patronage had contributed in an unmistakable manner to the triumphant careers of the two greatest French dramatists. For although the Church had maintained a nominal opposition to the theatre throughout the century, the question had not been brought into the open until the 1690s. Until then, ecclesiastical disapproval had been limited to formal sanctions against the members of the acting profession (although they obtained full civil rights in 1641, they remained automatically excommunicate, and forfeited the right to a Church burial unless they had made a formal recantation of their profession; the deaths of Molière in 1673, Rosimond in 1686, and Champmeslé in 1701 were occasions on which this sanction was applied). However, in the middle of the century and for the first decades of the reign of Louis XIV, the systematic attack on the theatre as an institution seems to have been suspended, and the campaign of the Compagnie du Saint-Sacrement against Molière in the 1660s was occasioned by the author's own temerity in treating the subject of religious hypocrisy in *Tartuffe :* the intemperate invective of Pierre Roullé, curé of Saint-Barthélemy, against 'un démon vêtu de chair et habillé en homme'[1] was a personal attack on Molière himself, rather than a denunciation of the theatre as a whole. The anathema pronounced on the members of what was officially regarded as an infamous profession did not prevent the faithful from going to the theatre to enjoy the products of their art,[2] and there is no evidence that

[1] *Le Roi glorieux au monde* (1664), quoted in Molière, *Œuvres,*'Grands Écrivains' edition (Paris, 1873-1900), X, p. 316.

[2] The following passage suggests that even the clergy occasionally found the theatre useful: 'Pourquoi me tairais-je de l'avantage que les orateurs sacrés tirent des comédiens, auprès de qui, et en public et en particulier, ils se vont former à un beau ton de voix et à un beau geste, aides nécessaires au prédicateur pour toucher les cœurs ?'—S. Chappuzeaux, *Le Théâtre français* (1674), p. 141.

at this period the Church made a serious attempt to denounce the theatre as a social evil.[1] But in the 1680s the climate at Versailles had changed, as the King's own conversion imposed an almost puritanical *dévotion* on his whole court. 'A l'heure qu'il est,' writes Mme de Lafayette in 1689, 'hors de la piété point de salut à la cour, aussi bien que dans l'autre monde',[2] and there is more than a grain of truth in the following remarks made by the Princess Palatine:

> Le malheur pour les pauvres coméd iens, c'est que le Roi ne veut plus voir de comédies. Tant qu'il y allait, ce n'était pas un péché; c'en était un si peu que tous les évêques y allaient journellement; il y avait une banquette pour eux, et elle était toujours bien garnie. M. de Meaux y était toujours.[3]

It is true that the Jansenist Nicole had published his uncompromising attack on the theatre in his *Traité de la comédie* as early as 1659, and the prince de Conti his *Traité de la comédie et des spectacles* (also written under Jansenist influence) in 1666;[4] while Racine's break with his past in ceasing to write for the professional theatre after *Phèdre* (1677) is also often attributed to Jansenist pressure, though it is open to doubt how far he was influenced by any such scruples in coming to this decision.[5] The Jesuits had on the whole been more favourably disposed towards the

[1] Fléchier, the future bishop, who attended the Grands-Jours at Clermont-Ferrand in 1665 in the capacity of secretary to M. Caumartin, one of the commissioners, watched the performances of a company of actors (cf. p. 52, n. 4) and comments as follows: 'Je ne suis pas de ceux qui sont ennemis jurés de la comédie, et qui s'emportent contre un divertissement qui peut être indifférent, lorsqu'il est dans la bienséance; je n'ai pas la même ardeur que les Pères de l'Église ont témoignée contre les comédies anciennes, qui, selon Saint-Augustin, faisaient une partie de la religion des païens, et qui étaient accompagnées de certains spectacles qui offensent la pureté chrétienne'—*Mémoires de Fléchier sur les Grands-Jours d'Auvergne*, ed. P. A. Chéruel (Paris, 1856), p. 126. This passage, written at a time when Fléchier was already in minor Orders and a 'prédicateur du Roi', forms a marked contrast to his attitude at the end of the century (see p. 217).

[2] 'Mémoires de la cour de France, 1688-9,' in *La Princesse de Clèves . . .*, ed. cit., p. 365.

[3] Princesse Palatine, duchesse d'Orléans, *Mémoires*, quoted by R. Picard, *La Carrière de Jean Racine,* p. 508.

[4] Conti's new-found hostility towards the theatre (he had been the patron of Molière's troupe before his conversion) was merely one manifestation of his intemperate zeal. Cf. a letter written by Racine from Uzès in the province of Languedoc, of which Conti was Governor (25th June 1662): 'M. le prince de Conti est à trois lieues de cette ville, et se fait furieusement craindre dans la province. Il fait rechercher les vieux crimes, qui sont en fort grand nombre. Il a fait emprisonner bon nombre de gentilshommes, et il en a écarté beaucoup d'autres. Une troupe de comédiens s'étaient venus établir dans une petite ville proche d'ici; il les a chassés, et ils ont passé le Rhône pour se retirer en Provence. On dit qu'il n'y a que des missionnaires et des archers à sa queue. Les gens de Languedoc ne sont pas accoutumés à telles réformes, mais il faut pourtant plier'.

[5] See the commentary to passage no. XVIII.

theatre, but the 'Querelle du théâtre' at the end of the century was to unite churchmen of all shades of theological opinion.

The controversy was set going, however, by a pamphlet written by an ecclesiastic in defence of the morality of the theatre, and published by the playwright Boursault in 1694 in the *Pièces de théâtre de M. Boursault, avec une lettre d'un théologien illustre par sa qualité et par son mérite consulté par l'auteur pour savoir si la comédie peut être permise ou doit être absolument défendue.* The 'théologien illustre' was an otherwise obscure priest, by name Caffaro, of the Italian Order of the Theatins; the Italian Church had always been more liberal in its attitude towards the theatre than its French counterpart, and indeed it is possible to see in this controversy a reflection of the much wider Gallican-Ultramontane differences which marked French ecclesiastical history throughout the reign of Louis XIV. Caffaro's general thesis is that the theatre as an institution is neither wholly good nor wholly bad, but that when dealing with the contents of plays, as with the private lives of actors, one can consider only specific examples, many of which are edifying; in particular, the French theatre during the second half of the seventeenth century had been thoroughly purged of the grosser elements of farce and indecency which had been characteristic of an earlier period. He argues that if it is permissible for bishops and clergy to attend private performances of plays, it cannot be harmful to watch them in public, and asks why, if plays and other works capable of arousing the passions can be read with impunity, it should be considered sinful to represent plays on the stage?

J'ai fait encore quelquefois une réflexion qui me paraît assez judicieuse en jetant les yeux sur les affiches qu'on lit au coin des rues, où l'on invite toutes sortes de personnes à venir à la comédie et aux autres spectacles qui se jouent avec privilège du Roi et par des troupes entretenues par Sa Majesté. Quoi! disais-je en moi-même, si l'on invitait les gens à quelque mauvaise action, à se trouver en des lieux infâmes, ou bien à manger de la viande les jours qui nous sont défendus, il est constant que les magistrats, bien loin de permettre la publication de ces sortes d'affiches, en puniraient sévèrement les auteurs qui abuseraient de l'autorité d'un Roi très-Chrétien et très-religieux, pour inviter les fidèles à commettre des crimes si énormes. Il faut donc, concluais-je aisément, que la comédie ne soit pas si mauvaise, puisque les magistrats ne la défendent point, que les prélats ne s'y opposent en aucune manière, et qu'elle se joue avec le privilège d'un prince qui gouverne ses sujets avec tant de sagesse et de piété, qui n'a pas dédaigné d'y assister lui-même, et qui ne voudrait pas par sa présence autoriser un crime dont il serait plus coupable que les autres.[1]

His most interesting argument is the one he advances against the authority of the Fathers of the Church, traditionally used by churchmen denouncing the theatre as a social evil. St Chrysostom and the other early Fathers, he says, could judge the state of the theatre only as it was in their own day, and their condemnation has no validity with regard to the very different theatre of seventeenth-century France:

> Comme le temps qui change fait tout changer avec lui, les gens équitables doivent regarder les choses dans le temps où elles sont. . . . Les médecins mêmes, dont les enfants remplissent des places considérables dans l'Église, dans l'Épée et dans la Robe, n'ont-ils pas été chassés de Rome comme infâmes? Et dans l'élévation où ils sont, reste-t-il le moindre vestige de leur infamie? Pourquoi donc y en aura-t-il dans une profession toute pleine d'esprit et qui est aujourd'hui, par les soins que tant d'habiles gens se sont donnés, moins l'école du vice que celle de la vertu?[2]

This is an example of historical relativism and independence of tradition rare indeed in a seventeenth-century churchman, and it is interesting to compare Caffaro's argument here with those advanced by the Moderns in the controversy with the Ancients on the subject of progress in the arts.[3]

The unfortunate Theatin's Preface was, however, to meet with a hot reception and from no less redoubtable a controversialist than Bossuet, who addressed an open letter to him demanding retractation of the opinions expressed in it. The letter, which was not published at the time, was circulated privately; and although Caffaro replied, denying authorship of the Preface, Bossuet expanded his own views into the *Maximes et réflexions sur la comédie* (also published in 1694). In the meantime (May 1694) Caffaro's Preface had been officially condemned by the Faculty of Theology, and had incurred the formal disapproval of the Academy, while the author himself had been suspended from his functions as priest by the Archbishop of Paris, Harlay.

Bossuet's treatise presents in an eloquent and persuasive manner the uncompromisingly stern judgment on the theatre of an austere churchman steeped in the authority of the Fathers of the Church. He cannot

---

[1] *Lettre d'un théologien illustre* . . . in C. Urbain and E. Levesque, *L'Église et le théâtre* (Paris, 1930), pp. 99-100.

[2] Ibid., pp. 93-4.

[3] See the commentary to passage no. XVII.

accept that the modern theatre is any less immoral than that against which they fulminated in their time, and all attempts to reform the theatre are misguided and bound to be fruitless. Taking illustrations from the plays of his time, Bossuet cites *Le Cid* as an example of tragedy arousing undesirable passions:

> Tout le dessein d'un poète, toute la fin de son travail, c'est qu'on soit, comme son héros, épris des belles personnes, qu'on les serve comme des divinités; en un mot, qu'on leur sacrifie tout, si ce n'est peut-être la gloire, dont l'amour est plus dangereux que celui de la beauté même,

and goes on to congratulate Racine on having renounced the theatre in order to turn to 'sujets plus dignes de lui'.[1] But his most forceful example is that of Molière, and he has been severely judged by posterity for the harshness of his attitude towards the author of *Tartuffe*. For however strong and sincere his feelings undoubtedly were on the subject of a playwright 'qui remplit encore à présent tous les théâtres des équivoques les plus grossières dont on ait jamais infecté les oreilles des chrétiens', there is a displeasing lack of Christian charity about his violent denunciation:

> Il a fait voir à notre siècle le fruit qu'on peut espérer de la morale du théâtre, qui n'attaque que le ridicule du monde, en lui laissant cependant toute sa corruption. La postérité saura peut-être la fin de ce poète comédien, qui, en jouant son *Malade imaginaire* ou son *Médecin par force* reçut la dernière atteinte de la maladie dont il mourut peu d'heures après, et passa des plaisanteries du théâtre, parmi lesquelles il rendit presque le dernier soupir, au tribunal de celui qui dit : «Malheur à vous qui riez, car vous pleurerez».[2]

Caffaro's Preface produced a number of other replies from champions of the orthodox Church attitude to the theatre; and although there is insufficient evidence for the precise dating of Bourdaloue's sermons, it is most likely that the sermon 'Sur les divertissements du monde' should be attributed to this same period.[3] Although the passage devoted to the theatre forms only a part of the sermon, Bourdaloue uses the same arguments as Bossuet in the *Maximes et réflexions;* he is merely replacing the issue of the morality of the theatre in the wider context in which it belongs, and judging the theatre, along with other *divertisse-*

---

[1] *Maximes et réflexions . . .* in Urbain and Levesque, op. cit., pp. 177, 194. Cf. the commentary to passage no. XVIII.
[2] Ibid., pp. 172, 185.
[3] Cf. Rousseau, *Lettre à d'Alembert*, ed. M. Fuchs (Paris, 1948), p. viii.

ments, from the absolute standpoint of one to whom all worldly activities which might distract the Christian from his goal of happiness in the next world are pernicious. It is not so much Bourdaloue's intransigent asceticism which makes a passage such as this difficult for a modern reader to sympathise with: one can still admire a quality which so impressed his contemporaries, reinforced as it was by the moral authority of 'le plus janséniste des jésuites';[1] for Bourdaloue was not a Prince of the Church, and was not so vulnerable to a satirist's jibes as Bossuet or the Archbishop of Paris:

> D'ailleurs tant qu'on verra des prélats fastueux
> Élever à grands frais des palais somptueux,
> En fait de mets exquis ne rien céder aux princes,
> Et de leur train pompeux éblouir les provinces,
> Contre la comédie en vain l'on écrira,
> De ces moralités le public se rira.[2]

Rather than the spirit which animates the passage, it is the kind of argument used by Bourdaloue that is alien to modern ways of thought.

The logical structure of his argument is impressive enough, but it is based on questionable *a priori* premises; when he appeals to the 'diversité des sentiments' (line 13) in order to justify abstention from pleasures of a dubious character—an argument which seems faintly to echo Pascal's celebrated argument of the 'wager' in 'n'est-il pas plus sûr... que je ne risque pas si légèrement mon salut?'—his conclusion is invalidated by the arbitrary dogmatism of 'les plus versés dans la science des voies de Dieu'. Above all, there is the unquestioning reliance on the established authority of the early Fathers: 'Suivant le conseil du Saint-Esprit, j'interrogerais ceux que Dieu m'a donnés pour maîtres; ce sont les Pères de l'Église . . . ils m'apprendraient des vérités . . . ' It may be true that 'ses divisions et subdivisions . . . s'inspirent, après tout, d'un principe cartésien';[3] but if Bourdaloue follows Descartes in this respect, he is resolutely anti-Cartesian in his unquestioning reliance on the doctrinal tradition handed down by the early Fathers. No Catholic priest could neglect that tradition with impunity, but Caffaro had shown himself much less bound by reverence for authority, as his feigned perplexity

---

[1] Sainte-Beuve, *Port-Royal*, ed. cit., II, p. 189.
[2] F. Gacon, 'Satire à Mgr. J.-B. Bossuet, évêque de Meaux, sur son livre touchant la comédie' (1694) in Urbain and Levesque, op. cit., p. 278.
[3] J. Vier, *Histoire de la littérature française*, XVIᵉ-XVIIᵉ siècles (Paris, 1959), p. 455.

at the contradiction between certain early Fathers and later scholastic authorities shows:

> Si je m'abandonne à la rigueur avec les Pères de l'Église, et que j'invective contre la comédie comme contre une des plus pernicieuses inventions du démon, je ne puis lire nos théologiens, ces grands hommes si distingués par leur piété et par leur doctrine, que je ne me laisse adoucir par la droiture de leur raisonnement et plus encore par la force de leur autorité. Vous m'avouerez, monsieur, qu'on serait embarrassé à moins, et que ce n'est pas une petite affaire de décider une question dont les sentiments sont si partagés,[1]

and even Bossuet had been prepared to meet Caffaro on his own ground, and to discuss particular examples taken from the seventeenth-century theatre, instead of relying entirely on the appeal to theological authorities of the past. But for Bourdaloue no sort of historical perspective seems to exist: he is content to accept the Fathers of the Church as divinely-appointed guides to Christian morality for all time, and his argument gains its dogmatic force from this simplification of the issue.

The 'Querelle du théâtre' remained a literary-theological controversy, with little effect on the general public. As an example of a secular writer treating the same theme of the morality of the theatre, we may cite P.-J. Brillon, whose *Ouvrage nouveau dans le goût des Caractères de Théophraste et des Pensées de Pascal* was published in 1697; in his chapter entitled 'Le Pour et le contre de la comédie', ostensibly an impartial review of the subject, this author in fact supports Bossuet and Bourdaloue in their criticism of the morality of the theatre. There were repercussions, too, in literary circles in England, where Jeremy Collier's *Short View of the Immorality and Profaneness of the English Stage* appeared in 1698. At Court, the atmosphere of austerity continued up to the end of Louis XIV's reign, but attempts by French bishops to proscribe theatre-going altogether in their dioceses (e.g. the *Mandements* of Rochechouart, Bishop of Arras, in 1695, and of Fléchier, Bishop of Nîmes, in 1708) seem to have met with little success. The most tangible effect of the controversy is to be seen in the increasingly repressive attitude of the Church towards the acting profession; in 1696, for instance, there was an appeal to Rome against the refusal of the sacraments to actors, but the case was referred back to the Archbishop of Paris, who upheld his clergy, even though it was made clear that the

---

[1] Urbain and Levesque, op. cit., pp. 68-9.

papal authorities did not favour the wholesale condemnation of the profession. The Italian actors in Paris benefited from the more liberal views prevailing in their own country, and were not regarded as excommunicate like their French colleagues; when they were expelled from the country, in 1697, it was not due to ecclesiastical but to political disapproval.[1]

After the death of Louis XIV there was a general relaxation of the prevailing austerity, and one of the first acts of the Regent was to invite the Italians to return to Paris. From now on there was no longer any support at Court for the Church's repressive attitude towards the theatre, and the religious discrimination practised against the actors themselves stands out all the more as a social anomaly. The case of Adrienne Lecouvreur, who died in 1730 and was refused Christian burial, caused considerable stir: Voltaire, for instance, drew attention to the very different attitude of the Church in England, where Mrs Oldfield had been buried with honour in Westminster Abbey;[2] but in France, the stigma of automatic excommunication was to remain in force until the Revolution.[3]

[1] The cause of their expulsion was satire of Mme de Maintenon contained in the play *La Fausse Prude*.

[2] See Voltaire, *Lettres philosophiques*, ed. cit., II, p. 159.

[3] In 1758 the theatre controversy entered on a new phase when Rousseau, in his *Lettre à d'Alembert*, attacked the project to establish a theatre at Geneva, not with the traditional arguments of the moral theologian, but on the grounds of social expediency based on a belief in the original goodness of human nature.

XXI

Fénelon

(1651-1715)

From *Télémaque*, Book X

Alors Télémaque ne put s'empêcher de témoigner à Mentor quelque surprise et même quelque mépris pour la conduite d'Idoménée. Mais Mentor l'en reprit d'un ton sévère.

«Êtes-vous étonné, lui dit-il, de ce que les hommes les plus estimables sont encore hommes et montrent encore quelques restes des faiblesses de l'humanité parmi les pièges innombrables et les embarras inséparables de la royauté? Idoménée, il est vrai, a été nourri dans les idées de faste et de hauteur; mais quel philosophe pourrait se défendre de la flatterie, s'il avait été en sa place? Il est vrai qu'il s'est laissé trop prévenir par ceux qui ont eu
10 sa confiance; mais les plus sages rois sont souvent trompés, quelques précautions qu'ils prennent pour ne l'être pas. Un roi ne peut se passer de ministres qui le soulagent et en qui il se confie, puisqu'il ne peut tout faire. D'ailleurs, un roi connaît beaucoup moins que les particuliers des hommes qui l'environnent: on est toujours masqué auprès de lui; on épuise toutes sortes d'artifices pour le tromper. Hélas! cher Télémaque, vous ne l'éprouverez que trop. On ne trouve point dans les hommes ni les vertus ni les talents qu'on y cherche. On a beau les étudier et les approfondir, on s'y mécompte tous les jours. On ne vient même jamais à bout de faire des meilleurs hommes ce qu'on aurait besoin d'en faire pour le bien public. Ils
20 ont leurs entêtements, leurs incompatibilités, leurs jalousies. On ne les persuade, ni on ne les corrige guère.

«Plus on a de peuples à gouverner, plus il faut de ministres pour faire par eux ce qu'on ne peut faire soi-même; et plus on a besoin d'hommes à qui on confie l'autorité, plus on est exposé à se tromper dans de tels choix. Tel critique aujourd'hui impitoyablement les rois, qui gouvernerait demain beaucoup moins bien qu'eux et qui ferait les mêmes fautes, avec d'autres infiniment plus grandes, si on lui confiait la même puissance. La condition privée, quand on y joint un peu d'esprit pour bien parler, couvre tous les défauts naturels, relève des talents éblouissants, et fait paraître un homme

30 digne de toutes les places dont il est éloigné. Mais c'est l'autorité qui met tous les talents à une rude épreuve et qui découvre de grands défauts.

« La grandeur est comme certains verres qui grossissent tous les objets : tous les défauts paraissent croître dans ces hautes places, où les moindres choses ont de grandes conséquences et où les plus légères fautes ont de violents contre-coups. Le monde entier est occupé à observer un seul homme à toute heure et à le juger en toute rigueur. Ceux qui le jugent n'ont aucune expérience de l'état où il est : ils n'en sentent point les difficultés, et ils ne veulent plus qu'il soit homme, tant ils exigent de perfection de lui. Un roi, quelque bon et sage qu'il soit, est encore homme. Son esprit a
40 des bornes, et sa vertu en a aussi. Il a de l'humeur, des passions, des habitudes dont il n'est pas tout à fait le maître. Il est obsédé par des gens intéressés et artificieux ; il ne trouve point les secours qu'il cherche. Il tombe chaque jour dans quelque mécompte, tantôt par ses passions et tantôt par celles de ses ministres. A peine a-t-il réparé une faute, qu'il retombe dans une autre. Telle est la condition des rois les plus éclairés et les plus vertueux.

« Les plus longs et les meilleurs règnes sont trop courts et trop imparfaits pour réparer à la fin ce qu'on a gâté, sans le vouloir, dans les commencements. La royauté porte avec elle toutes ces misères : l'impuissance humaine
50 succombe sous un fardeau si accablant. Il faut plaindre les rois et les excuser. Ne sont-ils pas à plaindre d'avoir à gouverner tant d'hommes, dont les besoins sont infinis et qui donnent tant de peines à ceux qui veulent les bien gouverner ? Pour parler franchement, les hommes sont fort à plaindre d'avoir à être gouvernés par un roi, qui n'est qu'homme, semblable à eux ; car il faudrait des dieux pour redresser les hommes. Mais les rois ne sont pas moins à plaindre, n'étant qu'hommes, c'est-à-dire faibles et imparfaits, d'avoir à gouverner cette multitude innombrable d'hommes corrompus et trompeurs. »

ed. A. Cahen (Paris, 1927), II, pp. 75-8

It was in 1689 that the future Archbishop of Cambrai, François de Salignac de la Mothe-Fénelon, was appointed tutor to the young duc de Bourgogne, grandson of Louis XIV, an appointment similar to that which Bossuet, the other great churchman of the century, had held from 1671 to 1680 in respect of the boy's father, the Grand Dauphin. Fénelon already enjoyed a considerable reputation for his piety, as well as for his talents as a preacher, and in a book published in 1687, *De l'éducation des filles*, he had given proof of his qualifications as an educationalist.

Louis XIV himself, by all accounts, had received a poor education. The following passage from Saint-Simon's portrait of the King is well known:

> L'esprit du Roi était au-dessous du médiocre, mais très-capable de se former. Il aima la gloire; il voulut l'ordre et la règle. Il était né sage, modéré, secret, maître de ses mouvements et de sa langue; le croira-t-on? Il était né bon et juste, et Dieu lui en avait donné assez pour être un bon roi, et peut-être même un grand roi. Tout le mal lui vint d'ailleurs. Sa première éducation fut tellement abandonnée, que personne n'osait approcher de son appartement. . . . Dans la suite, sa dépendance fut extrême. A peine lui apprit-on à lire et à écrire; il demeura tellement ignorant que les choses les plus connues d'histoire, d'événements, de fortunes, de conduites, de naissance, de lois, il n'en sut jamais un mot.[1]

It may be that this passage contains a good measure of characteristic exaggeration; but Fénelon himself was to write in similar terms about the evil effects of the King's education:

> Vous êtes né, Sire, avec un cœur droit et équitable, mais ceux qui vous ont élevé ne vous ont donné pour science de gouverner que la défiance, la jalousie, l'éloignement de la vertu, la crainte de tout mérite éclatant, le goût des hommes souples et rampants, la hauteur et l'attention à votre seul intérêt.[2]

As for the Dauphin, his education had certainly been thorough, but it seems not to have been geared at all to the modest intellectual capacities of the pupil, so that the results were most unfortunate. To quote Saint-Simon again:

> Monseigneur, tel pour l'esprit qu'il vient d'être représenté,[3] n'avait pu profiter de l'excellente culture qu'il reçut du duc de Montausier, et de Bossuet et de Fléchier, évêques de Meaux et de Nîmes. Son peu de lumière, s'il en eut jamais, s'éteignit, au contraire, sous la rigueur d'une éducation dure et austère, qui donna le dernier poids à sa timidité naturelle, et le dernier degré d'aversion pour toute espèce, non pas de travail et d'étude, mais d'amusement d'esprit, en sorte que, de son aveu, depuis qu'il avait

[1] Saint-Simon, *Mémoires*, 'Grands Écrivains' edition, vol. XXVIII (Paris, 1916), pp. 25-6.
[2] *Lettre à Louis XIV*, quoted by M. Daniélou, 'Fénelon éducateur' in *Bulletin de la Société d'étude du XVIIe siècle*, 1951-2, p. 182. For further discussion of this letter, see below, pp. 229 ff.
[3] Saint-Simon has previously described him as follows: 'De caractère, il n'en avait aucun; du sens assez, sans aucune sorte d'esprit'.

été affranchi de ses maîtres, il n'avait, de sa vie, lu que l'article de Paris de la *Gazette de France*, pour y voir les morts et les mariages.[1]

Fénelon's programme for the education of a young prince was to have a very different bias. The opening chapters of *De l'éducation des filles*, which deal with general educational principles, present a critique of traditional methods which has something at least in common with the liberal theories of Montaigne or of Rousseau. Like these other two enlightened thinkers, Fénelon believes that the educationalist should concern himself with the child's whole development, physical, moral and intellectual; and he is very much in line with modern ideas when he suggests that learning should be linked with pleasure:

> Remarquez un grand défaut des éducateurs ordinaires: on met tout le plaisir d'un côté et tout l'ennui de l'autre; tout l'ennui dans l'étude, tout le plaisir dans le divertissement. Que peut faire un enfant, sinon supporter impatiemment cette règle et courir ardemment après les jeux?
>
> Tâchons donc de changer cet ordre: rendons l'étude agréable, cachons-la sous l'apparence de la liberté et du plaisir; souffrons que les enfants interrompent quelquefois l'étude par de petites saillies de divertissement; ils ont besoin de ces distractions pour délasser leur esprit.[2]

Thus, whereas the text-books produced for the Dauphin had an austerely intellectual, even an academic character—the series of classical texts 'ad usum Delphini',[3] Bossuet's own *Discours sur l'histoire universelle*, or a translation of Erasmus's *Institutio principis christiani*—those which Fénelon devised for the Dauphin's son seem much more suited to a child's interests and capacities. 'Tout ce qui réjouit l'imagination,' he wrote, 'facilite l'étude';[4] and the three works which owe their origin to this phase of his career all have this in common, that they provide moral or political instruction indirectly, in an agreeable framework of narrative or dialogue.

The first two of these books, the *Fables* and the *Dialogues des morts* (a series of imaginary conversations between a most varied collection of historical personages, both ancient and modern) were designed for the early years of his pupil's schooling; but *Télémaque*, probably written in

---

[1] *Mémoires*, ed. cit., XXI (Paris, 1909), pp. 55-6. What Saint-Simon says is confirmed by Mme de Caylus: 'La manière dont on forçait Monseigneur d'étudier lui donna un si grand dégoût pour les livres, qu'il prit la résolution de n'en jamais ouvrir quand il serait son maître: il a tenu parole' (quoted by Daniélou, op. cit., p. 183).   [2] *De l'éducation des filles*, ch. v.

[3] We are told that the Dauphin knew a thousand words of Latin at the age of six—but not a single one at the age of twenty. Cf. Fénelon's views: 'On leur fait apprendre à lire d'abord en latin, ce qui leur ôte tout le plaisir de la lecture' (ibid.).   [4] Ibid.

FÉNELON

223

1695-6,[1] was addressed to a young prince already approaching manhood, and for this reason it has a much better claim to be considered as a work of art representative of the literature of its age. However, it must appear to the modern reader as one of the most dated of the works of that age, and it is not very easy for us to appreciate the stir caused by its publication in 1699. For *Télémaque* was received with widespread enthusiasm on account of its literary qualities; and even the hostile criticism it aroused, which represented the novel as politically subversive, would naturally enhance its interest for the contemporary reader.

Although Fénelon preserved a diplomatic neutrality in the controversy between the Ancients and the Moderns,[2] his own literary ideal looked back to the ancient world for its inspiration, to an antiquity Greek rather than Latin in character, but purified of its grosser pagan elements. With its harmonious blending of the instructive and agreeable, of the Christian ethic and the pagan 'merveilleux', *Télémaque* is almost the perfect expression of the seventeenth-century classical spirit in France. It abundantly satisfied the contemporary taste for the 'sublime', though in a manner which seems to us today rather colourless, over-didactic and trite.

The first edition bore the title *Suite du quatrième livre de l'Odyssée d'Homère, ou les Aventures de Télémaque fils d'Ulysse*; and the framework of the novel is provided by a longer and more episodic account of the young Telemachus's wanderings in search of his father (accompanied by the goddess Minerva, in the guise of the philosopher Mentor) than that given in Homer's narrative. In addition to its close connection with the epic literature of antiquity, however, Fénelon's novel had unmistakable affinities with the romanesque literature of his own day: both with the heroic novels 'à l'antique' of the mid-century such as *Polexandre* or *Le Grand Cyrus*, and with the more recent vogue of 'imaginary voyage' novels which catered for the dawning interest in the exotic. Whatever else of a more didactic nature—the moral portraits contained in the former, or the idealistic Utopias of the latter—such novels might offer the reading public, they shared a common element with all other

---

[1] The first edition appeared anonymously and Fénelon claimed that the manuscript had been delivered to a publisher, against his wishes, by the servant who had been instructed to copy it. The novel had already been circulated among the author's friends, in manuscript, and had presumably been used for its original pedagogic purpose; but Saint-Simon's suggestion that 'c'était les thèmes de son pupille qu'on déroba, qu'on joignit, qu'on publia à son insu' (*Mémoires*, ed. cit., XXI, p. 293) seems to be quite without foundation.

[2] Cf. his *Mémoire sur les occupations de l'Académie française* (1716), Letter X.

romanesque fiction of the age: they appealed to the imagination or the sensibility of the reader by their portrayal of amorous relations between the sexes. It was for this reason, of course, that the novel was condemned by stern moralists: we have seen that Bourdaloue classed the reading of novels among the 'divertissements du monde impurs de leur nature',[1] and Fénelon himself appears to take a conventionally censorious view in *Del'éducatio n des filles*.[2] *Télémaque* may seem to us today to be a pastiche of the classical epic rather than a novel, but it was certainly a novel by seventeenth-century standards, and to adopt this literary form was a bold choice on the part of an eminent ecclesiastic. Inevitably, he laid himself open to criticism on the part of his enemies within the Church: Noailles, the Archbishop of Paris, declared that '*Télémaque* n'est pas digne d'un prêtre, et ne convient point à l'éducation d'un jeune prince qu'on voulait élever chrétiennement',[3] and his brother, the Bishop of Châlons, and Bossuet both condemned the work in similar terms; though Bossuet was perhaps indulging in wishful thinking when he alleged that it was admired only by Fénelon's own 'party', the liberal sympathisers grouped round the duc de Bourgogne and his 'gouverneur', the duc de Beauvilliers:

> Il partage les esprits: la cabale l'admire; le reste du monde trouve cet ouvrage peu sérieux pour un prêtre.[4]

It was presumably not fear of this sort of criticism that made Fénelon try to stop the publication of *Télémaque*,[5] or that led the police to seize another edition published at Rouen in the following year. What was much more likely to disturb the authorities was the interpretation of the novel as an expression of the author's own political views, tendentious for their time and of particular interest now that the Archbishop was in political disgrace.

For between the writing of *Télémaque* and its publication, the young prince's tutor had completely forfeited the royal favour, and had been banished to his remote diocese of Cambrai, to which he had been appointed in 1695. It is not necessary here to go into the theological background of the Quietist controversy; briefly, Fénelon had become closely associated with the illuminist Mme Guyon, who enjoyed the

---

[1] See the commentary to passage no. XX.   [2] Ch. xii.
[3] Quoted in Bossuet, *Correspondance*, 'Grands Écrivains' edition, vol. XII (Paris, 1920), p. 6.   [4] Letter of 18th May 1699 to the abbé Bossuet, ibid.
[5] For details see the Introduction to the 'Grands Écrivains' edition of *Télémaque*, ed. A. Cahen (Paris, 2 vols., 1927).

protection of Mme de Maintenon, and whose teaching[1] had a considerable influence at Saint-Cyr round about 1690. But at the request of the Bishop of Chartres, Mme de Maintenon's 'directeur de conscience', Mme Guyon's writings were referred to Bossuet, who formally condemned them in 1695. The connection between Mme Guyon and Saint-Cyr was severed; Fénelon deferred to Bossuet's judgment, and his relations with Mme de Maintenon and with Bossuet himself remained perfectly cordial. However, after his nomination to the archbishopric, he returned to the defence of Mme Guyon, and when his book *L'Explication des maximes des saints* was published in 1697 he was promptly deprived of his office as tutor to the duc de Bourgogne, and banished to his diocese for life. Meanwhile, the controversy had been referred to Rome, and in 1699 came the condemnation of the *Maximes des saints*; when the King ordered that all the archbishops of the Church in France should give public support to the Pope's decision, Fénelon's disgrace became utter and complete. Complete, that is, except for two things: his own undoubted moral prestige, and the duc de Bourgogne's loyal attachment to his former tutor.

Contemporaries were well aware of the important political implications of this theological controversy; the Princess Palatine, for instance, wrote:

Je vous assure que cette querelle d'évêques n'a trait à rien moins qu'à la foi; tout cela est ambition pure; on ne pense presque plus à la religion, il n'en reste que le nom.[2]

Nor was it merely a quarrel of personalities: it involved not only the personal ambitions of the two protagonists, but their political ideas, the policies for which each stood, and the friends and associates of the two prelates near the King's person who supported those policies.[3] Bossuet's

[1] 'La quiétude' or 'la voie intérieure', had been defined by the Spanish monk Molinos (condemned as a heretic in 1687) as a state of complete passivity, in which the soul is given up to the contemplation of God, with consequent indifference to the 'works' (prayer, confession, etc.) by which, according to orthodox doctrine, the Christian should assist the operation of divine Grace. The crux of the debate about Quietism may be said to be the question of how far Mme Guyon and her sect followed Molinos in the more reprehensible developments of his doctrine.

[2] Quoted by F. Brunetière, 'La Querelle du quiétisme' in *Études critiques sur l'histoire de la littérature française, deuxième série* (Paris, 3rd ed., 1889), p. 60.

[3] Cf. Brunetière: 'La querelle . . ., en divisant toute la cour en deux camps, avait posé, pour ainsi dire, la question du gouvernement futur de la France, entre la coterie du Dauphin, fils de Louis XIV, et la cabale de son propre fils' (article 'Fénelon' in *La Grande Encyclopédie*, Paris, n.d.).

concept of kingship did not constitute a fundamental challenge to the absolutism of Versailles,[1] and his criticism was confined to energetic reminders of the King's duty to his people.[2] Fénelon's essential object, on the other hand, was to counteract the pernicious influence of Versailles, and to educate his young pupil above all to be a Christian king; and the political theory to which he subscribed envisaged an active and responsible aristocracy as a check to the monarch's prerogative. Fénelon and Beauvilliers attracted the support of those who like themselves saw much to criticise in Louis' absolutist régime, and for a time there had been a close sympathy between this group and Mme de Maintenon.

It was in these circumstances that *Télémaque* appeared; the privilege to publish was obtained shortly before the news arrived from Rome of the condemnation of the *Maximes des saints*, and it is easy to understand why Fénelon should have wished to prevent publication of a work which might aggravate his disfavour. Indeed, there is evidence in Saint-Simon's *Mémoires* that its publication did have that effect; speaking of the Archbishop's disgrace, Saint-Simon writes:

> Son fameux *Télémaque* . . . l'approfondit plus que tout et la rendit incurable ... M. de Noailles [the Archbishop of Paris] . . . disait au Roi alors, et à qui voulut l'entendre, qu'il fallait être ennemi de sa personne pour l'avoir composé.[3]

The critical problem presented by the allegorical interpretation of seventeenth-century works based on ancient history and mythology has already been touched on in commentaries on other passages;[4] *Télémaque*, as a work in which the author has deliberately set out to use the mythological subject-matter of the ancient world as a vehicle for the practical moral instruction of a young prince, in order to make him fit to rule in the contemporary, real world, poses the problem in an acute form. The general application of situations and events is clear enough; what is less certain is the extent to which they are meant to have a more particular application, and the question is an especially delicate one in respect of those passages whose interpretation as allegory, with a direct bearing on contemporary affairs, involves a serious personal criticism of Louis XIV.

Contemporaries saw fit to identify Louis with two characters in Fénelon's novel. One of these is the tyrant Pygmalion, ruler of Tyre, who

---

[1] See the commentary to passage no. XV.
[2] See the commentary to passage no. XIX.
[3] Ed. cit., XXI, pp. 292-3.
[4] See the commentaries to passages nos. VIII and XVIII.

is portrayed, with his mistress Astarbé, in Book III: a portrait so totally unsympathetic that it is impossible to believe that it can have been intended to represent Louis to his own grandson.[1] The case of the other character, Idoménée, King of Salente, is very different. To begin with, the portrait is by no means an unsympathetic one, and Idoménée's failings are treated with a certain measure of indulgence by Fénelon's mouthpiece, the wise Mentor. Moreover, they are unmistakably those failings—a wasteful love of splendour, unnecessary war-mongering, and neglect of his duty to the people—that his more critical subjects recognised in Louis himself, which is hardly true of the portrait of Pygmalion. In a passage at the beginning of Book X, for instance, which helps us to understand the tone of the extract under consideration, Mentor takes it upon himself to rebuke the King for his imprudence in planning to embark on a new war without just cause, when his people need a settled period of peace and prosperity, and of putting ideas of luxury and empty magnificence before the material well-being of his people as a whole:

> Pendant que vous aviez au dehors tant d'ennemis qui menaçaient votre royaume encore mal établi vous ne songiez au dedans de votre nouvelle ville qu'à y faire des ouvrages magnifiques. . . . Vous avez épuisé vos richesses; vous n'avez songé ni à augmenter votre peuple, ni à cultiver les terres fertiles de cette côte. . . . Il fallait une longue paix dans ces commencements, pour favoriser la multiplication de votre peuple. Vous ne deviez songer qu'à l'agriculture et à l'établissement des plus sages lois. Une vaine ambition vous a poussé jusques au bord du précipice. A force de vouloir paraître grand, vous avez pensé ruiner votre véritable grandeur.[2]

Idoménée is not a 'portrait' of Louis XIV, nor is the newly-founded state of Salente a portrait of Louis' France. But the contemporary reference of the allegory seems unmistakable; and if there are details which are deliberately introduced to obscure the resemblance, there are also suggestive touches which reinforce it. Thus, when Mentor says to Idoménée: 'Il ne tient plus qu'à vous d'élever jusqu'au ciel la gloire [de Salente] et d'égaler la sagesse de Minos, votre aïeul, dans le gouvernement de vos peuples',[3] it is surely not too fanciful to think of

---

[1] But cf. Saint-Simon's evidence: 'On avait persuadé au Roi qu'Astarbé et Pygmalion dans Tyr était sa peinture et celle de Mme de Maintenon dans Versailles; celle-ci n'y pouvait penser sans frémir de rage' (Écrits inédits, quoted in Mémoires, ed. cit., XXI, p. 293).

[2] Télémaque, ed. cit., II, p. 62.

[3] Ibid., II, p. 58.

Louis' own grandfather Henri IV, for whom Fénelon reveals his admiration in the *Dialogues des morts*.[1]

In the passage from Book X with which we are particularly concerned, Mentor assumes the role of defending counsel. Only the first part of the extract, in which he lays the blame for Idoménée's faults as a ruler on his education and on the ambition and flattery of his courtiers, is expressed in the form of a direct reference to Idoménée, however; from line 10 onwards he adopts a more general tone (*'les plus sages rois* sont souvent trompés', *'un roi* ne peut se passer...,' etc.), and apart from the apostrophe to Télémaque himself, the remainder of the passage consists of philosophical generalisations. But the whole forms part of a longer discussion of the mistaken policies of Idoménée, and the sentiments expressed in general terms are just as capable of containing allusions to contemporary affairs as the more specific references to Idoménée himself. Indeed, the warning against deceit and flattery leading up to the phrase 'Hélas! cher Télémaque, vous ne l'éprouverez que trop' bears a striking resemblance to a passage in *Athalie* in which the high priest Joad gives similar advice to the boy-king, and in which commentators have also seen a discreet topical allusion on the part of Racine.[2]

The charitable, if stern, tone adopted here by Mentor hardly seems likely, in the context, to have been more to Louis' taste than the more overt criticism of a ruler's power expressed at the beginning of Book X.

[1] Cf. the following passage, put into the mouth of Henri IV: 'J'ai fait la guerre avec vigueur; j'ai conclu au dehors une solide paix; au dedans j'ai policé l'État, et je l'ai rendu florissant; j'ai rendu les grands à leur devoir, et même les plus insolents favoris, tout cela sans tromper, sans assassiner, sans faire d'injustice, me fiant aux gens de bien, et mettant toute ma gloire à soulager les peuples' (*Dialogues des morts*, 'Henri III et Henri IV').

[2] Loin du trône nourri, de ce fatal honneur
Hélas! vous ignorez le charme empoisonneur.
De l'absolu pouvoir vous ignorez l'ivresse,
Et des lâches flatteurs la voix enchanteresse.
Bientôt ils vous diront que les plus saintes lois,
Maîtresses du vil peuple, obéissent aux rois;
Qu'un roi n'a d'autre frein que sa volonté même;
Qu'il doit tout immoler à sa grandeur suprême;
Qu'aux larmes, au travail, le peuple est condamné,
Et d'un sceptre de fer veut être gouverné;
Que s'il n'est opprimé, tôt ou tard il opprime.
Ainsi de piège en piège, et d'abîme en abîme,
Corrompant de vos mœurs l'aimable pureté,
Ils vous feront enfin haïr la vérité,
Vous peindront la vertu sous une affreuse image.
Hélas! ils ont des rois égaré le plus sage.
(*Athalie*, lines 1387-1402)

For the whole tenor of the extract is such as to bring down Idoménée to the level of other men, to stress the humanity of kings and therefore their fallibility; and this, for a king who was used to an adulation hardly less extreme than that given to the Roman emperors,[1] must have been a severe affront to his pride. Louis' reported comment on *Télémaque*: 'On ne peut pousser l'ingratitude plus loin: il a entrepris de décrier éternellement mon règne'[2] may be apocryphal; but in the literary climate in which Fénelon's novel was written, one may legitimately conclude that if an author's contemporaries were in general agreement in reading topical allusions into a work of an allegorical nature, then the author himself must have been aware of the probable interpretation of his allegory. We need not, therefore, set too much store by Fénelon's disclaimer:

> Il aurait fallu que j'eusse été non seulement l'homme le plus ingrat, mais encore le plus insensé pour y vouloir faire des portraits satiriques et insolents. J'ai horreur de la seule pensée d'un tel dessein. Il est vrai que j'ai mis dans ces aventures toutes les vérités nécessaires pour le gouvernement et tous les défauts qu'on peut avoir dans la puissance souveraine; mais je n'en ai marqué aucun avec une affectation qui tende à aucun portrait, ni caractère.[3]

In any case, the modern reader is in possession of evidence which was not available to the author's contemporaries, in the form of Fénelon's other writings on political subjects, which were published only during the course of the eighteenth century. The most interesting of these are the *Lettre à Louis XIV*, written in about 1694-5 (and therefore virtually contemporary with the writing of *Télémaque*) and the *Examen de conscience sur les devoirs de la royauté*, written after the retirement to Cambrai. The letter to the King, so outspoken in its terms that it is most unlikely that it was ever delivered, at least in the form in which it has been preserved,[4] covers very much the same ground as the criticism of

[1] Cf. Mignard's idealised portrait of the King 'à l'antique' in Plate VIII.
[2] Quoted in *Télémaque*, ed. cit., I, p. 40. [3] Ibid.
[4] There is a balanced treatment of this question in a note which prefaces the text of the letter itself in Fénelon, *Correspondance* (Paris, 1872), vol. II, pp. 329-32. Cf. also a modern historian's comment on the letter: 'Pamphlet haineux, qui n'a certainement jamais été lu de Louis XIV, puisque son auteur n'a pas fini à la Bastille, probablement jamais du duc de Beauvilliers ni de Mme de Maintenon, fort malmenés, puisqu'ils n'ont pas rompu avec le précepteur, et qui n'est sans doute qu'un épanchement intime de Fénelon'—R. Mousnier, 'Les Idées politiques de Fénelon' in *Bulletin de la Société d'étude du XVIIe siècle* (1951-2), p. 192. It is difficult to understand M. Mousnier's use of the adjective 'haineux': Fénelon's letter is inspired by humanitarian and patriotic motives, not by 'hatred'.

Idoménée, in particular the wasteful and unjust wars, and the abuse of arbitrary power by the King's ministers:

> Vous avez cru gouverner, parce que vous avez réglé les limites entre ceux qui gouvernaient. Ils ont bien montré au public leur puissance, et on ne l'a que trop sentie. Ils ont été durs, hautains, injustes, violents, de mauvaise foi. Ils n'ont connu d'autre règle, ni pour l'administration du dedans de l'État ni pour les négociations étrangères, que de menacer, que d'écraser, que d'anéantir tout ce qui leur résistait. Ils ne vous ont parlé, que pour écarter de vous tout mérite qui pouvait leur faire ombrage. Ils vous ont accoutumé à recevoir sans cesse des louanges outrées qui vont jusqu'à l'idolâtrie, et que vous auriez dû, pour votre honneur, rejeter avec indignation. On a rendu votre nom odieux, et toute la nation française insupportable à tous nos voisins.

As for the mass of the people, the following passage gives an eloquent picture of the ruinous effects of Louis' continual wars:

> Cependant vos peuples, que vous devriez aimer comme vos enfants, et qui ont été jusqu'ici si passionnés pour vous, meurent de faim. La culture des terres est presque abandonnée; les villes et la campagne se dépeuplent; tous les métiers languissent, et ne nourrissent plus les ouvriers. Tout commerce est anéanti. Par conséquent vous avez détruit la moitié des forces réelles du dedans de votre État, pour faire et pour défendre de vaines conquêtes au dehors. Au lieu de tirer l'argent de ce pauvre peuple, il faudrait lui faire l'aumône et le nourrir. La France entière n'est plus qu'un grand hôpital désolé et sans provision.

The *Examen de conscience* takes the form of a searching analysis of the policies and motives of a ruler; it is addressed to the young duc de Bourgogne, but the pitfalls and dangers which Fénelon's pupil is urged to avoid are those which the *Lettre* had reproved the King for succumbing to. Once again the connection with *Télémaque* is striking; the following passage from Book X, for instance, reproduces not only the content but also the catechistical form of the *Examen*:

> Si vous avez été trompé jusqu'ici, c'est que vous avez bien voulu l'être; c'est que vous avez craint des conseillers trop sincères. Avez-vous cherché les gens les plus désintéressés et les plus propres à vous contredire? Avez-vous pris soin de faire parler les hommes les moins empressés à vous plaire,

les plus désintéressés dans leur conduite, les plus capables de condamner
vos passions et vos sentiments injustes? Quand vous avez trouvé des
flatteurs, les avez-vous écartés? Vous en êtes-vous défié? Non, non, vous
n'avez point fait ce que font ceux qui aiment la vérité et qui méritent de la
connaître.[1]

Fénelon was not a radical reformer. He proposes no detailed programme
such as the scheme for fiscal reform put forward in Vauban's *Projet
d'une dîme royale* (1707); and even in *Les Tables de Chaulnes* (1711), his
most practical piece of writing on political topics, the society he en-
visages in a reorganised France is the same conventional hierarchical
society that he preaches as his ideal in *Télémaque*. He was above all a
Christian moralist, whose criticism of Louis' régime had a strong
ethical basis; and he strove earnestly to make of his royal pupil a conscientious Christian king who would never neglect his people's welfare.
At the same time, the *Lettre à Louis XIV* and the *Examen de conscience* are
not merely an individual's protest against the wasteful follies of Versailles;
they are also the articulate expression of the aspirations of the small
liberal 'opposition' grouped round the person of the duc de Bourgogne.
Fénelon has been accused of self-seeking, of looking forward to a day
when he might rule the country himself by playing the Richelieu to his
pupil's Louis XIII; this seems highly unlikely, however, for in the
1690s such an eventuality could be only a very remote one: the Grand
Dauphin himself was ten years younger than the Archbishop, so that
there were considerable odds against the duc de Bourgogne's succeeding
to the throne in his tutor's lifetime.[2]

Criticism of the régime was to grow in volume during the last two
decades of Louis' reign. Not all the criticism was as humane and disinterested as that of Vauban and Fénelon; the comments of Saint-Simon
and other nobles are often inspired by jealousies and frustrated ambition.
It does not seem that there was any tangible effect on the policies pursued by Louis and his ministers; indeed, the wars became increasingly
costly, the finances of the country increasingly disorganised, and the

[1] Ed. cit., II, p. 61.

[2] On the Dauphin's death in 1711, the duc de Bourgogne himself became Dauphin; bu
the hopes of Fénelon and his party were short-lived, as the Duke and his eldest son (the duc
de Bretagne) both died in 1712, followed by the Duke's brother (the duc de Berry) in 1714.
Louis XIV was thus left with the young duc d'Anjou, second son of the duc de Bourgogne,
as his only surviving legitimate descendant.

plight of the people increasingly desperate.[1] But it is difficult to believe that the accumulation of criticism did not make its mark with the elderly King, now more and more solitary amidst the empty ceremonial of Versailles; and in his death-bed 'confession' to his young successor we may surely see a belated recognition of his people's grievances, and an acknowledgment of the humane message of a work like *Télémaque*:

> Mon cher enfant, vous allez être le plus grand roi du monde. N'oubliez jamais les obligations que vous avez à Dieu. Ne m'imitez pas dans les guerres; tâchez de maintenir toujours la paix avec vos voisins, de soulager votre peuple autant que vous pourrez, ce que j'ai eu le malheur de ne pouvoir faire par les nécessités de l'État.[2]

[1] In 1697, national expenditure amounted to 210 million *livres;* the 'ordinary' revenue was only 60 millions, and the remainder had to be found by special levies, loans, 'exceptional fiscal measures', and 'affaires extraordinaires' ('privilèges, levées abusives, surtaxes, abus de toutes sortes'). In 1706, the total expenditure was 196 millions, of which 134 went to support the war; in spite of anticipating the following year's income to the extent of 22 millions, there was still a 22-million deficit; and in 1707, we are told, 'les fonds de l'année 1708 avaient été presque entièrement consommés d'avance'. See Vauban, *Projet d'une dîme royale*, ed. E. Coornaert (Paris, 1933), pp. xii-xiii.

[2] Quoted in Saint-Simon, *Mémoires*, ed. cit., XXVII (Paris, 1915), pp. 274-5. Saint-Simon's own version ('Ne m'imitez pas dans le goût que j'ai eu pour les bâtiments, ni dans celui que j'ai eu pour la guerre . . .') is considered less reliable.

Index

Black figures refer to main entries